# Postscript to the Past

## LOST MANSIONS AND HOUSES OF RENFREWSHIRE

DAN SWEENEY

First published in Great Britain 2015
by Windan Press

ISBN 978 0 9927148 4 0

Printed by James McVicar Printers, Glasgow
0141 774 5132
www.mcvicarprinters.co.uk

# Preface

For the purpose of this book, a companion volume to "Shadows of the City" (2013), which chronicles Glasgow's lost mansions and houses, Renfrewshire refers to the former county of the same name which disappeared following the Local Government (Scotland) Act of 1974. It was then incorporated into Strathclyde Region and subdivided into the three districts which became the basis for the unitary authorities which emerged from the subsequent reorganisation of local government in Scotland in 1994, viz. East Renfrewshire, Inverclyde and Renfrewshire.

The book describes sixty-seven properties which have been lost to a landscape which stretches from Wemyss Bay to Eaglesham. Some, at one time prominent county landmarks, represent major losses to the area's architectural heritage; others are more of interest because of their close association with the county's commercial and industrial growth and with its leading figures and families. While the main focus is on lost mansions and houses, the book also offers glimpses of the forces which shaped the county and sketches of some of its important personalities.

The American novelist William Faulkner famously wrote, "The past is never dead; it's not even past." So it is that many of these properties and the people associated with them are remembered locally in the names of housing developments, streets and parks.

Change is persistent and its rapid continuance makes it all the more necessary not to lose sight of the past. I hope that this book will help to bring readers to a deeper appreciation of history in their local areas and so stimulate their curiosity to learn more.

Dan Sweeney

2015

# Acknowledgements

I would like to thank Gerry Murtagh for his support and advice in the preparation of this book, Amanda Robb, Local Studies Librarian with East Renfrewshire Library Service, for her interest and assistance, and the staff of Paisley Central Library (Heritage Centre) and the Watt Library, Greenock, for their courtesy and help. Thanks are also extended to all those who made photographs available for the book, particularly East Renfrewshire Library and Information Services, Barrhead and Neilston Historical Association, Douglas Nisbet, Robert Humphrey and Andy Melvin. The majority of the illustrations have come from old postcards and photographs, and from books and periodicals listed in the bibliography and/or held in the above libraries. Photographs by Thomas Annan: pages 26, 32, 36, 54, 56, 58, 68, 70, 76, 92, 94, 100, 110, 114, 120, 122, 142. Cartoons from *The Bailie*, pages 16, 17, 63, 98, 99, 128, 129.

# Note

The relative values of the figures quoted in this book may be better understood by noting that, compared with 2011,

- £1 in 1750 would have had the same purchasing power as £182

- £1 in 1800 would have had the same purchasing power as £68

- £1 in 1850 would have had the same purchasing power as £110

- £1 in 1900 would have had the same purchasing power as £101

- £1 in 1950 would have had the same purchasing power as £28

(Source: House of Commons Research Paper 12/31, May, 2012)

# Contents

# List of Portraits

# Introduction

At the turn of the 20th century the county of Renfrewshire extended from the Firth of Clyde in the west to just beyond Cathcart in the east, and from Jordanhill, north of the Clyde, to beyond Eaglesham in the south. Geographically small, only twenty-seventh among the thirty-three Scottish counties in terms of area, it was both populous and highly industrialized, ranking fifth in order of population, contesting with Edinburgh the distinction of being the most densely populated county in Scotland, and sixth in the order of industrial importance.

The three principal pillars of the county economy were agriculture, shipping and shipbuilding, and textile manufacturing. Modern methods of farming, reclamation programmes and the application of science to agricultural processes had helped to ensure efficient and productive use of the land. Nearly two-thirds of the county's 250 square miles was under cultivation, and a cool, moist climate had helped to establish oats as the most important crop. More than 10,000 acres were given over to growing oats, more than seven times the area devoted to wheat. Renfrewshire was also one of the greatest dairy farming shires in Scotland and found ready markets for its milk in Glasgow and other large towns.

Shipping and shipbuilding hugged the coastal rim from Renfrew to Greenock. Foreign commerce had contributed to the prosperity of the county for almost two centuries. Port Glasgow, founded in 1688 when the magistrates of Glasgow addressed the problem of the non-navigability of the Clyde by feuing thirteen acres of ground known as Devol's Glen near Newark for a port and harbour, had in the early 18th century become Glasgow's point of entry for the products of the slave economies of the New World. Cargoes of tobacco, sugar and rum were then either transported upstream in shallow bottom boats or transferred by land. Dredging to deepen and widen the Clyde, resulting in traffic then progressing directly to Glasgow, dealt a hammer blow to the town, which turned its attention to shipbuilding, which became increasingly important from the end of the American War of Independence. By the turn of the 20th century Port Glasgow had become the greatest shipbuilding town on the Clyde. Although at this time it was still a major importer of Canadian timber and West Indian sugar, the town's mercantile role was much reduced, the baton having been picked up by Greenock, which as late as 1670 had been forbidden to engage in foreign trade – a privilege enjoyed only by royal burghs. When the restriction was removed Greenock transformed over time from the chief centre of herring fishing on the Clyde into a major 20th century seaport, with trading links with the West and East Indies, the Americas and the Mediterranean. In the process it also became a significant centre of shipbuilding.

Inland, cotton mills had proliferated along the banks of the Black Cart, White Cart, and Gryffe Rivers and their tributaries from the 1780s, providing employment for the inhabitants of the towns and settlements that had grown up around them, and stimulating growth in allied industries like bleaching and dyeing. By the late 19th century, however, the dominant force in the textile industry was thread-making, with Paisley, one of the largest manufacturing towns in Scotland, unchallenged as the global centre of thread production.

Beyond this trinity, the county's industrial footprint was broad and varied. Weaving was a shadow of its former self and sugar refining was going through one of the many periodic slumps which affected the industry, but their places as drivers of the county economy were taken by various branches of engineering - marine engineering in Greenock, sanitary engineering in Barrhead and machine tool engineering in Paisley and Johnstone. Chemical works and paper mills added to the diversity, while coal and ironstone continued to be mined in the heart of the county around Johnstone and Houston, and Giffnock's famous quarries were producing a white, fine-grained freestone to meet the demands of the West of Scotland building boom.

The profits from this economic activity were in large part responsible for the clutch of mansions and large houses which populated the county landscape at the time. While a number owed their existence to wealth repatriated from North America, the West Indies and India in the 18th and early 19th centuries, most were built with capital generated by local businesses. These properties varied quite significantly in style and importance, from fine examples of neoclassical Georgian and Scottish Baronial mansions by notable architects to modest properties of little obvious architectural merit, sometimes more noted for their attractive gardens and grounds. Structures transmit meaning. Whether built as focal points of country estates, convenient residences for mill owners and shipbuilders, marine retreats, or comfortable homes in expanding suburban environments, these properties sent unmistakeable messages to the community about their owners' wealth, status and influence.

The 20th century was to witness a diminution in the size of the county of Renfrewshire as well as in its pool of notable houses. Boundary changes to feed neighbouring Glasgow's voracious appetite for land removed areas like Cathcart, Pollokshields, Pollokshaws, Scotstoun, Jordanhill, and Govan in 1912, and Yoker, Cardonald and Nitshill in 1925. For a variety of reasons, moreover, many landmark properties were lost as the century progressed. Some succumbed to fire and subsidence. Others became victims of the thirst for land associated with the development of industry, transport and housing. Neglect and a lack of investment also took their toll, particularly where houses were the subject of requisition orders during the wars for the billeting of military personnel, hospitals, government operations, and children's homes, and were returned in a poor or ruinous condition to owners lacking the will or resources to restore them to their original state. At the same time fashions were changing and owners were reappraising the practicality of large houses and households, which became increasingly expensive to operate and maintain as industrial and commercial expansion challenged the market for domestic service, offering alternative employment opportunities at higher rates of pay. Changes in the political landscape also contributed. The introduction and extension of death duties, and the fact that a demolished house could not be valued for probate duty, provided an incentive to some owners to demolish a house rather than leave it standing. Vacant sites moreover were attractive to property developers, who could make a quick return by turning them over to tenements, terraces and detached houses.

Given the forces at work it may be considered surprising that so much of Renfrewshire's domestic architectural heritage has been preserved. Scores of mansions and houses continue to survive into the present century, among the more notable Ardgowan, Barshaw, Bishopton, Broom, Capelrig, Duchal, Eastwood, Erskine, Finlaystone, Glentyan, Greenbank, Gryffe, and Houston, many of course having been adapted for alternative use as hotels, council offices, schools, apartment buildings, and care homes. The regret must remain that they are not joined by many of the properties which feature in the pages of this book.

# RENFREWSHIRE

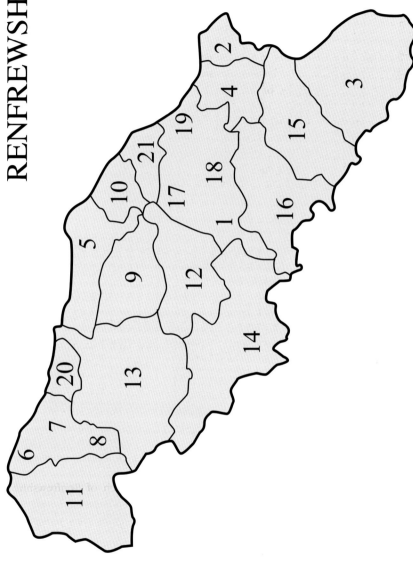

Parish Key:
1 Abbey (Paisley)
2. Cathcart
3. Eaglesham

4. Eastwood
5. Erskine
6. Greenock Middle

7. Greenock East
8. Greenock West
9.Houston and Killellan

10. Inchinnan
11. Inverkip
12. Kilbarchan

13. Kilmacolm
14. Lochwinnoch
15. Mearns

16. Neilston
17. Paisley High
18. Paisley Middle

19. Paisley Low
20. Port Glasgow
21 Renfrew

3

# Caldwell

## 1

## Barrhead and Neilston

*Caldwell*

*Carlibar*

*Cowdon Hall*

*Glanderston*

*Nether Arthurlie*

*Woodside*

The lands of Caldwell, straddling the Ayrshire and Renfrewshire boundary line near Lugton Water, close to the villages of Lugton and Uplawmoor, came into the possession of the Mure family through marriage in the 14th century. On the failure of the male line of the Mures of Caldwell, the lands in 1710 passed to William Mure, 4th laird of Glanderston, who was the first of seven William Mures to own Caldwell in a succession that extended into the 20th century. Long before he died childless in 1728 William Mure conveyed Caldwell to his nephew William Mure, an advocate, who around 1715 built a mansion house on the estate about a mile southwest of an old, ruinous tower house situated to the south-west of Loch Libo. After his sudden death in 1722, a few days after his election as MP for the County of Renfrew, he was succeeded by his infant son, also William Mure, born only four years earlier.

Mure studied law at Edinburgh and Leyden before travelling in France and Holland. In November, 1742, he was elected MP for Renfrewshire, a seat which he held until 1761 when he was appointed to the office of Baron of the Scots Exchequer. Three years later he became rector of Glasgow University. Mure's Parliamentary attendance was irregular; he was more interested in agricultural improvements, upon which he became a recognised authority. He was a close friend of historian and philosopher David Hume, and of Lord Bute, the Prime Minister, who trusted him not only with the management of his own estates but with a considerable amount of government patronage in Scotland, making Mure one of the most influential men in the country. Mure implemented major improvements at Caldwell, introducing many plants and trees, including the beeches that once lined the road from Caldwell House to Neilston Parish Church, and in 1754 building a large complex of coach-houses, stables and offices near the house. Moreover, he concentrated the family property portfolio around Caldwell, selling several properties such as Glanderston in 1755 and Capelrig in 1765, whilst purchasing contiguous properties such as Little Caldwell in 1753 and the lands of Cowdon in 1766.

In 1772 he commissioned Robert and James Adam to build an imposing country residence consistent with his status and position. Caldwell House, a five-bay, three-storey, castellated structure with decorative corner turrets, was built within a landscaped setting about 200 yards from the original mansion. It probably took around two decades to complete. Semple, in 1782, noted: "In the attick story of this superb building are two cisterns, viz. one at each end, for conveying the water, by roans, down the inside of this beautiful grand fabric; but there is very little of this elegant large modern house repaired within as yet."

Mure died at Caldwell in March, 1776, to be succeeded by his eldest son, Colonel William Mure. A friend of Sir John Moore, he served on the staff of Lord Cornwallis in the American War of Independence, during which he was wounded, taken prisoner and exchanged. He was present at the British surrender at Yorktown in 1781. He left the army early to devote his time to Caldwell, where he commissioned Paisley carpenter and builder Samuel Henning to carry out work on the mansion, which probably included the fitting of the staircase around 1790. Mure also converted the old house into stables and in 1799 laid out new gardens. Rector of Glasgow University in 1793, he died in February, 1831.

When he died the estate, which was rich in minerals, including lime, freestone and the coal which was being worked on the banks of Loch Libo, covered around 5,000 acres. His eldest son and successor, William Mure (1799-1860), yet another rector of Glasgow University (1847), was a distinguished classical scholar. He employed the Edinburgh designer and mural painter Thomas Bonnar to create Pompeiian interiors for the hall of Caldwell House in the 1840s. MP for Renfrewshire from 1846 until 1855, he died at his London home in April, 1860. The next laird, his son William Mure (1830-80), was a career soldier who had served in the Kaffir War in South Africa (1851-53) and in the Crimean War (1854-56), where he took part in the actions at Alma, Balaclava and Sebastopol. Retiring from active service in 1860 as Lieutenant-Colonel of the Scots Fusilier Guards, he settled at Caldwell, where he interested himself in politics, serving as MP for Renfrewshire from 1874 until his death in London in November, 1880, leaving a ten year old son, William Mure (1870-1912), who assumed management of

the estate in 1891, leaving briefly to serve in the Boer War. He was the last member of the Mure family to live at Caldwell. In 1909, having decided that the mansion was too expensive to run, he moved the family home to the nearby Hall of Caldwell, which he had extended and modernised, and leased the mansion. A noted breeder of Ayrshire cattle and a county councillor, he died in June, 1912, at Hall of Caldwell. His widow Georgiana gifted the Mure Hall in Uplawmoor in his memory. His only son David William Alexander Mure, born that same year at Eglinton Castle in Ayrshire, was raised in London and was the last family member to be born in Scotland.

In 1923 the 280-acre Caldwell Estate, including the mansion and offices, was purchased for £7,500 by the Govan District Board of Control, who subsequently spent £40,000 on extensive modifications before opening *Caldwell House Institution for Mental Defectives* on the site on June 6th, 1929. The interior suffered badly during the renovations, with the main staircase removed to accommodate an elevator. Further deterioration continued throughout the century with the continued use of the building as a home, which was eventually closed in 1985 when Strathclyde Regional Council considered it uneconomic to maintain. Two years later the estate was sold off in lots by the Secretary of State for Scotland. The house and around 95 acres were acquired by a developer with plans for a care village on the property, and the out-buildings were restored as a nursing home. The mansion was occupied until around 1990, after which it was left vacant. Neglect and vandalism soon told on the fabric and the structure. The nursing home closed in 1994, and the following January the northeast wing of the house was gutted in a suspicious fire which reportedly destroyed around 40% of the interior. Around 2010 JOK Developments acquired the Caldwell estate with a view to restoring and converting the then roofless and derelict mansion into flats and erecting a housing development in the policies. No action has since ensued, and the Grade-A listed building, situated about 1 mile southwest of Uplawmoor, remains in a ruinous condition and under serious threat of collapse.

# Carlibar

The village of Barrhead grew on the back of the textile manufacturing industry which developed along the Levern Water in the late 18th century. Bleachfields and printworks already existed in the area when a business consortium, which included Glasgow merchants Samuel Ramsay, John Livingstone and John Love, built Renfrewshire's first cotton spinning mill at Dovecothall in June, 1780, on land feued from the Earl of Glasgow. The three-storey structure was managed by Jonathan Haugh, a Lancashire man who applied to Dovecothall the knowledge he had imported of Richard Arkwright's water frame. The mill achieved a certain celebrity; in 1789 it hosted delegates of the French Chamber of Commerce anxious to learn how the cotton industry could be developed in rural locations. By then it had changed hands twice. In 1783 it was purchased by Glasgow merchant Richard Thomson, a significant figure in the emerging West of Scotland cotton industry. Apart from his mill on the Levern, he briefly owned the Busby Mill and was a partner in

William Gillespie's South Woodside Mill on the River Kelvin (1783). Around 1785 the brothers James and Henry Dunlop, partners in Stewart, Dunlop and Company, purchased the Dovecothall Mill, which quickly became obsolete as cotton spinning technology evolved, leading the Dunlops to build a much larger five-storey facility, the Levern Mill, on the opposite bank of the river in 1800. The Dunlop brothers carried out extensive spinning and weaving operations in the West of Scotland. Their success at Dovecothall prompted other ventures, including the Gateside (1789) and the West Arthurlie Cotton Mills (1795) in Barrhead, a mill on the waters of the River Cart at Linwood (1792) and, at a cost of £27,000, mills at Broomward in Glasgow's Calton district early in the 19th century. By this time James Dunlop had set up his own company. He had an extensive family of 12 children, including 10 sons, a number of whom in due course became partners in his expanding business.

There was an "exceedingly fine dwelling house" associated with the Dovecothall Mill in Thomson's time, and it is likely that this was the Carlibar House which was to be home to the Dunlop family for decades. James Dunlop's second son Robert Dunlop (1796-1825), a partner in the Levern Mill, lived in Carlibar House in the 1820s, and his fifth son Charles Dunlop (1802-51) lived there in the 1830s and 1840s. From 1853 it was owned by Dunlop's fourth son, Henry Dunlop (1799-1867) of Craigton in Glasgow, who stayed at the house only intermittently. A partner in the family business, Dunlop was noted for his interest in municipal and business affairs. He entered Glasgow Town Council in 1833 and was elected provost in 1837 after a bitterly disputed election. He was also chairman of the Glasgow Chamber of Commerce, with which he had a long association, held directorships in the City of Glasgow Bank, the City of Glasgow Life Assurance Company and the Glasgow Jute Company, and was a shareholder in 5 railway companies. During his time the grounds of Carlibar were altered and improved, and the house enlarged and rented out. In the 1850s it was occupied successively by two Sheriffs of Paisley, R. Robertson Glasgow and James Campbell.

Henry Dunlop died in 1867, leaving an estate valued at £28,158, and Carlibar was purchased from the Dunlop family in 1871 by Captain Robert Corse Glen and his wife Margaret Pollock Glen. Born Margaret Pollock at Malletsheugh Farm, Newton Mearns, she inherited a fortune on the death in 1864 of her uncle, Robert Craig, a native of Neilston who had managed the Nevsky Mills in St. Petersburgh. His legacy enabled Margaret Pollock and her husband to accumulate a property portfolio in Barrhead and Glasgow. Captain Glen died before the house was ready for occupancy, but his widow was to live at Carlibar for over 40 years, during which time she improved the house adding new conservatories, lodges, a stable and coach-house. Mrs Glen was a generous benefactor to the communities of Barrhead and Neilston, gifting the Glen Halls and the Volunteer Drill Hall to Neilston, a District Nurse's home to Barrhead, and a gold chain for Barrhead's provost. She also made financial contributions towards the costs of the municipal buildings in Barrhead, donated memorial windows in Neilston church, and offered bursaries for local schoolchildren. Her public and private generosity earned the respect of the community, who referred to her as "Lady Glen". She died at Carlibar House on 2 May, 1913, aged 89, leaving an estate valued at £40,472, most of which went to Glasgow hospitals and charities.

Her nephew, Major James Pollock (1852-1931), succeeded to Carlibar. A native of Barrhead, he was an enthusiastic curler and a skilful marksman who achieved distinction in 1892 by taking both the Gold Medal and the Queen's Prize at the National Rifle Association Bisley championship, the first occasion on which the two medals were won by one competitor. A banker by profession, he joined the Union Bank of Scotland in 1878 and was to become its agent in Barrhead, a position his father held before him. Later he also became the Union Bank's agent in Newton Mearns, joined the boards of Shanks and Company and the Barrhead Gas Company, and served on Barrhead Town Council and Renfrewshire County Council. He lived at Carlibar until the early 1920s, when he removed to a house in Craignethan Road in Whitecraigs which he named Carlibar. His son R. C. Pollock was also the agent for the Union Bank of Scotland in Barrhead, as in turn was his son, which must have established some kind of banking record – four generations of the same family controlling access to the funds of a single bank.

In 1922 Mrs. Glen's trustees sold the Carlibar property to the bowling green makers and recreation ground contractors Daniel and James Provan. On the death of the latter in 1947, Carlibar was sold to the burgh of Barrhead which over time utilised the property for a variety of purposes, including social security offices, a Parks Department base and a community centre. Despite having listed building status, Carlibar House was demolished by the council in 1975 and replaced with a new community centre, which in turn was demolished in 2006 to accommodate a new Carlibar Primary School.

# Cowdon Hall

The story of Cowdon Hall is inextricably linked with the Crofthead Cotton Works, which began construction in 1792 after Glasgow merchants Thomas Rankine and James Aitken acquired a 118-year lease of a two and a half acre site on the west bank of the Levern Water from Andrew Spreull, owner of the lands of Holehouse. Included in the lease was the use of the water of Levern that passed through Spreull's estate. The rural landscape of the area was being transformed at the time as the earlier bleachfields and print-works on the river banks gave way to cotton spinning mills. When Rankine and Aitken opened the Crofthead Mill around 1795 it was the seventh large mill to become operational along the Levern since the establishment of the Dovecothall Mill in Barrhead in 1780.

The mill was destroyed by fire in December, 1799, resulting in the insolvency of Rankine and Aitken's Crofthead Spinning Company. Three years later the company's trustees sold the property to the Glasgow textile manufacturers Kirkman Finlay and James Buchanan, who sold it on the following year to Stewart, Dunlop and Company, in which James Dunlop and his brother Henry were prominent partners. They rebuilt the mill in 1803. Control of the business soon passed to the brothers James and John Orr, and the company became Orrs, Dunlop and Company, and then simply James Orr and Company, which opened a second mill on the site in 1819. James Orr came from a prominent Paisley family. His father, William Orr, was a manufacturer in the town, and his brother John, in addition to being his sole partner in James Orr and Company, also owned the Underwood Cotton Mill in Paisley, which is said to have purchased the first James Watt steam engine in Scotland in 1799. Orr and his brother were also merchants and commission agents as partners in the well-known Paisley firm William Philips and Company.

In 1830, at a reported cost of £3,000, James Orr built a family home just south of the mill on two acres of the farm of Cowdenhall, which Orrs, Dunlop and Company had feued from William Mure of Caldwell in 1808. The 1837 New Statistical account described Crofthead House, the property of James Orr and Company, as a "handsome and elegant building". Orr died in 1846, but not before he had converted the lease of the site into outright ownership, when he purchased it from Andrew Spreull's son and heir in 1839.

In March, 1856, the firm, then managed by Orr's brother William, became insolvent, with liabilities of £14,000. Crofthead Mill, the mansion and various workers' houses were placed on the market and were subsequently acquired by James Orr's nephew Robert, who sold the Crofthead concern in 1859 for around £9,000 to R.F. and J. Alexander, a major player in the West of Scotland cotton manufacturing scene and owner, among others, of the large structure on the banks of the Molendinar Burn in Duke Street, Glasgow, which was later in the century to become the Great Eastern Hotel, a working men's hostel, and now survives as a condominium. Robert Orr assumed a seat on the board of Alexander's, for whom he continued to manage the Crofthead Mill. In 1865, near the site of his uncle's house, he built an elaborate four-storey mansion to designs by Glasgow architect John Honeyman, and surrounded it with attractive woodlands and pleasure grounds, which included a walled garden, croquet lawns, tennis courts, a bowling green and a boating pond with a boathouse. He called his new mansion Crofthead House, transferring the name from his uncle's residence which was demolished, despite being described in 1856 as "a superior mansion house". Orr's new home became known as Cowdon Hall in the early 1880s.

Crofthead Mill was rebuilt in whitewashed brick in 1883, after it had again been gutted by fire in February of that year, with damages estimated at £50,000 and, it is reported, inadequate insurance cover. When Alexander's was taken over by the English Sewing Cotton Company in 1898, Robert Orr, chairman of the firm at the time, immediately retired. The Orr family left the house and the area around fifteen years later, when Cowdon Hall Estate was given over to the recreation and welfare of a workforce which grew to around 1,500. The mansion saw temporary service during the Great War as an auxiliary hospital, following which it reverted to a company facility for the mill workers, who enjoyed access to the gardens, orchards and external sporting facilities, and held dances and events in the house, which in time came to be used for residential and retail purposes. Part of the mansion was converted into flats for mill workers, while the dressmaking firm, Diana Dresses, relocated from London just after World War Two, occupied premises in the building,

The house and outbuildings, including the stables, conservatories and glasshouses, were demolished in 1964. Of the property's main buildings, only the south lodge survives, now in private ownership. Nature has reclaimed the rest of the Cowdon Hall site, which stands on the south side of the A736 Lochlibo Road. Close to the boundary of the site can be found the ruins of the original Cowdon Hall, which was built by William Cochrane in 1630 on the brow of a hill a short distance south-west of Crofthead, near the junction of the Cowden Burn and the Levern Water. The Cochranes had acquired the lands of Cowdon in 1622 from James Spreull, whose family had owned them since the 14th century. Cowdon subsequently passed into the ownership of the 6th Duke of Hamilton in 1725, and was sold by the Hamiltons in 1766 to William Mure of Caldwell.

Crofthead Mill finally closed in 1992. After lying derelict and vandalised for several years, it was taken over in 1996 as the headquarters of J. and M. Murdoch and Son, a local recycling and haulage company. Under the Local Development Plan for Neilston it is envisaged that the structure, now B-listed, will be restored as part of a residential-cum-retail development, while the community will secure improved access to the Cowdon Hall site.

# Glanderston

In the 15th century the lands of Glanderston, a mile and a half south of Barrhead, formed part of the lordship of Neilston. They came into the possession of the Mures of Caldwell through the marriage of Lady Janet Stuart to John Mure, who transferred Glanderston to his second son William in 1554. The T-shaped Glanderston House was built in 1697 by William Mure, the 4th laird of Glanderston, around the foundations of an original tower house. Described in 1710 as "a pretty house of a new model, with several well-finished apartments", Glanderston House had a two-acre garden surrounded by a nine-foot high wall, orchards and large meadows.

In 1722 the lands of William Mure of Glanderston and Caldwell - he had inherited the Caldwell estates in 1710 - came into the possession of his grand-nephew William Mure (1718-76), later MP for Renfrewshire (1742) and Baron of Exchequer in Scotland, who sold the Glanderston estate in

1755 to Glasgow merchant John Wilson. Trade and commerce proved more profitable to Wilson than his early unsuccessful forays in the Clyde coalfields, and, like many merchants of the period, he translated his mercantile wealth into property. In addition to Glanderston, he owned the land in Glasgow known as St. Enoch Croft, a prime piece of real estate situated between present day Argyle Street and the banks of the Clyde, and in 1746 purchased the estate of Shieldhall on the Clyde, near Govan. Wilson, a professed Episcopalian, is reported to have had an uncomfortable relationship with his domestic staff at Glanderston because of their failure to give proper respect when he read prayers according to the Anglican rite. Wilson was succeeded in Glanderston and Shieldhall by his son Alexander Wilson, who served a mercantile apprenticeship in the West Indies between 1748 and 1750 prior to setting up as a West Indian merchant and engaging in a triangular trade involving Glasgow, Madeira and

Antigua. He went on to develop further trading links with Montserrat and Grenada. Sugar was one of his main interests, and in 1765 he was a promoter and founding partner, with Glasgow tobacco merchants Thomas Hopkirk of Dalbeth and Arthur Connell of Enochbank, later provost of Glasgow, in the Greenock Sugar House Company, Greenock's first sugar refinery. Alexander Wilson died in 1774, his financial affairs in disarray, and the following year the 630-acre Glanderston estate, which included Orr's Dyke, Over Balgray and Duncarnockcraig, 33 acres of woodland, and the right to vote in the election of a member of parliament, was sold for around £9,000 to Archibald Speirs, a relation of tobacco lord Alexander Speirs of Elderslie. The Shieldhall property soon followed, sold by Wilson's creditors in 1783 to the Glasgow tobacco importer and sugar refiner Alexander Oswald.

Around 1788 Hugh Cochrane, son of John Cochrane, a Paisley textile merchant, manufacturer and banker who was also town treasurer of Paisley, leased 54 acres of Glanderston from Speirs, including the mansion, policies and a bleachworks situated on the land. In or around 1798, the year his father built a flax or linen mill called Fereneze on the Levern Water, Cochrane built a new bleachworks and planted additional trees around the house, which had become the family home. When he became insolvent in 1803, his eldest son John not only continued the Glanderston bleaching business, in partnership with Matthew Andrew, but became a partner in another bleaching concern, Andrew Cochran and Company at High Arthurlie. The Glanderston bleachworks was to change hands a number of times, but the house remained home to the Cochranes, and it is recorded how John Cochrane's nine children would walk the two miles from Glanderston House to Neilston Parish Church on a Sunday under the watchful eye of their father. After his death at Glanderston in 1832, his sons Robert, William and Alexander continued to occupy the house until around 1838, when Robert's business failure necessitated surrendering the property. The house appears to have lain unoccupied for a period thereafter, before being marketed for letting by the Speirs family, the advertisement noting cryptically "the house will be put in a suitable state of repair". In 1856 the building was noted to be still intact and to retain a picturesque dignity. Over several of the windows the date 1697 could still be seen, with the initials T.W. and W.M. elegantly carved in the dark stone. The orchards had gone, but many of the old trees, including a fine avenue of beech, still adorned the policies. Because of its melancholy and desolate appearance, the house had acquired a rather sinister reputation locally. Although only occupied sporadically, it was rumoured that residents had heard occasional strange noises within its gloomy walls.

The last tenant of Glanderston House, from around 1858 until 1862, was Jackson Walton, a versatile Mancunian who was variously a merchant, wine dealer, sawmill owner, painter and photographer. One of his twelve sons, the Renfrewshire artist Edward Arthur Walton (1860 – 1922), a member of the famous 'Glasgow Boys', was born at Glanderston, which by 1865 lay abandoned, windowless and open to the elements. The derelict structure was demolished well before the turn of the century.

Glanderston House stood on a promontory immediately below the Glanderston Dam.

# Nether Arthurlie

In the late 1770s Paisley silk manufacturer John Lowndes (1735-81) purchased a portion of Allan Pollock's Arthurlie estate, 6 miles south of Glasgow, and began to build a fine country residence on the site. Lowndes was a leading figure in an industry that had only been established in Paisley as recently as 1759, when Humphrey Fulton established in Maxwellton a silk gauze weaving works creating imitations of the fabrics manufactured at Spitalfields, then the centre of the English silk manufacturing industry. The price and quality of Fulton's goods made them popular on the London markets and soon several of the Spitalfields producers, attracted by cheaper labour costs and the skill levels of the local workforce, opened manufacturing centres in Paisley. The Lowndes were probably among these mercantile emigres.

Lowndes died with his Arthurlie project incomplete, and it was left to his eldest son John to finish the house, which he sold in 1796 to his uncle James Lowndes (1744-1813). A partner in the family silk business William and James Lowndes and Company, which had branches in Paisley and London, James Lowndes also had interests in banking and was a founding member of the Paisley Bank, which opened in 1783. Following his death, his eldest son William Lowndes (1777-1849), a banker and partner in the family firm like his father, inherited Nether Arthurlie, where he lived with his brother Charles and their respective families into the 1840s. The Lowndes decided to vacate Nether Arthurlie in 1844, selling off the house furniture that year and placing the house and 20 acres of ground on the market. When they failed to attract a purchaser, the property was made available to rent. The first tenant was Graham Russell, a partner in the well-known Glasgow firm, Stirling, Gordon and Company.

On William Lowndes' death his eldest son James inherited the property. He retired from the family firm in 1850 and appears to have spent little if any time at Nether Arthurlie. He became a captain of militia and a member of Queen Victoria's Body Guard, and after his London marriage in 1859 went to live at Bosworth in Leicestershire. That year he sold Nether Arthurlie for £12,000 to Zechariah Heys of the South Arthurlie Printworks, who continued to lease the property. From

1868 until around 1874 Nether Arthurlie was occupied by shipbuilder William Ferrier-Kerr of the Glasgow Screw Steamship Company. It was subsequently taken on a 20-year lease by Zechariah Heys' son George Heys (1815-1887), a partner in the family firm, who lived at Nether Arthurlie until his death in 1887. His widow Catherine continued to live at the property until at least 1896.

In the early years of the 20th century Nether Arthurlie was the residence of William Shanks (1857-1929), senior partner in Shanks and Company, a local firm founded in 1855 by his uncle John Shanks which had grown to become a household name and a global brand. From its initial premises, a plumber's shop in Lowndes Street, Barrhead, it had expanded to occupy a seven-acre site, where the massive Tubal Sanitary Engineering Works manufactured, in addition to domestic bathroom ware, ship's fittings, specialized hospital and mortuary equipment, and laboratory accessories. Twenty different trades were represented within a workforce which was 1,000 strong by 1914, making it Barrhead's main employer. William Shanks, son of John Shanks' brother and partner, Andrew Ferrier Shanks (1831-1893), served an apprenticeship in the firm's workshops before becoming a partner in the company in 1878 and in due course taking over its commercial management. When John Shanks died in 1895 the family concern was converted into a limited liability company, with William Shanks and John Shanks Junior as joint managing directors. The previous year William Shanks had been elected the first provost of the new burgh of Barrhead.

In 1911 the Sisters of the Sacred Hearts of Jesus and Mary acquired the 34-acre property from Zechariah Heys' trustees, and established a convent and refuge on the site, the *St. Mary of Egypt Home* for friendless and homeless girls and women. The order enlarged the estate in 1918 with the purchase of a three acre plot of adjacent ground from the local builder, Hugh Leggat, and extended the premises with two buildings, one in 1916 and another in 1968, both funded by benefactors. When changes in government policy and new approaches to social care in the 1980s led to long-term institutional care being replaced by care in the community, the order began to relocate inmates in supported accommodation, a process completed by the Hospitaller Order of Saint John of God, which had acquired St. Mary's in October, 2001. The facility, then specialising in the care of people with learning disabilities and run by the Archdiocese of Glasgow, closed in April, 2004.

In June, 2006, East Renfrewshire Council approved plans for the demolition of the convent and home. The site had always held residential appeal. In 1953 Barrhead Town Council had tried to acquire almost 6 acres of St Mary's Home for housing but had its application refused by the Secretary of State. From the early 1980s, however, Nether Arthurlie was broken up piecemeal, and new housing estates including Lyoncross, Aursbridge and St. Mary's were created. The mansion was demolished in 2008, the year after Persimmon Homes had received planning permission for a new housing development in the former convent grounds.

Nether Arthurlie House was located in the vicinity of Lyoncross Avenue and St. Mary's Road. A memorial to James Lowndes and his wife Katharine, erected by their sons, is to be found in Paisley Abbey. Shanks and Company merged with Armitage Ware in 1969 to become Armitage Shanks, which was acquired in 1980 by the Blue Circle Industries group. In 1989 Blue Circle decided to close the Tubal factory, and, despite local protests, the works closed three years later with the business transferring to England.

# Woodside

Zechariah Heys (1796-1865) migrated from Milton of Campsie to Barrhead in 1841 when he acquired the South Arthurlie Calico Works from the bankrupt James Hendry and Company. At the time the works lay idle and semi-derelict as a result of one of the periodic recessions which afflicted the cotton industry. Under Heys' management the business began the march towards profitability, but not before a natural disaster had almost extinguished the fledgling company shortly after it had commenced production in 1842. On 30th December, 1842, Glanderston Dam, situated above the print-works, burst its embankment in the midst of a wild storm and sent a raging torrent cascading down the hill and through the South Arthurlie works, sweeping away two houses, drowning nine people and causing extensive damage. This reverse proved to be the catalyst for an important change, however. At that time power for driving the machinery in the works was provided by a huge water wheel, one of the largest in the Britain; when this was swept away by the flood, steam power was substituted, and the business began to grow and prosper.

Around 1850 Heys built the 26-roomed Woodside House south of the works for his son John, a partner in the family firm. Situated amid well laid out gardens and a grove of trees, from which the house derived its name, Woodside was destined to be a company house for its existence. John Heys (1815-1890), in tandem with his twin brother George and younger brother Henry, took over the reins of the family business in December, 1862, on his father's retiral, and turned it into a major player in the textile industry. By the end of the century the factory footprint had expanded until it was covering about 30 acres of ground, and the workforce of around 600 workers in its various departments was producing 18,000 miles of finished materials a year. An active partner in the firm over a 40 year period, John Heys retired from the company in December, 1883, at the same time as his brother George, leaving Henry and assorted nephews managing the business. He remained active in local affairs as an elder in the local parish church and chairman of Neilston School Board. A highly respected individual in the local community, on the day of his funeral business was suspended in Barrhead at midday, the parish bell was tolled and shops were closed, while crowds lined the streets to watch the 30 carriage cortege wind its way to the graveyard. His widow Susannah, the daughter of Glasgow drysalter and commission merchant George Heys, lived at Woodside till her death in May, 1897, while his eldest son, Zechariah John Heys, became provost of Barrhead in 1896.

The family business, including Woodside House, was sold on 30 September, 1899, to the Manchester-based Calico Printers' Association, a British textile company founded that year from the amalgamation of 46 textile printing companies and 13 textile merchants. Most of the leading companies in the industry had decided that amalgamation was necessary in order to survive, or as they put it "to preserve the tradition and standing of calico printing and to produce textiles of a high standard at reasonable prices." The company, which at its inception accounted for over 80% of Britain's output of printed cloth, leased the mansion to a succession of businessmen. From at least 1910 until 1928 Woodside House was occupied by William James Gavin, cashier of the East India merchant company, Milne and Company, an international business with branches in Glasgow and London. The amalgamation failed to secure the survival of the South Arthurlie Printworks in the dramatic global recession in the cotton trade in the 1920s, and the factory gates closed in 1930. The last occupants of Woodside House were Niels J. Neilson and his family, who left around 1961, following which the house was allowed to fall into disrepair. In 1962 the Calico Printers' Association, unable to afford the costs of securing and maintaining the dilapidated building, gifted the seven-acre site to Barrhead Town Council, who demolished the house in 1962 and established a play park on the site. Some of the house policies were incorporated in the upper Auchenback Housing Scheme.

Woodside House stood on Springfield Road on the site covered by Woodside Park to the north of St Luke's High School. The site is referred to locally as the Gerry Park, so-called, it is believed by some Barrhead residents, because German prisoners-of-war from detention camps in and around Glasgow laboured there during the Second World War.

*Baron William Mure (Caldwell)*

*"Lady Glen" (Carlibar)*

*Walter Crum (Thornliebank)*

*William Taylor (Crookfur)*

*Dr. Samuel Johnstone Moore (Busby)*

*Archibald Brownlie Watson (Redhurst)*

*Sir John Gilmour (Pollok Castle)*

*Harry Kemp (Dunavon)*

**Barcapel**

# 2

## *Eastwood, Mearns and Eaglesham*

*Barcapel*

*Busby*

*Crookfur*

*Dunavon*

*Eaglesham*

*Eastwood Hollows*

*Hazelden*

*Pollok Castle*

*Redhurst*

*Southfield*

*Stamperland*

*Thornliebank*

The Order of the Knights Templar was introduced to Scotland by David I around the middle of the 12th century, and quickly began to accumulate property across the country. In East Renfrewshire they are known to have owned land in Mearnskirk, Broom, Newton, and Capelrig ("chapel on the ridge or hill"), which was their main seat. Capelrig subsequently passed to the Knights Hospitallers, who are thought to have established a chapel on the lands, which reverted to the Crown at the Reformation. In 1765 Glasgow lawyer Robert Barclay bought the old Capelrig estate from William Mure of Caldwell and four years later built a modern residence which he named Capelrig House. Capelrig was to remain with Barclay's descendants into the 20th century.

In November, 1911, the produce importer Thomas Clement (1868-1956), the sitting tenant of Capelrig House, purchased 71 acres of the Temple lands of Capelrig from the Murdoch family and commissioned Glasgow architects John Watson and David Salmond to build a modern two-storey mansion on the property. Watson and Salmond had designed Netherton farmhouse on the Ayr Road for Clement's father Andrew Clement in 1901. Clement's house faced north to the Campsie Fells and the Kilpatrick Hills, and the grounds were laid out with tennis courts, lawns, extensive orchards and gardens. Clement called his property Barcapel to reflect the historical antecedents of the land. Barcapel was not the first venture into local property for Clement, who was not averse to trying his hand at property speculation. In June, 1900, he had purchased 129 acres of the Broom estate from the trustees of the deceased John Pollok of Fa'side, and began disposing of plots of land to Glasgow's business elite for the construction of the exclusive villa suburb of Upper Whitecraigs.

Thomas Clement was chairman of Andrew Clement and Sons, the largest wholesale dairy produce dealer in Scotland, with additional branches in London, Manchester and in the dominions. The

18

catalyst for the growing success of the company was the advent in the early 1880s of the refrigerated ship, which allowed perishables to be transported long distances. The family firm, founded in 1877, exploited this development and began importing large quantities of dairy produce from across the globe. Australia and New Zealand were the Clements' main markets, and Thomas Clement made numerous visits to both, establishing business connections and stimulating primary producers to turn to milk, cheese and butter production on a grand scale for the crowded industrial markets of Britain. Argentina, Canada, Italy and Russia were other sources for the company, and the Clements were pioneers in importing butter from Siberia in the years before the Russian Revolution.

Clement, eldest son of the firm's founder, was also very well known in farming circles. In 1918 he established the Clement Estates Company, one of the biggest arable farmers in Scotland, with 2,200 acres of farmland in Berwickshire, 800 acres in Kirkcudbrightshire, and extensive holdings in Renfrewshire near his home, among them Hazelden Farm purchased in 1917 and the 50-acre Netherton farm which he inherited on his father's death in 1908. Netherton became noted for a special breed of Ayrshire cattle, which was to turn the farm into a showplace. Clement's brother Andrew lived and farmed at Netherton, which was later to provide much of the land for Whitecraigs Golf Course as well as land for local housing. Thomas Clement's reputation as a leading authority on the British Empire's dairy industry saw him serve on various commissions and committees on commercial and agricultural issues during the First World War, including the Cheese and Butter Imports Committee. He was created a peer in 1919, and in the mid-1920s was a founder member of the Empire Marketing Board. He also operated on the local stage, being a director of the Glasgow Chamber of Commerce and president of the Scottish Provision Trade Association. He died at Barcapel on December 15, 1956. Andrew Clement and Sons, the company with which he had a 60-year association,

ceased to be a family concern five years later, when it was acquired by the conglomerate Scotcros, and it eventually went out of business in 1971.

On Clement's death Barcapel House reverted to the Clement Estates Company and was occupied by his nephew, the philanthropist Andrew Clement Wilson (1906-93). A friend of George Trevelyan, the "New Age" advocate of alternative spirituality, Wilson in 1965 used funds from the sale of the family business to establish the Truth Research Foundation, a charity with ambitions in the field of integrated health and complementary medicine. After his death it became part of the Barcapel Foundation, a family charity which continues to support works and projects in Scotland and beyond.

Barcapel House was destroyed by fire in 1965, and lay derelict and uninhabitable for some years afterwards. When the Barcapel estate was sold off in lots in 1971 the six-acre site containing the mansion and policies was acquired by Edinburgh building contractor James Harrison, who demolished the house and in July, 1972, began the construction of 30 luxury apartments on the site to designs by Edinburgh architect George R. M. Kennedy. Twenty one months later the apartments were available for purchase, at prices rising from £29,850.

A monolithic Celtic cross dating from the first millennium, a 7ft 7in sandstone shaft minus its top, stood on the Barcapel estate until 1926, when it was removed for preservation to the Glasgow Art Galleries and Museum. About 300 yards north-east of the site of the Capelrig Cross, in the adjacent Deaconsbank Golf Course, stands a well-preserved mediaeval, circular, stone doocot, which may have belonged to a vanished monastery on the lands of Capelrig. Robert Barclay's Capelrig House continues to stand within the grounds of Eastwood High School in Capelrig Road, while about a quarter of a mile to the north is situated Holm Farm, the original Templar residence on Capelrig

# Busby

The first cotton mill in Busby, then known as Newmill, was built in 1780 on the west bank of the White Cart by Glasgow textile merchant William Ferguson, on land feued from Sir Michael Stewart of Blackhall. Opening in July, 1782, and later to be known as the Upper Mill, it was acquired in rapid succession by Richard Thomson of the Dovecothall Mill in Barrhead (1783), Manchester merchant Richard Twyford (1786), and a fellow Mancunian James Doxon (1788), who in 1790 added a second mill nearby, the three-storey New or Lower Mill. In 1794 the mill complex was purchased for around £3,000 by the London cloth merchant and banker Thomas Everett (1739-1810) of Biddesden in Wiltshire, sometime MP for the borough of Ludgershall. Five years later, in 1799, Busby House was built on high ground overlooking the works by Malcolm MacFarlane, who took over the lease of the mill that year. After Everett's death, leaving an estate valued at £100,000, his trustees retained the Busby property, which was leased to a succession of tenants.

The house saw temporary service as a hospital in 1832, when the mill operator, William Kelly, permitted it to be used during a cholera outbreak. In 1843 the Busby cotton mills were leased by James Crum, younger brother of Walter Crum, head of the family calico-printing works at Thornliebank. Crum had resigned his partnership in the family firm J. and W. Crum earlier that year in order to go into business on his own. In addition to being a cotton spinner at Busby and a commission merchant in Glasgow, Crum was also a farmer, holding leases on the 76-acre Cartsbridge farm on the opposite side of the Busby Road from the mills and on the 80-acre Braehead farm at Thorntonhall. A well-known figure in Glasgow business and social circles, Crum took considerable interest in public affairs, serving as a director of the Chamber of Commerce, the Royal Infirmary, the Deaf and Dumb Institution and the Glasgow Eye Infirmary. He was also a sponsor and director of the Glasgow Polytechnic Institution, which opened in 1855 in Jamaica Street. Comprising a museum, fine arts gallery, exhibition halls and a hall for lectures, entertainments, and concerts, it aimed to provide the people of Glasgow with "useful instruction and innocent amusement". When it was destroyed by fire in September, 1857, James Watt's first steam engine was among the exhibits lost. Crum was a noted benefactor to the Busby community, and was an active supporter of the Busby Penny Bank, founded in 1852 to form and promote habits of thrift, economy and foresight among working people. His status changed from tenant to owner of Busby House in December, 1855, when he purchased the mill from Everett's trustees. He proceeded to modify and extend Busby House in 1858 to designs by Edinburgh architects Peddie and Kinnear. He died on 6th March, 1861, at the age of 55, leaving an estate valued at £63,839. His widow, Agnes Pollock Crum, daughter of Allan Pollock of Fa'side, continued to live at Busby House till her death on April 13, 1887. Her estate was valued at a mere £783, leaving one curious about the fate of James Crum's fortune. Robert McNair managed the Busby Mills on her behalf until 1874, when they were sold to the Busby Spinning Company.

Busby House was bought for £2,520 in February, 1888, by William McKenna, a Pollokshields master plasterer, who eight years later sold the mansion and its four acres of policies to the trustees of Dr. Samuel Johnstone Moore, who had been a very prominent figure in Glasgow medical and legal circles. A native of County Antrim, he taught in Paisley before studying medicine in Glasgow. He walked daily from Paisley to attend classes at the University in High Street, returning to the town each evening to teach night classes. Graduating in 1863, he was appointed pathologist to the Royal Infirmary, a post he held for seven years. He had started a private practice about 1864 in Glasgow's South Portland Street, which quickly became one of the largest and most lucrative general practices in the city, and through which he became an intimate friend and trusted adviser to many of the most influential families in the West of Scotland. He was later appointed Medico-Legal Examiner for Lanarkshire in 1877, a position which required him to conduct post-mortems and report on his findings to the courts. A consulting physician to the Glasgow Ophthalmic Institution, a

director of Glasgow's Training Home for Nurses, and Consulting Medical Officer to the Caledonian Railway Company, Moore died in 1894, aged 60. He clearly anticipated a longer life – his estate included 107 dozen bottles of wine, including champagne, Burgundy, port, and Chateau Lafite. A long-time supporter of initiatives for the provision and training of nurses, he left his estate for the foundation and support of *The Dr. Samuel Johnstone Moore Convalescent Home for Nurses*, which aimed to provide a temporary home for nurses whose health had temporarily or permanently broken down in the exercise of their profession. £12,000 was spent in buying the Busby property and making extensive improvements. The architect Frank Burnet modified the main house for use as a nursing home and an adjoining cottage was built for disinfecting and laundry purposes. The remainder of Moore's estate, around £30,000, was invested and used to cover operational costs. The home opened in May, 1898, with accommodation for 15 or 16 nurses, and operated on the site until its closure in 1956. The mansion was demolished in 1958 when the 6-acre estate was put on the market, eventually being sold by Moore's trustees in 1962 to the contractor, William S. Gordon, who opened the River Court apartment development on the site the following year.

Busby's Upper Mill was demolished in 1900. The Lower Mill, which was operated by the Busby Bleaching and Beetling Company from 1888 to 1942, continued to operate well into the 1960s. After lying empty for a period it was destroyed by fire in 1968. In 1982 a major renovation programme resulted in the site being adapted to provide business accommodation. It currently lies unoccupied and neglected.

A granite fountain donated to the City of Glasgow by James Crum in 1860 was once a feature of George Square. Removed temporarily in 2011 to facilitate popular entertainments, it has so far not been re-positioned.

# Crookfur

In 1838 the sugar refiner Peter Murdoch (1795-1871) and his wife, Barclay Brown (1800-1871), fourth daughter of George Brown of Capelrig, acquired 20 acres of the Broom estate, on the west side of the Glasgow to Ayr Road and one mile north of Newton Mearns village, from Allan Pollok of Fa'side. Soon after they built a mansion and named the estate and the house Langbank, after one of the enclosed fields on the property. Murdoch, son of James Murdoch of Auldhouse and a veteran of the Waterloo campaign, had earlier travelled to New South Wales in 1821 as aide-de-camp to Sir Thomas Brisbane. The following year he was appointed superintendent of the government agricultural establishment (a euphemism for a penal colony) at Emu Plains, before transferring in 1825 to Tasmania to establish a new penal settlement on Maria Island. By the time he left Tasmania to return to Scotland in 1837, he had accumulated 6,390 acres of Tasmanian real estate. Back home he became a partner in the family sugar business, Murdoch and Doddrell at the Port Dundas Sugar Refinery in Glasgow. Murdoch added to his Langbank estate by buying small parcels of local property as they became available, including

seven acres of Todhillbank in 1859. The Murdochs appear to have alternated between Langbank and Capelrig House following the death in 1850 of George Brown's widow, Mary Barclay Brown. Peter Murdoch died at Capelrig on 6 November, 1871, preceding his wife by a mere five weeks.

Langbank House, 16 rooms, plus servants' quarters and over two acres of policies, was purchased in May, 1871, by the grain merchant William Taylor. Taylor was a central player in Glasgow's momentous event of 1878, the collapse of the City of Glasgow Bank. A man with unimpeachable civic and business credentials, he was a Glasgow town councillor and magistrate, preceptor of Hutcheson's Hospital and a member of both the Glasgow School Board and the Mearns School Board. He was also chairman of the Glasgow Storage Company, a director of the Scottish Imperial Insurance Company, the State Line Steam Shipping Company and the Glasgow Corn Exchange, and sat on the board of the Clyde Navigation Trust. His business Henry Taylor and Sons, which imported grain for resale to customers, had an annual turnover of £650,000. About 1872

Taylor had become a director of the City of Glasgow Bank, then considered Glasgow's premier bank, with the third largest branch network of any British bank. It collapsed suddenly in 1878 in a financial scandal unprecedented in Scotland. The directors, including Taylor, were arrested in their homes by Glasgow police in October that year and charged with fraud and publishing balance sheets they knew to be false. The evidence at the trial which followed was damning, auditors reporting "…mismanagement, not merely frightful in its recklessness, but bristling with transactions of the most dubious character". Taylor, it was revealed, was in debt to the bank to the tune of £170,000, for advances against which the bank had obtained no security. The leniency of the sentences handed down – the directors got eight months - provoked a national furore. Depositors lost nothing, since it was before the time of limited shareholder liability, but after liquidation only 254 of the bank's 1,819 shareholders remained solvent. Taylor was ruined financially and socially.

Wine merchant John C. R. Marshall (1848-1910) purchased Langbank House in 1884, and two years later, perhaps to avoid an unhealthy association with Taylor, changed the property name to Crookfur, after another enclosure on the land. Marshall had a parallel career as a property speculator. In June, 1900, he purchased 144 acres of the Broom estate from the trustees of John Pollok of Fa'side for feuing, borrowing heavily to do so. He lived at Crookfur till his death in 1910. His son Walter sold the property in 1919 to the Rev. Archibald Templeton (1843-1923), son of carpet manufacturer Sir John Stewart Templeton. He had served as a United Free Church of Scotland medical missionary in Pachamba, Eastern India, between 1871 and 1876. On his return home he resigned his partnership in the family carpet-making business and became superintendent of the Oxford Street Dispensary in Glasgow set up by the Glasgow Medical Missionary Society. He retired in 1918 for health reasons and died in 1923. One of his sons, Kenneth Templeton, an enthusiastic aviator, was fond of flying his light aircraft around the district, using the present Crookfur Park as his airfield. One day in October, 1931, he actually struck the house while low flying. Archibald Templeton's widow died in 1947, and two years later the house, attractively laid out with a one-acre walled garden, two orchards, a vinery, peach house and fig house, was acquired by John Dickson Bain, owner of the Eglinton Arms Hotel in Eaglesham. It was subsequently acquired in 1955 by the structural engineering company, F.P. Caird, for office accommodation. The mansion was severely damaged by a fire on April 16, 1956, when the roof was destroyed and the two upper floors gutted. Shortly afterwards the house was declared uninhabitable and it was eventually demolished in 1960.

Caird sold the 14-acre Crookfur site in 1962 to Sir Hugh Fraser, who donated it to the Linen and Woollen Drapers Association, with a view to creating a Scottish Cottage Homes development for people who had retired from the drapery trade, along the lines of similar schemes in England. Planning permission for the project, designed by Sir Basil Spence, Glover & Ferguson, was obtained in December, 1962, and the foundation stone laid in 1964. The Crookfur cottage homes development, constructed by Barrhead contractor Hugh Leggat, comprised 50 cottages arranged in terraces around a central group of linked, two-storey blocks containing 20 flats, a small hospital wing, and a dining hall, and was formally opened by Lady Fraser of Allander in September, 1967, at a cost of £600,000. The scheme, which won a Civic Trust Award the following year, continues to serve retired personnel from the retail trade generally.

# Dunavon

The growth of Giffnock from a hamlet to a residential suburb began with the opening of a railway station on the Glasgow to Busby line on 1 January, 1866, and accelerated into the 1890s. As the extensive farmlands stretching south to Eastwood Toll were opened up for feuing, the estates of Eastwood Park, Orchard, Eastwood Mains, and Bagabout succumbed to villa development. Houses in a variety of shapes and styles were built of the local sandstone by contract and speculative developers for business and professional people eager to escape Glasgow's increasingly overcrowded and industrialised urban environment.

In 1893 Glasgow restaurateur and wine merchant William Wright sold just over an acre of ground directly north of Eastwoodhill House at Eastwood Toll, formerly part of a triangular field on Eastwood Mains Farm, to Glasgow architect and contractor Hugh Biggar, who built a large mansion on the property, to which he gave the name Celsa House.

Biggar, a partner in Steven and Biggar, bought out his business partner in 1897, and it may have been the costs associated with the buy-out that led him to sell Celsa House in 1898 to muslin manufacturer Hugh Taylor Brown, who renamed the property Dunavon. Brown was a partner in the Bridgeton firm John Brown and Son, which manufactured muslin draperies, Madras muslin, and harness muslin in their extensive weaving complex in French Street in Bridgeton. The production of muslin goods was an important feature of the Glasgow textile landscape at the time. Madras muslin was extensively used for light draperies at home and abroad, while harness muslin was used for dresses and for curtains.

Dunavon, through Taylor, had a link with an emerging technology which was to transform the world of communications at the time. Taylor was a sponsor and supporter of Nova Scotian Frederick George Creed in his efforts to invent a revolutionary telegraph machine which would enable Morse code signals to be punched into tape by means of a standard typewriter keyboard instead of by the laborious and time-consuming process of telegraph keying. A former employee of the Western Union Telegraph Company and the South American Telegraph and Cable Company, Creed came to Scotland in 1897 to work on his idea. With the aid of an old typewriter bought for fifteen shillings in a Sauchiehall Street auction sale, his vision began to take form. With no engineering training, and in the face of repeated advice from leading figures in Glasgow's scientific and engineering community to abandon the project, he persevered and finally came up with a prototype keyboard perforator. In 1898 Creed demonstrated that he could transmit the Glasgow Herald newspaper to London via telegraphy at a rate of sixty words per minute. His first commercial success followed in 1902 with an order for twelve machines from the British Post Office. Creed and Company, patentees and manufacturers of telegraphic apparatus, was then established in London, with Hugh Taylor Brown as a director. The Daily Mail became the first newspaper in the world to adopt the Creed System in 1912, when the entire newspaper contents were transmitted daily from London to Manchester for simultaneous publication. The following year the technology was being used to transmit London newspapers to other major centres in Great Britain and Europe.

In May, 1907, Dunavon was acquired by distiller Andrew Hair Holm (1859–1934). Holm had been a footballer as a young man, playing full-back with Queen's Park F.C., and winning international honours against Wales (1882 and 1883) and England (1883). He became managing director and a partner in Mackie and Company, which went on to become White Horse Distilleries in 1924. He lived at Dunavon until his death in January, 1934, leaving personal estate of £206,262. Dunavon was purchased later that year by Harry Kemp (1866-1972), an impresario known for his flamboyance and showmanship. Kemp had overseen the progress of the family business, established by his father George Kemp around the La Scala and Casino cinemas in Saltcoats, into the broader field of popular entertainment. During the 1922 summer season he introduced a series of popular concert parties, the first of the legendary Kemp Summer Shows, which ran for decades at the Beach Pavilion, Saltcoats, and at venues up and down the Ayrshire Coast, providing typical seaside entertainment specifically aimed at Glasgow holiday-makers. Kemp showed his flair for innovation in other ways too. He made possibly the first party political broadcast in Scotland in 1922, when *Vote for Harry Kemp* (1922) exploited the captive audiences in the family cinemas to drum up support for his successful campaign for election to Saltcoats Burgh Council. He could clearly be a bit of a character. In 1955 he was fined £4 for creating an obstruction with his car. Driving through Largs one Saturday evening at the height of the Largs Fair, with both sides of the street filled with parked cars, he came face to face with a double decker bus and refused to reverse his car into a space to let the bus pass. With cars backing up behind the bus, Kemp bought a newspaper, lit a cigarette and settled down to read the news. The police were not amused.

In 1946 Kemp sold Dunavon to the wholesale electrical manufacturer Henry Morris Robb, from whom it was acquired in 1949 by Myer Segal, owner of the leather goods firm Segal (Travelware), who sub-divided the villa for occupancy. In 1969 Dunavon, located at 234 Fenwick Road, was purchased by London-based Coleraine Properties, whose application to Renfrewshire County Council the following year for planning permission to erect a ten-storey, 250-bedroom hotel on the two-acre site was rejected. The house was demolished in 1971, when the site was earmarked for housing. It was subsequently acquired by building contractor John Dickie, who built the Hutchison Court flats on the site in 1979.

# Eaglesham

In 1835 the Eaglesham estate, a Montgomerie family possession since the 12th century, was put on the market by Archibald Montgomerie, 13th Earl of Eglinton, as the Eglinton family finances came under pressure. It was purchased in 1844 for £217,000 by the brothers Allan & James Gilmour. The acquisition was divided in two shortly afterwards, roughly in proportion to the amount each brother contributed. Allan, who had provided £148,534, acquired the larger portion, Eaglesham, while James took the smaller Polnoon property.

A native of Mearns, Allan Gilmour (1775–1849) in 1795 had owned a small local timber yard, from which he supplied Glasgow's building industry and Greenock's shipyards. He soon moved to Glasgow and expanded his operations, importing tar, hemp and flax but mainly lumber from the Baltic, Russia, and Norway, and around 1804 forming a partnership with two relations, John and Arthur Pollok, whom he had known at school. When Napoleon's Continental Blockade threatened timber supplies

to the domestic market, Parliament responded in 1809 by introducing a system of differential duties in favour of British colonies, leading the partners to switch their focus to the Canadian lumber trade. Following exploratory trips through Lower Canada, New Brunswick, and Nova Scotia, Gilmour decided to open a business in New Brunswick in 1812. Expansion followed, with branches quickly opened on the Canadian east coast, extensive forests acquired and saw-mills erected. Until 1830 Greenock was the main destination for their lumber, but after that date the ships unloaded at Liverpool, where the company maintained large storage yards for its timber cargoes and sold the wood to contractors participating in the construction boom of the period. By 1835 the firm was employing 5,000 people in its North American operations. Ship-owning was central to the business, which had the largest fleet of wooden hulled ships of any contemporary British firm. Many of the ships had names with local association, such as Mearns, Broom, Fingalton and Fa'side. Gilmour left the partnership in January, 1838, and applied his share of the firm's capital to establishing a property bank in the Mearns, purchasing Fingalton in 1838, Hazelden and part of South Muirhouse in 1839 and finally Eaglesham in 1844.

His nephew Allan Gilmour (1820-1905) succeeded to his properties, and to Polnoon when his father, James Gilmour, died in 1858. The following year he began work on a new house for his expanded estate. Designed by David Bryce in Scottish Baronial style, Eaglesham House was built at a cost of £70,000 on the site of Brackenrig Farm. A rectangular two-storey structure, with a three-storey tower at the north end, it was approached via a lodge house on the Glasgow road. The policies, which included a large walled garden with extensive glasshouses, a gas house, a curling pond and a trout hatchery on the Brackenrig Burn, extended to some 225 acres, and were laid out and planted with trees in the 1860s. Eaglesham House was to be the Gilmour family home into the 20th century. Gilmour sought to preserve the rural aspect and amenity of his lands by refusing to allow any railway to cross his lands, even though he was a railway investor with shares in the Glasgow and South-Western Railway. As he grew older he divested himself of his properties in piecemeal fashion. After gifting his eldest son and namesake the income from the Eaglesham estate in 1885, he gave him outright ownership of Polnoon in 1895 and of Eaglesham in 1898, and retired to Port Askaig, Islay, where he died.

Allan Gilmour of Eaglesham (1851-1917) practised law in London and seems to have returned to Scotland around 1885. Immediately after gaining possession of Polnoon and Eaglesham, he took out large loans totalling £83,000 on the security of his lands. He retired to Dunoon about 1914, transferring Eaglesham to his son Angus while retaining Polnoon. During the war a group of Belgian refugees were housed in Polnoon Lodge; the men among the group were found employment on the Eaglesham estate. The family properties were heavily indebted at this time. Polnoon, for example, valued at £57,440, had debts of £51,000 when inherited by Angus Cecil Gilmour (1882-1929), a Captain in the Argyll & Sutherland Highlanders and a veteran of the Boer

War. He sold the lands of Fingalton for £10,000, while Polnoon was sold by his father's trustees to William Douglas Weir, Baron Weir of Eastwood, but these disposals failed to avert a financial meltdown. When Angus died an invalid in October, 1929, his remaining lands, worth £87,000, were indebted to the tune of £55,382. It took the Gilmour trustees many years to dispose of the estate. Some tenants took advantage of the opportunity to buy the farms they were working, while builders and developers, attracted by the residential potential of the area, hoovered up large swathes of the property. One, John Smith, bought some 423 acres, comprising the farms of Windhill, Low Borland and High Borland, and a field known as the Front (Waterfoot) Park. Another, John Wotherspoon, a civil engineer in Glasgow, bought 303 acres comprising Castlehill and Bonnyton. Eaglesham House and its policies were part of a block of around 250 acres purchased by Glasgow builder Matthew Dickie, who had plans approved to build a country club, golf course and housing and retail units on the site. Eaglesham House lay temporarily unoccupied before being used as a transport depot by the army during World War Two. Dickie's plans failed to come to fruition, and following his death in 1944 his trustees sold the house and land to the Polnoon Estate Company, which established the Polnoon Grass Drying Company at the house in 1949. It grew grass on the estate then dried it to be used later as winter fodder. The house was destroyed by fire on May 26, 1954, when 300 tons of grass in an adjacent drying shed caught fire. The blaze quickly spread to the house, then occupied by an estate worker and his family. Despite the efforts of firemen from Glasgow, Paisley, Barrhead and Darnley, the house was burned to a shell.

Between 1985 and 1987 the London-based Richard Rogers Partnership, the architects responsible for the Pompidou Centre in Paris, designed an award-winning, state-of-the-art production facility on the site for Ivor Tiefenbrun's Linn Products, a company with a global reputation for audio technology.

# Eastwood Hollows

The Hollows, a three-acre triangle of property situated on the south-west corner of the crossroads created by the Thornliebank to Busby and Glasgow to Ayr roads, was an appendage of the Eastwood estate. Situated directly south of Eastwood House, it was purchased in 1819 from the advocate David Anderson Blair of Inchyra in Perthshire by John Dunn, a Glasgow fish hook maker, whose son, also John Dunn, a Glasgow property factor, inherited the small estate in 1850. He sold the Hollows, complete with a house, another building and a pew in the local parish church, in 1871 for £1,000 to the printer William Rankin, who died there in April, 1895.

Two years later the Hollows was sold by Rankin's daughter to John Sawers, who later that year commissioned architect Andrew Balfour to build a modern family villa on the site of the old house, which was demolished. Balfour's design for the Hollows, set within a landscape which included attractive gardens, a pond, a pergola and a greenhouse, featured in the journal, *Academy*

*Architecture*, in 1901. His firm Steel and Balfour was better known at the time for school and church architecture, being responsible for a number of public schools across Glasgow, including those in Govanhill, Battlefield, Langside and Newlands on the south side of the Clyde. The Eastwood Burn, which flowed down from Roddinghead through the Mains Estate and under the Ayr Road, separated the Hollows from Woodend, the next property to the west, which was owned by Sawers' father Thomas, with whom in 1876 he had established the family firm of fishmongers and game dealers which became one of Glasgow's best-known businesses, J. and T. Sawers.

The largest fish supplier in the west of Scotland, the firm had a customer base in the city and suburbs which was extensive and select, and included the city's principal hotels, restaurants and clubs, as well as private families. In 1890 new premises were opened in West Howard Street to designs by architect J. Winton Mackie. With hand-painted tile panels created by Doulton of Lambeth on the walls, marble and granite work fittings, an oyster bar, and a saloon at the rear, one publication of the time, *The Bailie*, noted that, "there is probably no more magnificent fish shop in Europe, and the splendours of the suggestive tiles and the granite slabs — to say nothing of the refreshing coolness experienced in the spacious refrigerator — must be inspected in order to be appreciated". The Howard Street shop, the only licensed fishmongers in Scotland, was much frequented by businessmen and apparently it was not unusual to see, sitting next to the women who cleaned the fish, bowler-hatted gentlemen having a lunch of oysters washed down with a bottle of Guinness. Sawers was the biggest buyer in the Glasgow Fish Market and, with its knowledge of the trade and contacts at the various Scottish ports, was even able to acquire shark, porpoise or turtle as centrepieces for its Howard Street displays. It also received large quantities of game from the owners of various sporting estates across Scotland, and many kinds of game not common to Scotland from Norway, Canada, and America. Deliveries were made by the firm's own transport fleet, which contained vehicles with names such as Miss Haddock, Miss Crab and Miss Plaice.

John Sawers was long-time chairman of the successor company Sawers Ltd., which came in due course to own twelve stores in Glasgow, in addition to having premises in Perth, Kilmarnock, Belfast, Dublin and Birmingham. It also had a number of subsidiary stores in other cities, like Edinburgh. Sawers, an artist in his leisure moments and a pioneer of colour photography, was also a collector of fine art, and in 1941 presented a watercolour by Charles Rennie Mackintosh, entitled *Pinks*, to the Glasgow Art Galleries. He lived at Eastwood Hollows until his death in April, 1945. The following year the property was purchased by manufacturer David Gardner, the occupant of neighbouring Hollows Cottage, for his wife Elizabeth.

The Eastwood Toll that Sawers left behind would have been significantly different from the one he knew in 1897. At the turn of the century houses were beginning to be built around the toll, stimulated no doubt by the opening of Giffnock Railway Station in 1866 and Whitecraigs Station in 1903, both of which enhanced transport links with Glasgow. The 1930s housing boom increased population density and traffic volumes in the district. When the steady build-up of traffic round the old crossroads led to calls in the 1950s for action to relieve congestion, Renfrewshire County Council decided in 1955 to build a new road and roundabout at Eastwood Toll, just west of the original crossroads. Eastwood Hollows, which stood in the direct path of the proposed development, was the subject of a compulsory purchase order by the Secretary of State for Scotland in 1959, and the house was subsequently demolished to accommodate the repositioning of the toll. The roundabout eventually opened in 1963. The Macdonald Hotel opened on the east of the Hollows site the same year. In 2001 the Macdonald Hotel was sold to property developers Bishop Lock Homes who replaced the hotel with luxury flats. What remained of the original Hollows site is now occupied by a luxury apartment development, completed by builder John Dickie in 1999.

Sawers was taken over in May, 1958, by the English-based Contanglo Banking and Trading Company, which sold off the remaining 28 Sawers branches. Sawers in Howard Street closed in 1960 amid regrets at the loss of its famous oyster bar. Prior to demolition of the building in 1989, Glasgow Museums salvaged the entire tile scheme as well as part of the mosaic fascia from the front of the shop.

# Hazelden

Reminiscing in 1842 on the Mearns he knew as a boy the essayist and critic John Wilson (aka Christopher North) wrote, "Not many gentlemen's houses in the parish – that is to say, old family seats: for of modern villas, or boxes, inhabited by persons imagining themselves gentlemen, and, for anything we know to the contrary, not wholly deceived in that belief, there is rather too great an abundance." Hazelden may have been one of the "boxes" he had in mind.

By the latter half of the 18th century the lands of Hazeldeanhead, situated to the south of Mearns Kirk, were sub-divided and shared among a number of owners. Glasgow brewer Patrick Reid owned two portions of the lands, one of which, the 25-acre property known as the South Park, was inherited in 1788 by his son Robert, who built a bleachworks on a spot on the north side of the Earn Water which was well served with copious supplies of spring and river water. The other plot passed to his other son, Patrick Reid, a Glasgow merchant. The lands were reunited by Robert Reid's son Patrick, who inherited his father's portion in 1811 and that of his uncle seven years later. Patrick Reid (1784-1858) had graduated in law at Trinity College, Dublin, and become a Writer to the Signet, an ancient society of Scottish solicitors which held special privileges in relation to drawing up legal documents. In 1818 he replaced his father's works with an extensive, improved factory, and north-west of his works he replaced an existing house with a modern mansion which he named Hazelden House. He remained at Hazeldon until early in 1839 when, apparently attracted by the opportunities that Australia seemed to present, he set sail for Melbourne with his wife and nine children, a retinue that included an old man servant and a nurse named Peggy, and a prefabricated house. His Australian adventure was financed by the sale of the bleach-works in 1836, and of Hazelden and other lands he owned in the Mearns. He was to die at his home, Hazel Glen, named after his Mearns property, on the Plenty River in Victoria, in July, 1858.

Reid's Hazelden and South Muirhouse lands were purchased in 1839 by the lumber merchant and ship-owner Allan Gilmour (1777-1849), who in the previous quarter century, in partnership with John and Arthur Pollok, had grown prosperous exploiting the opportunities presented by the Canadian timber trade. A rift developed between the partners around 1837, however. Gilmour was furious when the Polloks purchased the lands of Lochliboside over his head, renaging on a prior agreement to purchase the property jointly. Moreover, he objected to the Polloks spending the summer months on their Broom estate, which they had acquired in 1815 and where they had constructed a comfortable modern residence, Broom House (now Belmont School), rather than focusing on company business. In January, 1838, he resigned from the partnership, receiving £164,500 for his share, a considerable return for his initial investment of £1,000 thirty-four years earlier, but one he considered inadequate and unfair given the contribution he had made to the growth and development of the business. He used the money to become a landed proprietor in the Mearns, Hazelden and South Muirhouse forming only part of the property portfolio he soon amassed. Even after the purchase of the much larger Eagleham estate in 1844, he continued to manage his affairs from Hazelden House, where he died unmarried in March, 1849, leaving almost all his property to his nephew Allan, only surviving son of his brother, James Gilmour of Polnoon. Gilmour may have been an affluent landowner, but he appears to have lived a modest and unpretentious lifestyle at Hazelden House. A house inventory of 1849 valued his furniture and effects at a mere £394. It included no works of art or fine china, and showed his silver plate to be worth only £108.

Allan Gilmour (1820-1905) moved in to Hazelden House after his uncle's death. When his father died in 1858, he re-united Polnoon and Eaglesham, giving him ownership of around 16,500 acres in Renfrewshire and making him the second largest landowner in the county. He continued to occupy Hazelden House until shortly after 1861 when he moved to the new baronial structure he had built as the focal point of his enlarged Eaglesham estate. Hazelden House was leased around 1876 by Glasgow corn merchant John Anderson, and it remained his residence until 1915. Following the First World War it was occupied from 1919 until 1924 by Wilfred A. Henderson, a director of the well-known shipping firm D. and W. Henderson of Finnieston. In 1929 Angus Cecil Gilmour of Eaglesham sold Hazelden House and Lodge and 12 acres of ground to local garage owner James Allen of Shawhill, Newton Mearns, who established Hazelden Nurseries on the grounds. Allen disposed of plots of land on the property for housing and the mansion was subdivided for letting. In 1951 Hazelden House and two acres of grounds were purchased for £2,750 by the Hazelden School of Equitation, whose owner Robert Young demolished the old house as he established his business in the policies of the house. Hazelden Equitation Centre and Saddlery continues to occupy the site on Hazelden Road.

As the 19th century progressed Patrick Reid's bleach-works was adapted in turn for a calico works and a silk works, but was eventually to close in the 1930s when it proved unable to compete with cheap imports from the Far East.

# Pollok Castle

Pollok Castle occupied a prominent position on a rocky crag above the Clyde and Cart valleys, about one mile north-west of Newton Mearns. Originally a plain medieval keep, it was rebuilt between 1686 and 1693 by Sir Robert Pollok, who was knighted for his services to William III and the "Glorious Revolution" of 1688. Sir Robert, MP for Renfrewshire from 1700 to 1722, created "a stately large house of a new model." Four storeys high, with a spacious courtyard and surrounded by high walls with several ornate gateways flanked by carved masonry elephants and greyhounds, it was entered from the south and approached by a handsome staircase with stone balustrades.

The last representative of the Pollok main line was Robina Pollok (1737-1820), daughter of John Pollok of Balgray and wife of Sir Hew Crawfurd of Kilbirnie and Jordanhill, who inherited the baronetcy and the 4,810-acre estate in 1807. She was succeeded by her son Robert Crawford-Pollock, who died childless in 1845 leaving the estate to his nephew Hew Crawfurd, who assumed the surname Pollok. Hew Crawfurd-

Pollok (1794-1867) added a north wing to the structure about 1856. At the time of his death he had been long estranged from his only son Hew Crawfurd who had disappeared without trace in May, 1865. Detectives were employed to find him and notices placed in the *London Standard* offering a reward of £200 for information on his whereabouts. Apparently a headstrong and wilful individual who was well-known at Cheltenham for his love of hunting and steeplechasing, he is said to have absconded to the United States and enlisted in the Fifth US Cavalry under the name of Johnston. One night in 1867, it is reported, while in camp in Texas, he read a death notice for his father in an old newspaper he was using to light his pipe, and immediately made himself known to his commanding officer. Diplomatic intervention in Washington saw him secure an army discharge, and he returned to Scotland to claim his inheritance.

Trouble appears to have dogged the footsteps of Sir Hew Crawford-Pollok (1843-1885). In 1871 he married Annie Elizabeth Green, a barmaid with whom he fell in love during a visit to Hull. Two years later the new Lady Pollok successfully sued him for separation and aliment, citing his abusive and violent conduct. He denied the charges, attributing his actions to the unfortunate drinking habits he had developed in the United States. Lady Pollok returned to Hull after the hearing. Five years later, following a court case in Paisley, he agreed to pay £160 and expenses to a 17-year old domestic whom he had seduced with promises of marriage and left with child. Further misfortune ensued on July 31, 1882, when Pollok Castle was destroyed by fire, with only a few paintings and the family plate being salvaged. The alarm was raised shortly after 8 p.m. when the fire, the cause of which was never determined, was confined to the roof of the house. Mounted messengers were despatched to Pollokshaws and beyond for a fire engine which, delayed by the heaviness of the roads and the steepness of the hill at the entrance to the Pollok estate, did not reach the house until 10 p.m. The supply of water from a nearby burn proved ineffectual and soon after the roof collapsed carrying with it all the floors to the basement. By midnight nothing remained of the picturesque structure but the external walls. The damage, estimated at £30,000, was covered by insurance. The last baronet travelled a great deal afterwards, before dropping down dead in the coffee room of the Castle Hotel in Dover in December, 1885, the coroner's verdict attributing his death to alcoholic poisoning.

In the absence of an heir the estate, then extending to 2,855 acres and providing an income in excess of £3,300 p.a., was inherited by his sister Jean Johnston Crawfurd Pollok (1845-1893), who had married the solicitor and one time Benares indigo planter, William Fergusson (1825-1908), in 1867. They assumed the name Fergusson Pollok upon inheriting the property. In 1889 the old house, after lying bleak and desolate for some years, was rebuilt and extended by the Fergusson Polloks to designs by architect Charles S.S. Johnston. The 80-room structure contained many features of the old house, including a 56-feet high castellated tower. On William Fergusson Pollok's death in 1908, his eldest daughter Jane Dunlop Fergusson Pollok (1869-1950) succeeded to the estate. Around 1910 she leased Pollok Castle to John Gilmour (1876-1940), recently elected Conservative

and Unionist MP for East Renfrewshire. A native of Fife, Gilmour saw active service and was decorated in both the Boer and the First World Wars. When part of his constituency was transferred to Pollok in 1918, he stood for the Glasgow seat, which he held until his death. Gilmour held a number of Cabinet posts between 1924 and 1940. As Secretary of State for Scotland he authorised the release of Oscar Slater, albeit in the face of a relentless public campaign for his freedom. He was also the highest ranking member of any British Government to have been a member of the Orange Order. He occupied Pollok Castle until 1920, when he succeeded to the title and estate of his father, Sir John Gilmour of Montrave in Fife. The following year Miss Fergusson Pollok put the estate on the market, and realised £17,000 in disposing of a number of lots including Netherplace House and Bleachworks. Having failed to dispose of the castle, she made it her residence, and continued to occupy one wing when it was requisitioned by the British army for ammunition storage during World War Two. In 1944 she moved to her South Ayrshire residence, Pinmore House in Pinwherry, where she died in April, 1950, leaving Pollok Castle, Pinmore and around £100,000 to her nephew, a sawmill worker in British Columbia whom she had not seen since he was a child and about whose life she knew little. At this time Pollok Castle was considered uninhabitable.

Miss Fergusson Pollok's trustees continued the disposal of the estate, selling the 79-acre Corslet Farm in 1951, and the 91-acre Green Farm the following year, both to sitting tenants. When consideration of tax and death duty liabilities persuaded Robert Hew Fergusson-Pollok (1907-1967) that the property would be too costly to retain, the castle and surrounding lands were sold early in 1952 to Maybole builder and civil engineer Myles J. Callaghan for £8,000. The castle, which stood in the area of present day Aurs and Stewarton Roads, was demolished soon afterwards, most of the stone reportedly sold and used as hard core for an extension to the runway at Edinburgh Airport. All that remains of Pollok Castle are some old foundations, the West Lodge on Aurs Road and private residences created from some of the surviving estate buildings in the grounds, which also contain a new, detached property called Pollok Castle House.

# Redhurst

The rural landscape of Giffnock, four miles south of Glasgow, began to open up to industry in the early 1830s and by 1836 there were three quarries operating in the area, employing between them around 100 quarriers and labourers, who worked ten hour shifts, six days a week, for weekly wages of fifteen shillings and ten shillings respectively. The quarries became the largest source of building stone in the Glasgow area because of the quality of their liver rock, a blond sandstone much used in the construction of villas, tenements and schools. It was also a feature of some of Glasgow's landmark structures. It provided the column under the statue of Sir Walter Scott in George Square, and contributed in varying degrees to Glasgow University, Kelvingrove Art Galleries, the former Post Office building in George Square, the Glasgow Savings Bank in Ingram Street and the Scottish Cooperative Building in Morrison Street. It was also exported to cities such as Belfast, where it was used in the construction of the Customs House and Assembly Buildings, and some was even transported as far as America and South Africa for both building and monument construction.

By mid-century creeping industrialisation found Giffnock also housing coal works in Burnfield Road, the Orchard Lime Mine on Florence Drive, a small forge, and a brick and tile works. This was located east of Eastwood Toll, established in 1833 where the Kilmarnock road crossed the Paisley to East Kilbride road. These lands formed the farm of Eastwood Mains which, together with the adjoining lands of Bagabout, stretched to 170 acres. Here in 1849 James Baird established the Eastwoodmains Brick and Tile Work. Around 1861, on land adjacent to his works and fronting the East Kilbride Road, Baird built a new and commodious family home which he named Eastwood Vale. The house was unusual for the period in that it was not built of the increasingly popular Giffnock sandstone but of bricks and tiles. Baird died there in March, 1863, at the age of 43. His tile-works business was sold off two months later. Eastwood Vale was marketed by his trustees in 1867 with an asking price of £850, and was sold the following year to William Smith Yuille, owner of a tobacco and snuff manufacturing business on Trongate, Glasgow. After his death at Eastwood Vale in May, 1892, the property, then comprising a seven-roomed villa, coach-house, stables, one acre of policies and an adjacent cottage, Vale Cottage, was purchased by A. B. Watson, who renamed the property Redhurst. Watson was married in the house that December.

Archibald Brownlie Watson (1856-1940) was born in Pollokshaws, the son of Duncan Watson, a provision merchant and provost of Pollokshaws in 1860. He was a prominent figure in the surveying profession in Glasgow, a member of the Council of the Institute of Measurers. Measurers, the forerunners of quantity surveyors, were the individuals who prepared standardised schedules for building projects which quantified all of the construction materials, labour activities and the like, against which competing builders could submit priced tenders. Around 1880 he founded the firm of A.B. Watson and White, and in his career secured numerous important surveying commissions, including those for the Royal Hospital for Sick Children, Scotland Street School, Thornliebank Public School and the electricity power station at Dalmarnock. Watson, actively interested in municipal politics, became Deacon of the Incorporation of Wrights in 1915, but never stood for election to Glasgow Corporation. After his death at Redhurst in January, 1940, his widow continued to occupy the property for another decade.

The last owner of Redhurst was Richard Lindsay, who acquired the house in 1955, shortly after his wife Agnes purchased a newsagent and tobacconist shop in nearby Seres Road. He remained at Redhurst until 1967, when the property was acquired by Stakis Holdings which demolished Redhurst House and built the Redhurst Hotel on the site in 1968. At the time the chairman of the company, Reo Stakis,

was embarking on an ambitious programme of hotel construction and acquisition. An immigrant entrepreneur, he had arrived in Britain from Cyprus in 1928 aged 14 with a suitcase of his mother's lace, which he sold door to door. The money he made enabled him to move into the hospitality business after the war, when he opened his first restaurant, the Victory, in St Vincent Street, Glasgow, in 1947. During the 1960s he went on to open a chain of steakhouses, which had a formative influence on the eating habits of Glaswegians of the period, before branching out into casinos. In 1967 he opened Scotland's first casino, the Chevalier, the first of an eventual chain of twenty two. Following this he moved into hotels, at a time when the government was subsidising hotel building to boost the tourist trade; hotels were also able to circumvent Scotland's strict licensing laws, which prohibited serving alcohol on Sundays. The Stakis empire of hotels, health clubs and casinos was subsequently sold to Ladbrokes in 1999 for £1.2 billion.

Redhurst House stood at 27 Eastwoodmains Road. Vale Cottage came in time to be renamed Ingleneuk, and can still be seen today, though much modified and modernised, at the corner of Broomley Lane and Eastwoodmains Road. By 1900 the only Giffnock quarry still in operation was Baird and Stevenson's New Braidbar quarry, which employed about 280 workers. It had become a major tourist attraction, with visitors coming to tour its massive underground galleries, in places 40 to 50 feet high and some 16 feet wide, connected by an elaborate tunnel network which was lit with naptha lamps carried on metal cradles. Quarrying ended in Giffnock in 1912, a result of flooding and the high cost of extracting stone. Following failed attempts to use the quarries for purposes such as mushroom growing, they were used for tipping slag from steel foundries in the 1930s before being filled in and landscaped after 1940.

# Southfield

In the late 13th century Southfield was a Templar estate associated with Sir James Sandilands, head of the Knights of St. John and preceptor of Torpichen Priory. In 1771 the Temple lands of Southfield, located a short distance southeast of the village of Mearns, about 7 miles from Glasgow, were acquired by Jamaican merchant Alexander Hutcheson (c.1725-1788). It may have been Hutcheson, or his immediate predecessor James McGilchrist, who built Southfield House. Hutcheson died at Southfield in 1788 when the estate passed to his brother Hugh. The Hutchesons were an Ayrshire family with plantation and slave interests in Jamaica, and Hugh Hutcheson (c.1730-1813) was long associated with Maybole where he became a bailie in 1770. Like his brother he died at Southfield without a direct male heir, leaving his estate to his grandson Hugh Doig (1790-1815), who took the surname Hutcheson on succeeding. Doig-Hutcheson was to have a very brief enjoyment of his inheritance, however. He

died in December, 1815, only six months after his marriage, and his only child Charlotte Niven Doig-Hutcheson (1816-1902), born about four months after her father's death, fell heir to the property. She married Thomas Montgomery-Cuninghame of Corsehill in Ayrshire in 1832. The Hutcheson connection with Maybole was to pay off handsomely for Lady Montgomerie-Cuninghame in 1844 when her grand-uncle William Niven, a farmer, banker, bailie of Maybole, and, prior to the 1832 Reform Act, the only townsman in Maybole to have a vote, died leaving her over £100,000, including his Ayrshire properties.

The Montgomerie-Cuninghames divided their time between the family residence, Kirkbride House in Ayrshire, their home in London and other estates in the Home Counties, with the result that the 325-acre Southfield mansion and estate, described in one 1851 advertisement as "a fine old commodious house" standing "in a lawn of rich old pasture, surrounded with fine old timber", were regularly rented out. When Sir Thomas died at his Hyde Park residence in 1870, his widow Charlotte was his main beneficiary, inheriting all his personal effects including his estates in Buckinghamshire and elsewhere in England.

The last tenant of Southfield was shipbuilder Arnold James Henderson (1876-1913). His father, John Henderson, was instrumental in establishing the Anchor Line, a leading transatlantic emigrant carrier with a network of services from the Mediterranean to New York, as well as up to three sailings per week on its Clyde-Northern Ireland-New York service. It was also a major operator in the Glasgow-Liverpool-Mediterranean and Glasgow-Liverpool-India trades. Henderson, a director in the family firm, died at Southfield House on 6th March, 1913. That year Glasgow Corporation paid £17,000 to Lady Cuninghame's trustees for Southfield House and its policies, together with the neighbouring farms of Hazelden Head, Westfield, Eastfield and Langrig, with a view to establishing a sanitarium and hospital for children at risk from non-pulmonary tuberculosis, a scourge which often flourished in large, densely populated cities at this time. The stimulus for the authority's action was the National Health Insurance Act of 1911, which provided a substantial government contribution towards the costs of hospital construction and maintenance. The original plan was to keep Southfield House as an administrative building and to build accommodation for 300 beds for children and 160 sanatorium beds for adults. Building operations were delayed by the First World War, however, and by the end of hostilities the condition of the mansion had deteriorated to the extent that it had to be demolished in 1919.

In 1921 Glasgow Corporation's Public Health Department began construction of the hospital on 78 acres of the Southfield site. When Mearnskirk Hospital opened on 9 May, 1930, at an estimated cost of £400,000, it had 500 beds for children under 15. Parliamentary records show that in 1932

the weekly cost of a patient at Mearnskirk was just under three pounds and fifteen shillings. During the Second World War children were evacuated to the Garrison Hospital, Millport, and Mearnskirk was used firstly as an Emergency Medical Service Hospital and later as a Naval Auxiliary Hospital. It never subsequently regained its role as a hospital primarily for children, and in 1946 the Surgical Thoracic Unit was opened. When improvements in child health and advances in medical practice saw tuberculosis became less prevalent, the hospital diversified, admitting children with long-term orthopaedic conditions and making beds available for any outbreak of infantile paralysis. A showcase hospital in a prime rural location, Mearnskirk attracted a host of visitors and entertainers, including stars of stage and screen, among them Judy Garland, Danny Kaye, Dorothy Lamour, Roy Rogers and Terry Thomas. In 1959 the status of the hospital was changed from sanitarium to general hospital, and its cardio-thoracic service came to be recognised as the principal cardio-thoracic referral centre for the southwest of Scotland. By the late 1980s, however, Mearnskirk was operating solely as a geriatric unit.

Greater Glasgow Health Board decided on the closure of the hospital in July, 1990, as part of its plans for rationalising services. Most of the Mearnskirk complex was closed, to be demolished two years later. In 1995 Bryant Homes negotiated the purchase of the hospital grounds and buildings from Greater Glasgow Health Board, and led a consortium of developers, including John Dickie Homes and Stewart Milne Homes, in building 261 houses and 107 flats in the Mearnskirk Hospital development. A long-term continuing care hospital, Mearnskirk House, was opened on the hospital site in 1998.

# Stamperland

Stamperland, about four miles south of Glasgow, formed part of the old lands of Midlee, which were acquired in the 1660s by James Maxwell and combined with surrounding lands including Netherlee and Bogton to form the estate of Williamwood. The Maxwell family wealth, derived from their extensive arable farmlands, was augmented in the 18th century by the coal mines and lime quarries opened to exploit the estate's mineral resources. Williamwood limestone in particular, used for cement and building purposes, was noted for its excellent quality. Coal mining ceased on the estate in 1822, to be replaced as a source of income by quarrying, as the Stewart family, who had acquired Williamwood in 1817, joined the ranks of local landowners turning a profit from providing local sandstone to meet the Glasgow building boom. In 1859 Bishopbriggs builder Francis Brown, leasee of the Colston quarry in the north of the city, opened the Williamwood quarry, which quickly joined the quarries of Orchard, Braidbar and New Braidbar as a major producer of Giffnock

sandstone. Around three years later Brown built a large villa adjacent to the farmhouse on the 93-acre Stamperland farm, which straddled the Glasgow to Busby turnpike road. Brown vacated Stamperland House around 1872, while continuing to hold the lease of the quarry. In 1875 Stamperland House and one and a half acres of policies were purchased by the bedding manufacturer Catherine McCrae, whose Camlachie works employed over 100 people making beds and iron bedsteads. Catherine McCrae lived at Stamperland until her death in 1906.

Stamperland House was acquired in 1910 by Robert Paterson, a partner in R. Paterson and Sons, manufacturing chemists and "sole proprietors" of Camp Coffee. The firm had been founded in 1849 by his grandfather Robert Paterson (1820-1874), who provided preservatives, essential items for Victorian households in the days before refrigeration. After his son Campbell joined the business in 1868, it began to diversify into sauces, ketchup and fruit wines, and eight years later, following the death of its founder, the family business launched the first instant coffee: Camp Coffee, an essence of coffee-beans, chicory and sugar poured from a distinctive, square, eight and a half fluid-ounce glass bottle, rather like the HP Sauce bottle. Camp Coffee is believed to have originated following a request to Campbell Paterson from the Gordon Highlanders for a coffee drink that could be used easily by armies in the field in India, the regular process of grinding and brewing coffee beans considered too time-consuming for a military field kitchen. Camp Coffee was produced in Paterson's Charlotte Street factory in Glasgow, built in 1891, and the product proved so popular that three large additions had to be made to the structure between 1893 and 1908. The label of the product is said to bear the portrait of the Victorian military hero Major-General Sir Hector MacDonald, known as 'Fighting Mac' for his exploits at the battle of Omdurman, which were said to have saved Kitchener from embarrassment. A crofter's son who rose to the top of his profession and earned a knighthood, MacDonald shot himself in a Paris hotel in 1903 following a whispering campaign insinuating inappropriate conduct with young men.

Robert Paterson had moved from his home in Orpington back to Glasgow in 1909 when his father turned the family firm into a private limited company. In the fourteen years following his purchase of Stamperland House he steadily built up his land holding in the area, buying small parcels of land as they became available. A noted cattle breeder, in 1923 he turned his attention to the breeding of Clydesdale horses, founding that year the award-winning Stamperland Stud on his lands. Deciding for health reasons to make Stonehurst in Sussex his home, he sold his Stamperland estate, then around 110 acres, to Glasgow builder James Wright in 1924, and instructed his trustees to disperse his stud. Wright planned to use the land for a housing development on the garden city model. By this time the area was becoming accessible to Glaswegians looking for homes in the country. Clarkston station, on the Glasgow to Busby railway line, had opened in 1866, and in August, 1921, Glasgow's tramway system was extended outside the city boundary climbing from Muirend, through Netherlee and Stamperland, to Clarkston. Stamperland House, described at the time as "a small but convenient house, with attractive garden and policies and home farm", was occupied by Wright, who continued Paterson's legacy of dairy farming and cattle breeding. His plans for 500-600 semi-detached houses on the land were approved in September, 1929, and his garden suburb was well under way when he died in 1933. His trustees disposed of the Stamperland herd in October that year, and in 1935 sold his undeveloped Stamperland lands to the builder and developer John Lawrence, who immediately demolished Stamperland House and began to lay out a housing estate of terraced and semi-detached villas. A three-apartment terraced house could be had for £400, payable by means of a £22 deposit and a 25-year mortgage at fifteen shillings a week, whilst a semi-detached villa was available for £430, or a cash payment of £24 and repayments of sixteen shillings and threepence per week for 25 years. The farm buildings were used by Lawrence while erecting the terraced homes in Stamperland.

The last owner-occupant of Stamperland House, which was situated where Orchy Gardens now stands in the middle of the Oval, was Wright's son James Moffat Vennard Wright. The bungalow which presently stands in Stamperland Gardens, in the hollow below the edge of Stamperland Hill, was formerly the gatehouse to Stamperland House. Stamperland farmstead survived until the 1940s.

Williamwood quarry had a relatively brief existence and had gone out of production by the turn of the century. The Glasgow Camp Coffee works closed in the 1970s and Camp Coffee is now produced in Paisley by the company's present owners McCormick Foods who, in response to criticism from campaigners that it perpetuated racial stereotypes, changed the bottle label to show a Sikh soldier sitting drinking Camp Coffee with an army officer, as opposed to standing serving the coffee to a seated officer.

# Thornliebank

The 105-acre lands of Brocklees formed part of the extensive Eastwood estate sold off in 1810 by Hugh Montgomerie, 12th Earl of Eglinton, to pay for his ruinously expensive projects in Ayrshire. In 1829 Dugald Bannatyne (1755-1842) acquired a 27-acre parcel of Brocklees, comprising the grounds and farm of Birkenshaw Cottage, and soon after constructed a modest residence on the site. An accountant by profession, Bannatyne was also a merchant, a hosiery manufacturer, and a property developer who played a principal role in the development of Glasgow's New Town. Recognising the growing prosperity of the city and its rapid increase in population, in 1786 he helped to form the Glasgow Building Company, 'for the purpose of erecting a class of houses designed to meet more fully the growing wants of prosperous city merchants'. The company went on to build most of George Square, Brunswick Street, John Street, and Hutcheson Street. A prominent figure in Glasgow business circles, Bannatyne was a long-serving secretary of the Chamber of Commerce and Postmaster of Glasgow. He lived mainly in Glasgow, and between 1832 and 1835 the 2-storey, 7-room mansion on his Birkenshaw Cottage estate was leased by local industrialist John Crum.

In 1839 John Smith, the next tenant of Birkenshaw Cottage, paid Bannatyne £3,000 for the property. A native of Alloa, Smith, who had collaborated with architect David Hamilton in the construction of Glasgow's Royal Exchange Square, built another mansion south-east of Bannatyne's house, and by 1841 his family and that of his son James were living at Birkenshaw House and Birkenshaw Cottage respectively. James Smith (1806-63), an architect and builder, had married David Hamilton's daughter Janet in 1833, and took over his father's construction business about 1837. His eldest daughter Madelcine was to achieve notoriety in her celebrated trial in 1857, when accused of poisoning her Jersey lover, Pierre L'Angelier. The Smiths went bankrupt in 1843, probably due to sluggish sales in the Royal Exchange development, and the Birkenshaw property was sold in 1844 for £4,250 to Glasgow merchant John Slater, following whose death in February, 1848, the estate was put on the market with an asking price of £4,500. In May, 1852, it was acquired by J. and W. Crum, owners of the Thornliebank textile mills and dye and calico print-works, which had become the largest of its kind in the country under the management of Walter Crum (1796-1867), who pioneered the application of chemistry to calico printing, earning academic and social distinction in the process. He was elected a Fellow of the Royal Society in 1844, president of Glasgow's Philosophical Society in 1852, and served as president of Anderson's University from 1847 to 1865. When he failed to secure the required investment for his original plan for a paper mill on the site, Walter Crum decided to make Birkenshaw his family home. In 1858 he commissioned architect Charles Wilson to modify and expand Smith's mansion, which he renamed Thornliebank House, although for some time it was also known as Rouken, after the Rockend Mill on the banks of the nearby Auldhouse Burn. When Prince Albert visited Crum's Thornliebank works in October, 1863, for example, the Glasgow Herald noted that "preparations for lunch were made at the Rouken, the hospitable mansion of Mr. Crum." By this time the Crums had accumulated many properties in the area, including the lands of Davieland on the west side of the Glasgow to Kilmarnock Road and Wood Farm on the north side of the Thornliebank to Busby Road.

Walter Crum died in May, 1867, leaving an estate valued at £29,919, and his eldest son Alexander Crum (1828–1893) succeeded to the property, which he improved and extended. Between 1872 and 1875 he carried out significant alterations to the house to designs by architect Alfred Waterhouse, and built a new stable complex, which incorporated Birkenshaw Cottage. Although retiring by nature, he had a high public profile, being Liberal MP for Renfrewshire (1880-1885), a Renfrewshire county councillor, chairman of Eastwood School Board, and a director of both the Caledonian Railway Company and of the Union Bank. A significant benefactor to the local village, Alexander Crum died suddenly on the platform of Thornliebank railway station on 23 August, 1893, when waiting for the 10.09 train to Glasgow. He left an estate valued at £106,603. The following year the 350-acre Thornliebank estate was put on the market but failed to attract a buyer. William George Crum (1836-1926), who had spent most of his adult life in England managing the Manchester branch of the family firm, followed his brother and eventually disposed of the property in 1904. 190 acres, comprising the lands of Davieland and Wood Farm, were sold for £22,000 to the trustees of Hutcheson's Hospital for feuing. The mansion house, cottage and 136 acres of land were purchased for £24,000 by politician and philanthropist Archibald Cameron Corbett (1856-1933), Liberal MP for Tradeston and occupant of Thornliebank House since 1898, who donated them to Glasgow for a public park. Two years later Cameron Corbett (later Lord Rowallan), who made his money chiefly in property development in Ilford and Eltham in London, gifted the city the 14,740-acre Ardgoil estate on Loch Long. An active temperance campaigner, a stipulation of both donations was a prohibition on the sale of alcohol for all time.

On May 25, 1906, Rouken Glen Park, the name agreed by Glasgow Corporation, was formally opened to the public and rapidly became a popular destination for day-trips, family picnics and works outings, especially as the Corporation extended the city's tramway network to the park gates that year. Tearooms were opened in the mansion and the cottage to cater for visitors. Various uses for the mansion were considered at the time. A Glasgow School Board recommendation that it be used as a home and school for crippled children was rejected in 1907, and a proposal to house Glasgow's first zoo on the site was dropped with the outbreak of the First World War, during which plans to turn the mansion into a general hospital were abandoned due to the costs of required alterations. Instead the mansion was used to accommodate Belgian refugees, for whom Glasgow Corporation was the distributing authority in Scotland. The people of Glasgow and the West of Scotland were able to enjoy the amenity of the park in the interlude between the wars, but in May, 1940, the park was requisitioned by the War Office and the mansion and other buildings provided residential and office accommodation for the army while the parkland was used for military exercises. The condition of Thornliebank House deteriorated significantly, and in the absence of any interest or investment in the post-war period it was demolished by Glasgow Corporation Parks Department in July, 1965. Birkenshaw Cottage, however, continues to stand inside the main gates of the park, which is now managed by East Renfrewshire Council, Glasgow City Council having leased it in 1984 to Eastwood District Council for 125 years.

# Barochan

## 3

### Houston, Inchinnan and Erskine

*Barochan*

*Blackstone*

*Burnbrae*

*Craigends*

*Eastbank*

*Linwood*

*Park*

*Southbar*

*Walkinshaw*

*Wester Rossland*

For six centuries Barochan, situated north-east of the village of Houston, was the family seat of the Flemings, one of the principal families of Renfrewshire. William Fleming of Barochan, James IV's sheriff of Lanark, was slain at the battle of Flodden in 1513 with his six sons. Towards the end of the 16th century a tower house was built on the lands by Janet Sempill, widow of Alexander Fleming, to replace an original structure which had been accidently destroyed by fire. This tall square tower, retained when the house was considerably extended and improved during the 18th and 19th centuries, extended twenty feet above the rest of the house to dominate the centre of the structure.

Malcolm Fleming (1745-1819), who saw military service before inheriting Barochan in 1766, had to sell part of the property to pay the debts left by his father. In 1780 Fleming, later to become a colonel of a volunteer regiment and a magistrate, married Elizabeth, eldest daughter of William Fergusson of Doonholm in Ayrshire. He sold a further part of the Barochan estate to Archibald Speirs of Elderslie in 1818, and died in November the following year, to be succeeded by his son William Malcolm Fleming, who had earlier been a judge in the Bengal Civil Service. A pioneer of agricultural chemistry, he was noted for his estate improvements. Fleming, a bachelor, lived at Barochan with his three unmarried sisters, who created a bit of a stir in 1840 when they voluntarily renounced annual pensions of £49 which they had been receiving since 1792 because of their father's military service. This may have had to do with their brother coming into money. William Fleming was an executor of the will of Henry Douglas of Patna in Bengal, a life-long employee of the East India Company, who died in 1839 leaving £155,000. If Fleming benefited from his friend's estate, this may help to explain the improvements made to Barochan House in the 1840s.

Fleming died in 1852 and Barochan became the responsibility of his sisters. When the sole surviving sister Catherine, the last of the Flemings of Barochan, died in November, 1863, at the age of 78, the property passed to a distant relative, William Charles Stewart Fleming Hamilton of Craighlaw in Wigtonshire, from whom it was purchased by John Charles Cuninghame of Craigends.

The 1,125-acre Barochan estate was subsequently purchased from Cuninghame in May, 1895, by Charles Bine Renshaw (1848-1918), the sitting tenant at Barochan since 1883, who at the same time purchased the nearby 883-acre Boghall estate. Between 1895 and early 1897 Renshaw extensively rebuilt Barochan House to plans by Edinburgh architect Charles Stewart Still Johnston. While carefully preserving the older features of the house, including the vaulted cellars and kitchen, the tower with its turnpike stair, and a priest's hiding-place, Johnston added a large block of buildings on the north side, comprising an entrance hall, kitchen, upper hall, billiard-room, and suites of bedrooms. The new entrance courtyard was enclosed on two sides by a massive, red sand-stone balustrade. Renshaw, in addition, erected a new gate lodge and gates, and an ornamental stone bridge over the burn which flowed through the grounds.

The son of an extensive landowner in his native Sussex, Charles Bine Renshaw migrated north in 1868 to join Arthur Francis Stoddard, who had acquired Elderslie's Glenpatrick Carpet Factory in 1862. When his main American market was threatened by punishing import duties, Stoddard began searching for new markets for his products and in 1870 Renshaw travelled across Europe establishing new agencies, returning home in 1872 to marry Stoddard's daughter and take his place as a partner in the firm. Following Stoddard's death ten years later, Renshaw took control of the company and began supplying other export markets, especially Australia, New Zealand, and South Africa. Renshaw, who took the firm public in 1894 with himself as chairman, was very active in both business and public affairs. He was chairman of the Caledonian Railway Company and a director of the Callander and Oban, and Cathcart Railway Companies. When the Education Act was passed in 1872, he was elected a member and later chairman of the Abbey School

Board of Paisley. He became a member of Renfrew County Council in 1899 and served as convener of the council and chairman of its Committees on Secondary Education and Technical Education. Later he was to be the first chairman of the Association of County Councils in Scotland. Conservative MP for the Western Division of Renfrewshire (1892-1906), Renshaw received a baronetcy in 1903, taking the title Renshaw of Coldharbour after the paternal estate in Sussex. Latterly Renshaw divided his time between his Cadogan Square residence in London, Coldharbour, Garvock Lodge in Greenock and Barochan, where he died in March, 1918, leaving an estate valued at £154,427.

Barochan was purchased in 1924 by Charles Millington Collins (1876-1942), chairman of Edward Collins and Son at the Kelvindale Paperworks in Glasgow. A breeder of cattle and horses and an enthusiastic agrarian improver, Collins was a well-known figure in Scottish agricultural and sporting circles and attained national celebrity in 1930 as the purchaser of the 10,000-acre Ben Lomond estate on Loch Lomondside. He lived at Barochan until his death in 1942. In February of the following year the 800-acre property was acquired by the well-known jeweller Matthew Maclaren Henderson (1861-1947), founder of M.M. Henderson which had branches across Scotland. Henderson at the time also owned two Glasgow restaurants, the Angus Restaurant in Argyle Street and the Ca'd'oro in Union Street, which he acquired in 1943, dropping the licence and turning it into an alcohol-free establishment. Henderson used the three Barochan farms to supply his restaurants with milk, vegetables and flowers. Due to general decay and dry rot most of Barochan House, including the square tower, was demolished around 1947, when the remainder of the house was renovated. The Hendersons continued to occupy Barochan until its sale in 1998.

# Blackstone

The lands of Blackstone were situated about two miles north-west of Paisley on an extensive plain on the west banks of the Black Cart River. In pre-Reformation times they belonged to the Abbey of Paisley and George Shaw, the Abbot of Paisley, built a summer residence here in the reign of James III. With the secularisation of church property which followed the Reformation, Blackstone came into the possession of the Maxwell family in the first half of the seventeenth century. Catherine, daughter of John Maxwell of Blackstone, married Alexander Napier, grandson of John Napier of Merchiston, the renowned mathematician and inventor of logarithms, and in this way the property passed to the Napiers who occupied the lands until 1843.

Captain Alexander Napier of the Scots Greys succeeded to the lands early in the 18th century. After the old house was accidentally destroyed by fire in 1730, Napier constructed on the site a substantial pavilion-roofed, south-facing mansion, and surrounded it with trees, extensive orchards and ornamental grounds. Napier paid the price for his loyalty to the Hanoverian cause during the 1745 Rebellion, when he commanded a party of county militia to harass the rebel army. On Prince Charles' retreat north in 1745 a raiding party of between 200 and 300 soldiers was despatched to Blackstone from Glasgow, where Charles' army was stationed. Anticipating their arrival, Napier drove his cattle to hideaways in the hills around Lochwinnoch, hid the house valuables and made himself scarce. After demanding six tons of hay and a large quantity of corn from Napier's wife, the Highlanders plundered the house before returning to Glasgow.

Napier died in 1750. At this time the Blackstone estate comprised Over and Nether Blackstone, Middleton, Linwood and part of Candren. His son Alexander extended and improved the lands, replacing a portion of Blackstone Moss with a fir plantation. On his death in 1801 the estate passed to his eldest son, Colonel Alexander Napier, a career soldier who saw service in various parts of the globe. He became

Lieutenant-Colonel of the 92nd Regiment in Egypt in 1801, and was killed at Corunna in 1809. His brother William Napier succeeded to Blackstone. More interested in business than a military career, he was a partner in a company which began to build one of the largest cotton-spinning mills in the country on his Linwood lands in 1792. He was also principal partner in William Napier and Company, otherwise known as the Renfrewshire Bank, a small private bank founded in 1802 with its head offices in Greenock. After prospering for a brief period it began to lose business to competitors and was sequestrated in 1842 with debts of £226,545. The following year Napier was obliged to sell Blackstone, which was acquired by Thomas Speir of nearby Burnbrae. Thomas Speir (1801-74) and his brother Robert had established the Glasgow merchant and manufacturing firm R. and T. Speir around 1822, and had a close connection with the London-based Cockerell, Trail and Company, which was heavily involved in the East India trade. While young men they went to India where they enjoyed considerable commercial success which permitted them on return to Scotland to invest part of their new-found wealth in property, Thomas in Blackstone, and Robert in the purchase of the estate of Culdees in Perthshire. Blackstone House was leased out by Speir, who lived at Burnbrae House, and was occupied until around 1856 by Robert Robertson, Sheriff-Substitute of Glasgow. Matthew Wilson, the factor on the Blackstone estates, was the tenant from 1857 until his death in 1875.

Speir made lots of improvement to the Blackstone estate, including around 1855 turning 130 acres of Blackstone Moss into arable land. He also began the exploitation of the mineral properties of his estates. In 1872 he leased a large portion of the minerals to William Black and Sons of Airdrie, who formed the Blackstone Mineral Company to work the ironstone, coal and shale on the land. Leases for working shale, coal and fire clay were also granted to James Liddell and Company of the East Fulton Oilworks. By 1875 the estate was taking in £1,479 annually in lordship from minerals. This development had a significant impact on the amenity of the lands, however, with the orchards and plantations giving way to the detritus of mining. Speir was very active in public affairs, and was convenor of the County of Renfrew from 1865 until 1874. On his death Blackstone was inherited by his nephew, Robert Thomas Napier Speir of Culdees and Burnbrae (1841-1922). The Napier in his name was that of his mother Mary Napier, eldest daughter of Sir William Milliken-Napier of Milliken. Robert Speir was actively involved with the Scottish Episcopal Church, and for forty years was chairman of its Executive Committee and Home Mission Board. As an amateur architect, moreover, he was responsible for designing a number of small Episcopalian churches across Scotland. He died at Culdees in April, 1922, following which his trustees began to dispose of the Blackstone estate.

Blackstone House and policies were acquired in 1930 by Glasgow accountant Alexander Wilson who converted the mansion into apartments for leasing. It later lay unoccupied for a period before coming into the possession of James Pinkerton, who demolished the house in 1939 to expand the turkey farming business he established on the site. His brother George, a farmer at Houston and a member of the Glasgow auxiliary air squadron, received the Distinguished Flying Cross for shooting down a German plane over the Firth of Forth in the first air raid in Scotland on 16th October, 1939. Blackstone Farm closed after James Pinkerton's son John failed to block a runway extension at Glasgow Airport in 1972. Blackstone House was located directly south of the redundant farm buildings of Blackstone Mains Farm on Blackstone Road.

# Burnbrae

Burnbrae, situated opposite Linwood on the south bank of the Black Cart River, east of the Old Patrick Water, came into the possession of the Speir family early in the 18th century and remained in the family for almost two hundred years. Farming was the foundation of the estate economy but the fortunes of the family were transformed by the sons of the third laird of Burnbrae, Robert Speir (1752-1841). His eldest son William ventured to India where he became a founding partner in the merchant firm Groves, Speir and Company, based in Calcutta. Back in Scotland his younger brothers Robert Speir (1801-53) and Thomas Speir (1801-74) were forming the manufacturing firm R. and T. Speir in Glasgow around 1822. During the 1820s they began to work closely with the London firm Cockerell, Trail and Company which was extensively involved in trade with the East Indies and was turning its attention to the export of British manufactures. With an obvious eye for an opportunity, the brothers ended up in Calcutta in the late 1820s working with their brother William. Robert owned a silk print-works, where he

experimented with indigo and various other dyes, while Thomas, considered an expert in chemicals, had a dyeing factory. The brothers were to become bit players in the greatest mercantile collapse in Indian history in 1830, when the giant of the East India trade, John Palmer and Company, which traded with Britain and the whole of south-east Asia and dominated the opium trade, was liquidated with debts of £2.8 million. Cockerell, Trail and Company, owed £400,000 by Palmer, foreclosed on the debt and precipitated the collapse. Robert Speir was able to organise credit worth £100,000 in Glasgow to enable Cockerell and Trail to sustain its Scottish business during this crisis. A combination of private enterprise and agency work for Cockerell and Trail ensured lucrative returns for the Speir brothers, all of whom were shareholders in the Bengal Bonded Warehouse Association, founded in 1838.

Around 1838 the brothers returned to Britain, richly rewarded for their Indian endeavours. William opted for life in Brighton while Robert and Thomas returned to Burnbrae where their Indian wealth paid for Burnbrae House in the late 1830s. Built on the site of an earlier house and enclosed by woodlands and landscaped gardens, it was a Gothic-style structure with a turreted roof, stone-carved balustrades, pillared porches, bay windows and balconies.

Robert Speir, an original member of the Glasgow East Indian Association, founded in 1829 to promote free trade with the East Indies, married Mary, daughter of Sir William Milliken Napier of Milliken, at Burnbrae in 1839. He succeeded to Burnbrae on the death of his father two years later. In 1842 he purchased the 1,629-acre Culdees estate, 4 miles from Crieff, for around £50,000. Active in public life and a director of both the National Fire and Life Insurance Company of Scotland and the Scottish Central Railway Company, Robert Speir died in 1853 at Burnbrae, which was placed in the trust of his brother Thomas, who had earlier employed some of his Indian capital purchasing the Blackstone estate near Burnbrae in 1843. Thomas Speir fully exploited the Burnbrae lands, opening up a freestone quarry at East Fulton in 1854, reclaiming about 40 acres of bog-land for farming in 1860 and leasing the mineral rights to coal and oil shale on the property to Glasgow coal-master James Anderson in 1866. Speir shared Burnbrae House with a number of his sisters and his nephew Robert Thomas Napier Speir, his brother Robert's only son, who succeeded to Burnbrae on reaching his majority in 1860, and to Blackstone on his uncle's death in 1874, giving him possession of 1,527 acres of land in Renfrewshire. Robert Thomas Napier Speir (1841-1922) of the Culdees, Blackstone and Burnbrae, was a captain in the 4th Battalion, Argyll and Sutherland Highlanders, prior to inheriting the estates. A church architect when not administering his huge estates, he built several small Episcopal churches in Scotland, including St. Mary the Virgin in Bridge of Weir. A stained-glass window to his memory can be found in Paisley Abbey.

The Speir family residential connection with Burnbrae ended with the death of Agnes Speir at Burnbrae House in 1886. The property was later occupied by the widow of Robert Kerr of Crookston, who lived there until around 1902. Her daughter Bertha married William Hodge Coats of the Paisley thread-making dynasty at Burnbrae in 1891. Burnbrae House was occupied in the years prior to the First World War by the widow of farmer and horse-breeder Walter B. Longton. Robert Speir's eldest son Guy Thomas Speir (1875-1951) preferred life in North Berwick to Linwood or Perthshire. A lawyer by profession, he was Private Secretary to the Secretary for Scotland (1899-1905) and Chief Conservative Agent for Scotland (1906-11) before serving in the British Expeditionary Force in the early stages of the Great War, becoming Lieutenant-Colonel of the 6th Battalion, South Staffordshire Regiment. The Burnbrae estate passed in 1930 to his son Robert Cecil Talbot Speir (1904-80), later a wing commander in the Royal Air Force Volunteer Reserve.

Burnbrae House, situated north of Burnbrae Bridge to the west of Burnbrae Road, was demolished around 1940 and the site was later occupied by the carpark of Rootes Motors, which produced automobiles at Linwood from 1963 until 1981.

Early in 2010 the supermarket chain Tesco uncovered the Speir family vault in an old parish church hall which it was planning to demolish to build a new store, as part of the regeneration of the former Linwood Shopping Centre. The crypt contained the remains of five members of the Speir family in lead-lined coffins. The store was given authority to open the vault and remove the corpses for cremation and re-interment near the family home in North Berwick.

# Craigends

The estate of Craigends, near the village of Houston, given in 1479 by the first Earl of Glencairn, Alexander Cuninghame, to his second son William Cuninghame, was held in direct succession by the same family until the 20th century. The original Craigends mansion was probably built around this time and stood for nearly four centuries on the banks of the River Locher.

The estate was almost lost to the family in the 18th century. When William Cuninghame (d.1765) succeeded as 10th laird in 1742, he found the Craigends estate irretrievably embarrassed, the result of his father Alexander Cuninghame standing surety for the bad debts of his father-in-law, John Houston of Houston, who had died in 1722. The family fortunes were restored by Alexander Cuninghame's second wife, Katherine Campbell, who recovered the property for the family by purchasing it at a judicial sale. She was a sister of Sir James Campbell,

the West Indian plantation owner and merchant who had acquired the neighbouring Houston estate around 1730, and of Agnes Campbell, who had married Alexander Cuninghame's brother William. After Sir James Campbell's death in 1731, his 3,500-acre Grandvale sugar plantation in Jamaica came in due course to his sisters and so into the possession of the Cuninghame family, who enjoyed its revenues well into the 19th century. William Cuninghame, who extended the boundaries of Craigends, went on to work coal and lime on the estate, opened quarries, the stone from which he used around 1760 to build stables and house offices, planted trees on the south side of the River Locher and enclosed his land. His eldest son Alexander (1756-1790), the 11th laird, who married a daughter of William MacDowall of Garthland and Castle Semple, continued his father's improvements, creating a fine orchard and 3-acre garden in 1777, adding more trees and, curiously, planting five acres of tobacco.

In 1858 William Cuninghame, the 15th laird of Craigends, sold the estate to his uncle Alexander Cuninghame (1804-66), who demolished the original house, having decided it was unsuitable for a man of his wealth and position, and replaced it fifty metres to the south with a modern mansion, designed extravagantly in Scottish Baronial style by David Bryce using local Craigends stone. Cuninghame had made his fortune in iron and steel. In 1838, in partnership with James Merry, he established the Carnbroe Iron Works, just as railway mania, with its relentless demand for iron and steel, began to sweep Britain. Their purchase of the Glengarnock Iron Works in Ayrshire five years later was the prelude to a rapid expansion which saw the iron and steel works of Merry and Cuninghame, with their linked colleries and ironstone pits, become the most extensive in Scotland. Religion preoccupied Cuninghame in his later years. He maintained a large staff of missionaries for various projects, held religious services on the Craigends lawn nearly every Sunday afternoon and donated generously to a range of religious and charitable causes. At the time of his death it was estimated that he had a personal fortune of £600,000, exclusive of his extensive property portfolio.

His son John Charles Cuninghame (1851-1917) was the 17th and last laird of Craigends. He became actively involved in the running of his father's company in 1876 and consolidated his control when buying out his partner's share for £250,000, just before James Merry died in 1877. He was to remain chairman and managing director of Merry and Cuninghame and of the Glengarnock Iron and Steel Company for most of his life. Railways were a key factor in the success of the firm and Cuninghame became a director of the Glasgow and South Western Railway, the South Yorkshire Junction Railway and the Lanarkshire and Ayrshire Railway companies. Actively interested in politics, he served two terms with Renfrewshire County Council but failed in three attempts to enter Westminster. He shared the Cuninghame's voracious appetite for land. To the estates of Craigends, Walkinshaw, Crosslee, Barochan, Clippens and the 13,000-acre Upper Foyers in Inverness, all of which he inherited from his father, he added in 1876 the 7,438-acre

Dunragit estate in Wigtonshire, for which he paid £241,000, and in 1877 Boghall, near Craigends, which cost him £40,000. A major in the Renfrewshire militia and a noted breeder of Clydesdale horses, he lived at Craigends only intermittently. When not commuting between his Mayfair residence and his Scottish estates, he was travelling extensively in Europe, Australia, China, and Japan.

In 1901 he married his cousin Alison Pearson, a widow, but died childless in London in January, 1917. His estate, valued at £817,500, was placed in trust, and his widow awarded life-rent of Craigends. His trustees tried to off-load the property in 1927, when they unsuccessfully offered Craigends's 586 acres for £22,500 to the governors of the West of Scotland Agricultural College, who were looking to concentrate all college activities on a rural site near Glasgow. Except for a period during and shortly after World War II, when the estate was requisitioned for army use, Mrs Cuninghame lived in the mansion with her sister Helen Laura Pearson until her death in November, 1959. Following Miss Pearson's death in 1961, the house contents were sold by auction. In the absence of a buyer the property then lay vacant and neglected, and local people were given freedom to access the house and grounds. Taylor Woodrow acquired Craigends for housing around 1970 and as building began in 1971 the old mansion, then derelict and vandalised, was demolished, despite local demands for its retention and inclusion in the new housing development. The front entrance was left standing, only to be deemed dangerous and demolished in 1980. By this time Taylor Woodrow had completed more than 500 houses on their Craigends estate.

Little remains of the grandeur of Craigends, bar a stone archway now situated in nearby Cuninghame Gardens and the Craigends Lion, a stone figure from the structure, now repositioned at the entrance to Houston's Carrick Centre.

# Eastbank

Gleddoch formed part of the barony of Finlaystone-Maxwell, alias Newark, which was confirmed in the possession of Sir Patrick Maxwell by royal charter in 1670. The 750-acre Gleddoch estate, which included the lands of Langbank, subsequently came into the possession of William Hamilton of Wishaw, from whom it was purchased in 1795 by Thomas King (1772-1802), youngest son of Port Glasgow merchant and ship-owner James King of Drums (1725-1809), who was also a founding partner in Port Glasgow's first sugar refinery built in 1777. Thomas King, an advocate who had a fortune independent of his father, built Eastbank House shortly after on the lands of Easter Langbank on the south bank of the Clyde opposite Dumbarton. He was already a landowner in the county, having inherited the estate of Millbank on the death of his elder brother Matthew in 1793. He increased his possessions further in 1801 with the purchase from John Cuninghame of Craigends of the lands of Park Erskine, lying contiguous to Drums and Millbank. By this time he had abandoned the practice of law

to give his time and attention to rural affairs and the improvement of his estates, and in 1797 had married well. His wife Christian was the daughter of the tobacco and sugar merchant John Wallace of Kelly, one of Glasgow's mercantile elite. On King's death in 1802, at the premature age of 30, his widow took their three children to live in Devonshire. His eldest son James succeeded to his properties, and also inherited Drums in 1809 on the death of his grandfather, who had outlived all of his four sons. The estates of Park Erskine, Gleddoch, Millbank, and Drums, over one thousand acres in total, of which 720 were prime arable land, were purchased for £49,000 around 1825 by the trustees of the late Duncan Darroch of Gourock (1740-1823), who had been empowered to purchase land to augment the family's property portfolio in the county.

In 1840 the Glasgow, Paisley and Greenock Railway Company, which had been established by Act of Parliament in 1837 and had bought up swathes of Darroch's land for the Paisley to Greenock stretch of the line, sold 9 acres of Easter Langbank, including Eastbank House to Glasgow solicitor Dugald John Bannatyne (1805-63), for whom it became a summer retreat. Born into a distinguished Glasgow family, his father Dugald Bannatyne was Postmaster of Glasgow as well as being a merchant, hosiery manufacturer, and a property developer who had played a significant role in the development of Glasgow's New Town in the late 18th century. Bannatyne had trained in law, and in 1830 set up business with his brother Andrew in A. and D. J. Bannatyne, later to become Bannatynes and Kirkwood, one of Glasgow's premier law firms. He developed a masterly grasp of parliamentary business and was eagerly pursued by early railway companies anxious to steer railway bills through Parliament in the 1830s and 40s. He was particularly associated with the various extensions to the Glasgow and Edinburgh, the Ayrshire and the Dumfries lines. He was also instrumental in the formation of the Clyde Navigation Trust, and was largely responsible for the Glasgow Police Act of 1862. An agent for the Western Bank, and a member of the Highland and Agricultural Company of Scotland, Bannatyne died of constipation of the bowels in December, 1863, at the family's Bath Street home in Glasgow.

Eastbank House, which featured 18 rooms, two stables, a coach house, a walled garden with a vinery and peach house, and a bowling green, then stood in just over 11 acres of well-wooded ground. It had lain vacant for three years when Bannatyne's eldest son and namesake Dugald sold the property in 1864 to the seed merchant and chemical manufacturer David Cross (1813-84), senior partner in Alexander Cross and Sons, one of the largest agricultural supply firms in Europe. The firm, founded by his father in Glasgow in 1830 to supply seeds and seed grain to British farmers, expanded over time, adding the import and manufacture of fertilisers and feedstuffs to their core business. In 1848 it pioneered the introduction of Peruvian guano (bird-droppings), the properties of which as an agricultural fertiliser were just being recognised in Britain, and quickly established an important foothold in this trade. Other fertilisers followed, such as nitrate of soda, and in 1872 the company opened an extensive chemical works at Port Dundas, Glasgow, devoted to the production of various chemical fertilisers. Cross expanded his property holdings with the purchase of the Inglestone estate near Bishopton and the Knockdon estate in Maybole. After his death at Eastbank in December, 1884, his eldest son Alexander Cross (1851-1921), a leading agriculturalist, secretary of the Highland Agricultural Society, and a noted breeder of Clydesdale horses, Border Leicester sheep and Ayrshire cattle, succeeded his father in the business. Chairman of Langbank Conservative Association (1888-1913), he purchased the estate of Horninghold near Uppingham in Leicester in 1916, where he had been tenant for the previous 20 years.

His brother Thomas Cross sold Eastbank House in 1922 to the Glasgow engineering and automobile accessory dealer George Millar Smith, from whom the property was purchased in 1947 by Alexander Rayner McCallum of Parklea Farm in Port Glasgow, who established a hotel on the premises. The mansion was gutted in a devastating fire in March, 1961, and was demolished soon after. The site remains in the ownership of the McCallum family. A flatted development now occupies the site of Eastbank House.

# Linwood

In pre-Reformation times the lands of Linwood, three and a half miles west of Paisley on the left bank of the Black Cart River, formed part of the extensive possessions of the Abbey of Paisley. After the Reformation the lands and revenues of the Abbey were secularised and erected into a temporal lordship for Lord Claud Hamilton, who was created Lord Paisley in 1587. The lordship remained in his family until 1652, when it was purchased by the Earl of Angus, who sold off most of the lands. By the end of the 18th century Linwood belonged to the Napiers of Blackstone.

In 1792 a consortium comprising William Napier, James Dunlop, James Kibble of Whiteford, Paisley manufacturer Robert Orr and his sons William and John Orr, began to build a large cotton spinning mill on a five-acre site on the banks of the Cart on Napier's lands at Linwood. Dunlop was one of the pioneers of the native cotton spinning industry. In partnership with his brother Henry he had acquired the Dovecothall Mill in Barrhead

around 1785, built the Gateside Mill nearby in 1789, the West Arthurlie Mill in 1791 and was later to be responsible for cotton mills in the Calton in Glasgow. The Linwood Mill, three hundred and forty feet long and six storeys high, each floor reaching to a height of ten feet, was one of the largest mills in the country at the time and was described as "the most splendid establishment in the cotton spinning business perhaps in Britain". Linwood House, built directly north-west of the works, became the family home for Dunlop, who managed the mill. His third son Henry Dunlop, later of Craigton, and a future provost of Glasgow, was born at Linwood House in 1799. In 1795, the year after the mill was completed, the property was put on the market. This may have been due to a recession in the industry and the fact that capacity well exceeded demand. The mill was capable of employing 1,800 workers, but for a period only 75 worked there. No buyers appear to have emerged, however. While Dunlop was still a key figure in the Linwood Cotton Mill, it burned down in December, 1801, leaving the owners significantly out of pocket, the insurance cover of £11,000 falling well below the damage valuation of £20,000. The partnership was dissolved that year and the mill again put up for sale.

By this time a village was beginning to form around the mill, which was acquired and rebuilt in 1805 by James Brown, whose Linwood Cotton Spinning Company operated the mill for over sixty years. James Brown, the principal partner, son of Matthew Brown of Crossflat in Paisley, occupied Linwood House for much of this period, making additions to the mill in 1824. Over time he was joined in the business by his brothers, Andrew Brown of Auchentorlie and Hugh Brown of Broadstone in Beith, and by John Stirling Napier of neighbouring Merchiston. The Brown family were extensive cotton spinners in the area, also owning mills at Johnstone and Elderslie. By the mid-nineteenth century, the population of Linwood had risen to around 1,400, mostly employed in cotton-spinning either at the Linwood Mill or at Henderson's smaller cotton mill, or at Paterson and Neilston's Paisley shawl factory. The Linwood Cotton Spinning Company was dissolved in 1859, after the deaths of James, Andrew and Hugh Brown. The business was carried on by the remaining partner, Alexander Malloch, who occupied Linwood House from around 1858 until 1879.

The British textile industry never recovered from the impact of the American Civil War and the Cotton Famine of the early 1860s, and the Linwood Mill was among many which suffered. In 1879 Malloch sold the property, including Linwood House and various mill-worker houses, for £16,000 to a partnership comprising George Wood Richardson of Ralston, and Storer and Sons, mill-owners at Thornhill, Johnstone. The following year Richardson bought out Storer and began to invest in an equipment upgrade. Production was clearly downscaled after 1879, because that year part of the large Linwood Mill was taken over and converted for paper production by Robert and William Watson, who had established a paper mill in Linwood six years earlier. When Richardson wound up the Linwood Cotton Spinning Company in 1894 and sold off the mill's cotton spinning equipment, the whole building, adapted for papermaking, became the property of the Watson brothers, whose firm operated on the site until the 1970s, manufacturing a wide range of paper products for industrial and commercial use, including telephone cable insulating papers, jacquard card material, linson paper, (used as a book binding material), labels and envelopes. The mill building was demolished in 2009.

Robert and William Watson lived most of their adult lives at Newfield House in Johnstone. From 1879 Linwood House was leased by a succession of businessmen, including Glasgow solicitor Samuel Marshall Thomson, a partner in the Wishaw Coal Company, from 1894 until his death in 1903. During the First World War the tenant was the research chemist Arthur Villers St.-Armande. A director in two chemical works, he was jailed for one month in 1917 for a serious assault on his wife in Linwood House, in the course of which, in a drunken stupor, he terrified her by firing a rifle and revolver and then beat her all night until exhaustion made him stop. The leniency of the sentence may have had something to do with the fact that he was apparently engaged at the time in work of national importance. Robert Watson Junior, of the Dalmarnock papermakers Brown, Stewart and Company, occupied the house from 1936 until 1939.

Linwood House, which was situated on the north side of Napier Street, was last owned in the 1970s by local coach hirer Brian Hicks. It was demolished shortly after he sold it, and the site is now occupied by a small private housing estate.

# Park

Park was situated on the south bank of the Clyde, around 3 miles north-west of Renfrew, near Inchinnan. Extending from the river to the Old Greenock Road, the property was acquired from James MacGilchrist of Northbar around 1734 by Jamaican merchant John Somerville, after whose death in 1767 it was purchased by Greenock-based West Indian merchant Colin Campbell (c.1733-1793). Campbell built Park House around 1780 and made considerable improvements on the property. After his business experienced difficulties during the American War of Independence, Campbell petitioned for bankruptcy and sold Park to textile manufacturer William Fulton, son of Humphrey Fulton (1713-79), who had pioneered silk manufacturing in Paisley. Fulton had inherited his father's business, and was to remain at Park for almost half a century. He opened freestone quarries on the Park estate around the turn of the 19th century, and this stone was used to build the 1812 bridges across the River Cart at Inchinnan. He also constructed Fulton's Quay on the river, whence large quantities of paving whinstone were shipped to Liverpool.

Fulton sold Park in 1838 for £16,200 to the businessman and philanthropist John Henderson (1780-1867). Henderson, the son of a Bo'ness merchant and ship owner, had started in business as a drysalter in Glasgow with his elder brother Robert. Subsequently they established the East India merchant business R. and J. Henderson which, based in London and Glasgow, became one of the largest businesses of its type in the country, making both brothers very wealthy in the process. In May, 1842, Robert Henderson died in a freak accident. In company with his brother, Dr. King, minister of Greyfriars' Church, and a female servant, he was landing from the river steamer *Windsor Castle* opposite Park House, when the boat carrying the party to the shore capsized following a collision with another steamer. John Henderson and Dr. King successfully reached the shore, but Robert and the servant drowned. John Henderson, with the aid of several of his nephews, carried on and expanded the family business, which became very active in South-East Asia. The firm was closely allied to the Calcutta-based agency George Henderson and Company, and was one of the British companies which put up capital to finance the operations of the Eastern Archipelago Company which in 1850, in collaboration with the first Rajah, James Brooke, secured the monopoly rights to trade between Sarawak and Britain. It was later to promote the Borneo Company, set up to exploit the metal and mineral resources of the island. By 1860 the shareholding of the Hendersons in Borneo Company Limited had grown to 35 per cent, and family members continued to hold at least one quarter of BCL shares in the period up until the First World War.

Henderson was one of those 19th century businessmen who combined commercial acumen with religious zeal. A strict Sabbatarian, he bought up most of the stock of the Edinburgh and Glasgow Railway Company and divided it among friends whom he knew would oppose the running of trains on the Sabbath. Sunday trains between Glasgow and Edinburgh only started running when the amalgamation with the North British Company in 1865 placed Henderson and his supporters in a minority. He maintained several religious newspapers, and on one occasion spent £4,000 sending every railway worker in Britain a copy of a publication denouncing the evils of Sunday work. Henderson was deeply affected by his brother's death and this was reflected in his support for various religious and charitable causes, which he personally supervised. Within his business premises he had a department for receiving aid applications and determining amounts to be granted. It is estimated it disbursed between £30,000 and £40,000 annually. From 1847 he was involved with the United Presbyterian Church, especially in their overseas work and the advancement of missions in India and on the continent. Ecumenical in outlook, he was instrumental in establishing the Evangelical Alliance, an association concerned with aligning the various Protestant denominations. He established the National Bible Society of Scotland, and bought and maintained a number of mission churches and religious buildings in and around Glasgow. Park Church and manse in Inchinnan were built by Henderson in 1849 for the Free Church Congregation who had left the parish church following the Disruption of 1843.

Henderson died childless at Park in May, 1867, following an attack of influenza, bequeathing a total of £82,750 to religious and charitable bodies. The residue of his estate was left to his nephews and nieces. The 550-acre Park estate was left to his brother's grandson, George W. Henderson (1854-1934), who worked in the family business and lived in London. John Henderson's widow continued to occupy Park until her death in 1877, following which the house furniture was auctioned off and the mansion leased to a succession of businessmen. Glasgow hemp and sail cloth manufacturer Malcolm Colquhoun Thomson, the tenant from 1890 until 1903, carried out renovations to the property. William Fleming, director of the Highland and Agricultural Society, occupied Park House from 1906 until his death in 1923, following which his family retained the tenancy.

In 1913 George Henderson, a director of the Bank of England for 27 years and chairman of the Borneo Company for 28 years, transferred Park to the banker Edward Charles Grenfell (1870-1941) on the occasion of Grenfell's marriage to his daughter Florence Emily Henderson. Grenfell had in 1904 become a partner in J. S. Morgan and Company, later renamed Morgan, Grenfell and Company to reflect his position. Like his father and grandfather before him, he was a director of the Bank of England, and was also on the boards of the Sun Assurance Group and the White Star Line. Conservative MP for the City of London from 1922 until 1935, he was raised to the peerage as Baron St Just, of St Just in Penwith in Cornwall. In 1932 Grenfell's trustees sold the Park estate to the Department of Agriculture, which had earmarked the site for a 30-plus smallholding scheme. Most of the homes vanished piecemeal as Erskine new township encroached upon the lands from 1969. The condition of the mansion deteriorated rapidly after it was vacated by the Fleming family. By 1945 it lay unoccupied. In May that year it was used by villagers to celebrate the end of the war in Europe, and was demolished the following year.

# Southbar

The 530-acre Southbar estate, located on the south side of the Old Greenock Road, one mile west of Inchinnan, was in the possession of the Maxwell family for almost three hundred years. George Maxwell, the last of the Maxwells of Southbar, built the original Southbar house in 1757. Positioned on rising ground and surrounded by fine woodland, the house commanded open views over fields and countryside. Maxwell died in 1785 with debts outstanding, and his creditors sold Southbar later that year to Boyd Alexander, recently returned from India.

Boyd Alexander (1758-1825), the third son of Claud Alexander of Newton, was typical of the young men from impoverished gentry families who travelled to India to seek their fortune. His elder brother Claud Alexander (1752-1809) had gone to Calcutta in 1771 as a clerk in the East India

Company, and progressed to the lucrative post of Military Paymaster-General. The ability of company officials to supplement meagre salaries by private trades and commissions enabled him to amass a £50,000 fortune, which he used on his return to Scotland to buy the Ballochmyle estate in Ayrshire in 1782    Boyd Alexander went out to Bengal in 1776 and two years later became Deputy Paymaster to the garrisons at Patna. The considerable reserves he accumulated enabled him upon his return home to purchase the estates of Southbar and Boghall. Active in politics, he was chosen MP for the County of Renfrew in 1796, and was returned as representative for the Glasgow burghs in 1802. Alexander was also a banker, a founding partner in the Renfrewshire Banking Company (1802). He improved both the house and grounds at Southbar, in the process creating "a most beautiful property, with an elegant mansion that overlooks the whole country". He died childless at Southbar in 1825. In August the following year Southbar House was burned down while his widow was occupying the premises. Only one wing was saved. The house was not rebuilt until 1846 when Alexander's successor, his brother Claud's eldest son, William Maxwell Alexander (1790-1853), built a new south-facing residence, comprising a three-storey main block flanked on the east by a two-storey wing and on the west by a large conservatory. Formerly a London merchant, he carried out extensive agricultural improvements at Southbar during his tenure. He inherited his father's Ballochmyle property in 1845 and died unmarried in 1853, to be succeeded in his estates by his brother Boyd Alexander (1796-1861).

Brighton-born John Hobhouse Inglis Alexander (1832-1875), second son of Boyd Alexander, inherited Southbar in 1861. A career naval officer, he had joined the Royal Navy in 1844, attaining the rank of captain. He served in the East and West Indies, in the Crimea, in China during the Opium wars and in the Japanese war, in which he was severely wounded. An aide-de-camp to Queen Victoria, he was made a Companion of the Bath and an officer of the Legion of Honour. When he died his properties were put into the trust of his brother Claud Alexander of Ballochmyle for the benefit of his children. During this time Southbar House and policies were leased to a succession of West of Scotland businessmen. James Clark of the Anchor Thread Mills in Paisley was the occupant when the mansion was partially destroyed by fire in February, 1879. The fire started in an upstairs room and was able to take hold because the fire brigades rushing from Paisley were hampered firstly by bad roads and then by an insufficient supply of water from two local streams. The east wing of the house was entirely gutted and considerable damage caused to some of the rooms in the main block. Damages, estimated at £20,000, were mainly structural, most of the furniture, plate and Clark's fine art collection being rescued. A newspaper report noted that the Paisley police and Renfrewshire constabulary were among the early arrivals at the scene, "and their services were much needed to repress the rapacity and vandalism of the crowd."

In 1897 the Southbar estate was purchased from Alexander's trustees by Robert Sutherland (1833-1924), principal partner and chairman of the distiller Bulloch, Lade and Company, which sold blended whisky mainly to the United States and Australia. He restored the mansion-house sometime after 1898 to designs by architect Robert Alexander Brydon and modernised the estate, renovating or rebuilding the farm steadings and enclosing the lands. In June, 1921, there was yet another serious fire at Southbar, which lasted for three days and totally destroyed the house. Water was pumped into the fire for 40 hours; family legend has it that the fire brigade discovered Sutherland's whisky cellar and rendered themselves incapable of dousing the flames. This time the house was not rebuilt. Instead, Sutherland, who died three years later leaving an estate valued at £133,572, built a temporary timber-framed house nearby which the family occupied until 1944, when his daughter Annie died, after which the property was sold. The ruins of Alexander's Southbar House were eventually removed around 1950, and little or no trace it remains.

The Scottish Milk Marketing Board acquired Southbar around 1948 and operated a centre for cattle breeding and artificial insemination research on the property until 1985. Stevenson's replacement Southbar House lay vacant and derelict from the late 1990s and was destroyed by fire in December, 2003, to be replaced by another private dwelling. The farm steading survives and has been converted into apartments.

# Walkinshaw

The Walkinshaw estate, which stood south of the Black Cart River near its confluence with the River Gryffe about a mile east of Houston, was in the possession of various branches of the Walkinshaw family from the middle ages until being sold in 1683 by Gavin Walkinshaw to Glasgow merchant James Walkinshaw, second son of John Walkinshaw of Barrowfield. Credited with making improvements on the property, he may have built the original Walkinshaw House, described in the early 18th century as 'one of the pleasantest seats in the county'. About 1769 his grandson James Walkinshaw sold the estate to Dr. William Miller (d.1790), the son of a Paisley minister, who had made a fortune from sugar plantations and the practice of medicine in Antigua. His nephew Alexander Millar sold the estate around 1790 to the merchant and banker Day Hort MacDowall (1753-1809) who in 1791 commissioned Robert Adam to design and build a distinctive country residence. The 36-roomed Walkinshaw House had an unusual geometric shape; it was one of the few triangular country houses built in Britain. There were five bays on the entrance front of the two-storey building, three bays each on the shorter sides, and three-storey octagonal towers at the angles of the house. In 1806 MacDowall added to his properties with the purchase for £100,000 of the Castle Semple estate from the trustees of his brother William MacDowall, who was ruined when the great West Indian firm Alexander Houston and Company went into liquidation in 1800 in one of the greatest financial collapses in Scotland's business history. Although unaffected by the reverse which befell his brother, MacDowall clearly had overreached himself, and by 1809 was having difficulty repaying the loans he had taken out to purchase Castle Semple. In July that year he drowned himself in one of the fishponds on his Castle Semple estate, following which the 900-acre Walkinshaw estate was put on the market with an asking price of £85,000.

It was purchased from MacDowall's trustees in 1811, possibly for its mineral potential, by Boyd Alexander of Southbar and Francis Redfearn of Langton Lodge in Yorkshire, colleagues from their time in the Bengal Civil Service and now business partners. Neither viewed Walkinshaw House as a potential residence and in due course the property came into the possession of Alexander's nephew William Maxwell Alexander, who also neglected the property. By 1845 it was noted that the house "has not been regularly inhabited for some time and has gone much into disrepair'. Eleven years later the iron-master Alexander Cuninghame bought Walkinshaw from Boyd Alexander for £75,000, only months before he purchased Craigends, the ancient family seat, for £38,000. He made improvements to Walkinshaw House, turning it into 'a superior dwelling house", but his home became the magnificent baronial mansion he had built by David Bryce on Craigends in 1857. Cuninghame began working ironstone on Walkinshaw in the mid-1850s. To accommodate the workers needed for his Abercorn and Douglas pits, he built a new village close by, which was named Inkerman after the British victory in the Crimean War, which was in progress at the time. When he died in 1866, he was succeeded by his son John Charles Cuninghame (1851-1917), the 17th and last laird of Craigends.   An extensive landowner, principal partner in his father's company Merry and Cuninghame, an officer in the 4th Battalion Argyll and Sutherland Highlanders, a Renfrewshire county councillor and a breeder of Clydesdale horses, in 1883 he leased the right to work the shale and ironstone from the Abercorn and Douglas fields to the Walkinshaw Oil Company, following the demise of which in 1890 he opened  another pit to the north east of the original ones, and signed contracts for the construction of a mineral railway line from Inkerman to near Walkinshaw House to serve it. Plans, however, for a new racecourse on the lands fell through in 1900, because Cuninghame failed to reach agreement with the Paisley Race Committee.

Walkinshaw House, which was approached by a magnificent avenue from a boathouse at the juncture of the Rivers Cart and Gryffe, was destined to be unloved by its owners and was leased out throughout the Cuninghames' tenure. John Weems of the Perseverance Iron Works in Johnstone was the tenant of Walkinshaw from 1868 until his death at Walkinshaw House in 1894. It was then occupied by Alison Pearson, the cousin whom John Charles Cuninghame was to marry in 1901. Walter B. Longton, a farmer and horse-breeder from Lancashire, who occupied the house from 1900 until his death in November, 1907, was probably the last private tenant of the property. In 1914 it was noted that the seeds of decay had settled on the building, which was then occupied by the mine overseer. Great yawning cracks extended from the basement to the roof, the result of underground coal workings. The mansion lay derelict and crumbling for a considerable time before being demolished in 1927.

The site of Walkinshaw House, directly west of Glasgow Airport, is currently occupied by the remains of Walkinshaw Gardens, a former farm building with a shed and walled garden.

# Wester Rossland

From the end of the 16th century until 1876 the Rodger family held title to Wester Rossland, which lay south of the village of Bishopton and, according to a 1796 map of Renfrewshire, contained a house, an old castle and the hamlets of Roslin and Roslin Town. The initial property had come into the family's possession in 1599, when a member of the Rodger family, descendants of the Rogers of Ochiltree, obtained a charter to Fergushill's Rossland (or Roslin). These lands were augmented in 1736 with the purchase of the Rossland estate of the deceased George Brisbane. Comprising the farms of Hay Hill, Long Meadows and Gladstone, this extended the Rodger's Wester Rossland estate to around 130 acres. The estate revenues derived mainly from farming, although a stone quarry was opened on the lands in the early 19th century and a tile-works at Gladstone in the 1840s, the clay on the land being considered of excellent quality for the manufacture of tiles and bricks. By the time

the Glasgow, Paisley and Greenock Railway cut across Wester Rossland in 1841, Matthew Rodger, a shareholder in the railway company, appears to have opted for life in Glasgow.

In 1845, directly west of the railway line and near the site of the old house, Rodger built a modern mansion which he immediately began to let. Wester Rossland House may be rare in the annals of country mansions in that it appears that it was never occupied by the family which built it. Among early tenants were Glasgow calico printer James Gourlie and manufacturing chemist Ernest Smith, of Paisley's Craigielea Chemical Works.

Matthew Rodger died in 1867 at the Garnethill home of his second son Robert, a Glasgow commission merchant. The Wester Rossland estate was inherited by his eldest son, the Rev. Matthew Rodger (1830-98), minister of the parish of St Leonards in St Andrews, who sold the mansion and 160 acres of land in 1876 for £22,000 to Glasgow builder Thomas Kay, who had plans to build villas on the property. Kay's ambitions for Wester Rossland appear to have been short-lived, however, for in 1882 he sold the property to William Houston, a former Glasgow merchant then operating from London.

Wester Rossland House continued to be let at this time. Its most notable tenant from around 1880 was Robert Simpson, founder of the drapery warehouse Robert Simpson and Sons, which long occupied the corner site at Jamaica Street and Argyle Street, Glasgow, and which, acquired by Fraser, Sons and Company in 1936, was amalgamated two years later with the adjoining drapery store belonging to Arnott and Company to form the business Arnott-Simpson, for a long time one of the West of Scotland's most popular stores.

Another tenant, from 1913 till at least 1933, was cotton broker Frederick Mann Hannay. Also a noted sportsman, Hannay played curling, golf and tennis, but his first sport was hockey, where his skill earned him international caps against all three of the home nations in 1903. He later became president of the Scottish Hockey Association in 1910. Hannay, who in 1914 commissioned building contractor Henry Wilson to make alterations to the property prior to his occupation, was descended from a Liverpool family of cotton dealers who had developed commercial interests in the Far East. His father Douglas Mann Hannay, a cotton broker and commission agent, was also a director of the Tenom Borneo Rubber Company, Champdany Jute Company in Calcutta, the Glasgow Cotton Spinning Company and the Consolidated Tea and Lands Company. When he died in 1929, the family home, Broom House, Newton Mearns, and 65 acres of the Broom estate were inherited by Frederick.

William Houston died at his Sussex home, Sachel Court in Horsham, in February, 1918, aged 89. In 1937 the Government began the compulsorily purchase of over 2,500 acres of farmland in the Bishopton area for a new munitions factory. In March of that year William Houston's trustees sold the 130-acre Wester Rossland estate to the Secretary of State for War. The Bishopton Royal Ordnance Factory opened over the winter of 1940/41 with a workforce of 20,000. Wester Rossland House, which stood in the grounds of the factory, was used until 1976 as a social club-house for the workers and as an events venue for the people of the village. It lay vacant thereafter. The cost of upgrading and renovating the house being considered prohibitive, the Ministry of Defence decided to demolish the mansion in 1980. An annexe continued to be used as a recreation and social club. The Bishopton Royal Ordnance Factory was privatised in 1984, and sold to British Aerospace in 1987.

*Thomas King (Eastbank)*

*John Charles Cuninghame  (Craigends)*

*John Henderson (Park)*

*Sir Charles Bine Renshaw (Barochan)*

*William MacDowall, 2nd (Castle Semple)*

*Archibald MacKenzie (Milliken)*

*Archibald W. Finlayson (Spring Grove)*

*Sir Lionel Fletcher (Muirshiel)*

# 4

## *Johnstone, Kilbarchan and Lochwinnoch*

The town of Johnstone developed on the back of the thread and cotton mills built on the banks of the Black Cart River to the north of the town. In 1825 there were about 13 mills in the Johnstone area. One of the earliest was the Cartside Mill, built in 1794 under the direction of the successful cotton spinner, Robert Burns, whose partners in the venture, William Macdowall of Garthland and George Houston of Johnstone, had earlier been responsible for a cotton mill at Lochwinnoch in 1788. A large, 6-storey building, Cartside Mill was considered one of Scotland's finest, early water-powered cotton mills. The original Cartside House, a compact 8-room structure with servants' quarters, standing a short distance east of the mill on high ground on the south bank of the Black Cart, was built about this time for the mill manager. It appears to have become a temporary home for the Napiers of Milliken after 1801, when the old house of Milliken was destroyed by fire. Colonel Robert Milliken Napier (1765-1808) made Cartside his home in 1802 on his retiral from the army. He had entered the British Army in 1779 and over the following twenty-two years saw active service in Holland, Ireland, the West Indies and India, where he commanded the siege of Mangalore. Obliged to retire from military service due to the severity of wounds received in battle, he died at Cartside House in February, 1808.

The original mill partnership, Houston, Burns and Company, was dissolved with the death of George Houston in 1815, and the mill, house and 19 acres of Cartside became the responsibility of his second son William, who operated the business as George Houston and Company. William Houston (1781-1856) lived at Johnstone Castle with his elder brother Ludovic, who had become laird in 1815, before moving into Cartside House shortly after his marriage in 1845. His eldest son George Ludovic Houston, who was to succeed his uncle as laird of

Johnstone in 1862, was born at Cartside in 1846. Houston extended the mill, making an addition in 1825 which nearly doubled its size. In addition to being a successful cotton-master, Houston is credited with transforming canal travel in the 1830s. Previously unacquainted with boats and untutored in boatbuilding, he designed swift, iron boats which were introduced as passenger vessels on the Glasgow, Paisley and Ardrossan Canal, which had opened in 1809. Pulled along at twelve miles per hour by a single horse, they enabled the canal company in 1839, when there were 13 boats sailing daily between Glasgow and Paisley, to carry over 400,000 passengers, twice as many as were transported on the Forth and Clyde Canal. The business flourished only for a very brief period, however, declining rapidly after a faster and more convenient mode of travel arrived with the opening of the Glasgow and Paisley Joint Railway in 1840.

After Houston and his family moved to Johnstone Castle in 1862, Cartside House, with about 8 acres of policies, was regularly leased out. From 1862 it was occupied by the Glasgow East India merchant Archibald Glen. Following losses in his business with Singapore, Malaya and the Philipinnes, Glen went bankrupt in 1874 with liabilities of £150,000, and died at Cartside House in December, 1875. Around 1877 the paper manufacturer Peter McLaurin moved into the house with his family. McLaurin in 1849 had founded the Glasgow firm Smith and McLaurin, which pioneered the manufacture of gummed paper. In 1869 he had purchased the Houstons' Cartside Cotton Mill, which he converted into a paper mill to produce a wide range of paper products - gummed tape, pasteboards, cardboard and label cloth paper suitable for envelopes and books. Shortly after moving into the mansion, in December, 1878, a fierce explosion shook the house. The gas boiler in the kitchen exploded after a feed pipe which had frozen in a severe frost thawed, sending a stream of cold water rushing into the heated and empty boiler cylinder. The kitchen, which was occupied at the time, was badly damaged, with the ceiling and windows destroyed, walls split and part of the kitchen wall thrown across the room. The cook

died in hospital, while two of McLaurin's children were severely burned. This accident may have been the catalyst for McLaurin's rebuilding of Cartside House in 1881, in Scottish Baronial style to designs by Paisley architects Andrew Robb Scott and John Albert Rennison.

Peter McLaurin had nine children, three of whom emigrated in the late 19th century to the United States, where they established a successful paper business. After McLaurin's death in 1909 one of these sons, Duncan McLaurin, returned to join his brothers in the family business. He was living at Cartside House in 1914 with his widowed mother and his brother Alexander.

In 1931 Johnstone Town Council, driven by the housing needs of the burgh, acquired Cartside House and grounds for housing, and the following year extended the burgh boundaries to include the property. Five years earlier it had purchased neighbouring Linn House and policies, and now brought forward proposals to build 220 houses for over 900 people on the joint 32-acre site. Cartside House, which stood at the junction of Cartside Avenue and Beech Road, was demolished soon after.

The McLaurin family sold the business in 1964 to the Guardbridge paper company, from whom it was purchased in 1984 by the James River Corporation, an international force in the paper industry. Smith and McLaurin remains a leading manufacturer and global supplier of paper products. The Cartside Mill, including the original 1794 block, was demolished in 1992. A two-storey stone structure, the last remaining fragment of the works complex, continues to serve as an office block for the company.

# Castle Semple

In 1727 the extensive Castle Semple estate on the north bank of the Castle Semple Loch, owned by the Semple family since 1474, was sold for £10,000 by Hugh, 11th Lord Semple, to Colonel William MacDowall (1678-1748), a planter, slave owner and sugar merchant recently returned from the Leeward Islands. MacDowall, the fifth son of Alexander MacDowall of Garthland in Wigtonshire, had travelled to Nevis around 1695 with his friend James Milliken as an apprentice overseer on a sugar plantation, and progressed to become a plantation manager, an agent for absentee landlords and owner of a number of plantations, including the 800-acre Canada Hills plantation on St. Kitts. In the process he amassed a fortune, which he augmented with a marriage to Mary Tovey, the daughter and heiress of Nevis planter Richard Tovey. She had inherited land and houses in Charlestown, Nevis, and all the slaves on her father's Nevis plantation. MacDowall took a prominent part in the island's affairs, becoming an officer in the island militia and a councillor, and, with the fleet of ships he assembled with Milliken, became a major player in the Caribbean sugar industry. His involvement in slavery was

considerable; he bought, sold and transported black Africans, several hundred of whom were exploited and maltreated on his plantations, where he proved parsimonious in his expenditure on their health, food and accommodation. He returned to Britain in 1724, immensely rich and determined to establish himself among a business elite much impressed by his fortune and his military position. In late 1726 he became a partner in Daniel Campbell's South Sugar house in Glasgow and in the St. Christopher Sugar Warehouse in Edinburgh, and co-founded with his friend Milliken the West India firm James Milliken & Company. Having decided that "sugar will sell as well at Glasgow as in any other part of Britain", in 1728 he began switching some of his sugar ships from London to the Clyde and effectively initiated the city's extensive West Indian trade. MacDowall brought a number of Africans from St. Kitts to Scotland in the 1730s to work on his Castle Semple estate and in his Glasgow home. This was the source of much dissension in the MacDowall household, Mrs MacDowall making it patently clear she was unhappy with a coloured presence in the home. The matter was only resolved when MacDowall threatened to leave her if she did not moderate her attitude.

Between 1727 and 1730 MacDowall commissioned extensive estate improvements. William Boucher was employed to landscape the grounds of Castle Semple and John Watt, uncle of the engineer James Watt, to drain the loch. In 1735 he demolished an older house and used the rubble to build on the site a house commensurate with his status and wealth. His elegant Palladian mansion was constructed by Robert Hunter with more than a passing reference to Daniel Campbell's prestigious Shawfield mansion in Glasgow, which MacDowall had purchased in 1727 for his town house and then rebuilt and renovated following the damage it had suffered during the Shawfield Riots of 1725. At the time of his death at Castle Semple in October, 1748, MacDowall was described as "the most notable man in Glasgow".

His eldest son, also William MacDowall (1719-1784), inherited a vast commercial empire based on sugar, rum and the slave trade, together with extensive properties in Renfrewshire, Glasgow, and the West Indies. He added the ancestral lands of Garthland to the family property portfolio in 1760, as well as estates in Lanarkshire and Ayrshire. At Castle Semple he improved the estate, planting trees, landscaping park-land, adding a bowling green and spending around £3,000 on loch drainage to reclaim a further 250 acres of estate land for farming. In 1749 he diversified into banking, becoming a founding partner of the Ship Bank, Glasgow's first native bank. He in turn was succeeded by his son, another William MacDowall (1749-1810). MP at various times and for various constituencies, and rector of Glasgow University (1795), he was a leading political figure of his day. It was said of him that "with his influence and connections in Renfrew and also at Glasgow, (he) used to swallow the whole patronage of the Clyde as quick as a bottle of claret". By the end of the 18th century his West Indian possessions included sugar plantations on other Caribbean islands such as Antigua, St. Vincent, Tobago and Jamaica. His fortunes declined, however, when the firm co-founded by his grandfather, then trading as Alexander Houston and Company, went into liquidation in 1800 and the assets of the partners– including Castle Semple– were seized to pay the creditors.

William's youngest brother, Day Hort MacDowall of Walkinshaw, borrowed heavily to purchase the estate from the Houston trustees in 1806 for £100,000, but unable to maintain repayments, he drowned himself in the fishponds on the Castle Semple estate in June, 1809. When William MacDowall died in May, 1810, the family estate was then broken up to facilitate a sale. The Castle Semple portion of the estate was purchased in 1813 for £73,000 by Major John Harvey whose family, like the MacDowalls, had extensive business interests in the West Indies.

When John Harvey died in 1820 the estate passed to his daughter Margaret, wife of Major James Octavius Lee, who assumed the name of Harvey. A career soldier like his father-in-law, Lee Harvey served with the Gordon Highlanders in the Napoleonic and Peninsular Wars, retiring from active service in 1814. Three of his sons inherited Castle Semple in succession, all dying childless, to be followed in 1883 by his grandson James Widdrington Shand (1853-1922), the eldest son of Sir Charles Farquhar Shand, Chief Justice of Mauritius, where the family owned large sugar plantations. Shand Harvey, as he became, enjoyed a comfortable life-style on annual estate revenues of £5,560, and was active in local affairs and a member of Renfrew County Council. A reported addiction to gambling resulted in insolvency, however, and Shand sold Castle Semple in 1908. The mansion were converted into apartments and the property broken up into smaller agricultural holdings, a process which accelerated in May, 1937, when the 1,100-acre estate was acquired by the Department of Agriculture for £11,300 for a land settlement project under the Government's "Home for Heroes" programme.

The house was largely destroyed by fire in 1924, but the ruined shell was allowed to stand until work began on its removal in November, 1970. The lodge and stable block have since been converted into private homes.

The Castle Semple estate now forms the Castle Semple Country Park.

# Garthland

In 1759 Hamilton Adam of Kersehead, near Dalry, acquired the lands of Burnfoot on the western edge of Lochwinnoch from John King of Garpel and went on to open a bleach-field on the property. His son James Adam, a solicitor, inherited his father's properties and sold Kersehead to fund the purchase of the Garpel estate where in 1796 he commissioned architect David King to build a mansion, which he named Barr House. Around 1807 Adam moved to Perth when appointed factor of the Drummond estate at an annual salary of £400. Within a few years, without any meaningful capital to back his investments, he began to speculate heavily in land, buying property to the value of £70,000, including in 1810 the estate of Barr and other lands belonging to William MacDowall (1749-1810) of Garthland and Castle Semple. On Barr he began an ambitious programme of land reclamation which involved improving the embankment and drainage of the Barr Loch. He became so preoccupied with the project that he gave up his charge of the Perth estate and brought his family to Garpel in the spring of 1815. The rising costs of the work, reaching around £7,000, took him to the verge of insolvency, and in 1820 he sold the Barr estate to William MacDowall, originally of neighbouring Skiff Park. The following year MacDowall added Adam's other Lochwinnoch properties, Burnfoot, Garpel and Carsefauld, to his Barr estate.

A Glasgow merchant and Controller of Customs at Greenock, William MacDowall (1770-1840) had earlier in 1810 inherited the Garthland estate in Wigtonshire from his uncle, Wiliam MacDowall of

Castle Semple, only to sell the ancestral lands the following year. He retained the title, however, which he now transferred to his new estate at Lochwinnoch where, between 1820 and 1830, he extensively modified and extended Adam's "excellent" house, creating a fine residence, notable features of which included diamond-shafted coped chimney stacks, carved dormers and bay windows. He landscaped the policies, adding attractive gardens and lawns, trees and shrubs. He renamed the mansion Garpel, and then Garthland, and lived there until his death unmarried in 1840. Adam, meanwhile, after the sale of Garpel, practised law in Edinburgh before moving to Stornoway in 1824 to become factor on the great Seaforth estate, then held by Mary Mackenzie. A man of many talents, Adam also boasted being a merchant, a coal-master and a lime-burner, and was reportedly the first person to provide a planned survey for a railway line between Edinburgh and Glasgow, which, unfortunately for him, was rejected. He died in 1849.

MacDowall's successor at Garthland, his half-brother Lieutenant-Colonel Lawrence MacDowall (1791-1842) of the Madras Army, also died unmarried and the estate was inherited by their cousin, Lieutenant-General Day Hort MacDowall (1795-1870), another career soldier who also died without an heir, at which point Garthland fell to his brother Henry MacDowall of Carruth (1796-1882). The last of the family to live at Garthland was his son Henry MacDowall (1845-1927) of Garthland and Carruth, upon whose death the estate was inherited by his Canadian-born nephew, Henry Charles Victor MacDowall (1891-1947), who sold the 50-acre property in 1935 to St. Joseph's Foreign Missionary Society of Mill Hill, London, who planned to use the mansion as a missionary college and centre. Garthland was renamed St Joseph's College, and work began almost immediately on altering and expanding the structure. A three-storey dormitory block linked to the mansion was added in 1936, and seven years later a red-brick chapel was built, to designs by architect Thomas Smith Cordiner. This served as a place of worship for the local Catholic community until the construction of Our Lady of Fatima Church in 1955.

When the college closed in 1985, the house and estate were acquired by Caledonian Nursing Homes who in 1986 opened the 84-bed *St Joseph's Nursing Home*, a facility for the elderly, those with long-term needs and those in need of recuperative care. The home operated on the site until its closure in 2004, its then owners Craegmoor considering it incapable of being adapted to meet the exacting standards which had been introduced for care home provision. Around this time two purpose-built, single-storey residential care units were built north of the mansion for adults with learning and or physical disabilities. Concerns for the fate of the abandoned mansion, which lay derelict and vandalised, led to the house and chapel being Category C listed in 2006. Two years later planning permission was granted for a flatted conversion of the house and a selective demolition of the outbuildings, but no action followed and eventually, in April, 2013, Garthland House was demolished.

Latterly the old mansion developed a reputation for being haunted. Strange happenings were reported, including the opening and closing of doors, plates and dishes falling from tables and pictures dropping from walls. There were also tales of spectral horses galloping up and down the avenue at dead of night. Following the closure of the college, moreover, when coffins from a priests' cemetery in the grounds were exhumed and reburied in sacred ground elsewhere, there were reports of phantom clerics wandering over the former graveyard.

# Johnstone Castle

In the early 18th century the lands of Johnstone and Easter Cochrane (or Quarrelton), separated by the Black Cart River, were owned by George Houston, eldest son of Glasgow tobacco merchant Patrick Houston. In 1729, to repay his father's debts, he sold the open farmlands of Over and Nether Johnstone on the north side of the river to Major James Milliken. Houston reserved the title Johnstone, however, which he transferred to his Easter Cochrane estate. An old tower on the property, dating from around 1600 and known as Easter Cochrane Tower, became his residence. A central rectangular structure with two wings, a walled garden to the rear, and a long tree-lined avenue leading north, the tower was surrounded by coal and lime pits. In 1757 his great-grandson George Houston (1743-1815), the 4th laird, then aged 14, succeeded to the estate which then comprised the lands of Cartside and Hag, in addition to the 105 acres of enclosed farmland on Quarrelton, and provided an annual income of around £3,500. It also boasted a "tolerable good mansion", suggesting modifications had been effected to the old tower in the interim. Houston made further alterations to the mansion-house in 1777 and 1812, the latter development attributed to the architect James Gillespie Graham, to create an elegant, castellated structure. Typical of the landowners of the period, Houston fully exploited the resources of his estate. Described in 1802 as a man "of great experience and professional knowledge in coal matters", he had extended and developed his Quarrelton coalfield, which by 1792 was yielding 20,000 tons of coal per year. He also opened additional lime works at Floor Craig. To provide accommodation for his workers, Houston in January, 1782, began to plan the layout of a new town. He also began to encourage the development of the cotton industry on his lands that same year when he feued 13 acres of his estate to the Paisley textile merchant Robert Corse to build Johnstone's first cotton mill. Two years later he built his own spinning mill downstream from Corse's mill, and established his own company to operate it. George Houston and Company established further mills at Cartside and Hag. By now a wealthy landlord and industrialist, Houston diversified his business interests, becoming in 1788 a founding partner in the Union Bank of Paisley, and in 1809 a sponsor of the Glasgow, Paisley and Ardrossan Canal, which crossed his lands.

Convener of the County of Renfrew, he died in December, 1815, and his property and business interests were inherited by his elder son Ludovic Houston (1780-1862), who further improved and enlarged the house. The grand turreted mansion in its landscaped parkland setting, described in 1837 as "one of the chief ornaments of the county", played host in September, 1848, to Frederick Chopin, who had tutored the wife of the 5th laird in Paris. The family had earlier faced a succession crisis in September, 1843, when Ludovic's only son George Houston (1810-43), MP for Renfrewshire, dropped dead on the moors when out shooting in Aberdeenshire. An heir was provided when Ludovic's younger brother William Houston (1781-1856), a 63-year old bachelor at the time, married Marion Douglas Russell, forty years his junior, in July, 1845, and proceeded to have a family of four children.

William's eldest son George Ludovic Houston (1846-1931) succeeded to Johnstone Castle and found himself a significant landholder in Renfrewshire, owning 1,841 acres of land. He initially travelled a great deal and Johnstone Castle was leased from 1864 until 1885 by Glasgow cotton manufacturer Andrew Galbraith. Conservative and imperialist in politics, Houston took an active interest in South African affairs. He was present when Henry Rider Haggard raised the Union flag over Pretoria when Britain annexed the Transvaal in 1877, and was later one of the conspirators behind the Jameson Raid, the illegal and ill-fated attempt to overthrow President Paul Kruger of the Transvaal Republic in December, 1895. In the latter stages of the Boer

War, in 1900, Houston was arrested by the Boers as a British spy, but was soon released. He was friends with Haggard whom he invited to manage the vineyards on his estate in Cyprus, purchased in the early 1880s during his travels. Business meetings were held at Johnstone Castle, but nothing came of the project. Among his other correspondents were Alfred Milner, High Commissioner in South Africa, H.H. Kitchener and A. J. Balfour, who became Prime Minister in 1902. Unimpressed by the social and financial reforms of the Liberal Government under Lloyd George, Houston abandoned Johnstone Castle around 1913 and retired to Cyprus, where his lifestyle was financed by estate revenues and land disposals to the expanding town. The 6th and last laird of Johnstone died childless in Kyrenia, Cyprus, in September, 1931. His only brother William having drowned in a boating accident at Castle Semple Loch in September, 1866, when just 17, and his two sisters dying unmarried, his estate was left to his wife, Ann Douglas Stirling (1865-1950).

The last tenants of Johnstone Castle were the Watson family of the Linwood Paper Mill in the 1930s. During World War II the estate was requisitioned for military purposes, and barracks were erected in the grounds. Polish servicemen were billeted there, and later it was used for training Allied troops, detaining prisoners of war and housing returning British servicemen. When Ann Houston died in Cyprus in 1950, Johnstone Castle became the property of her only sister, Charlotte, Lady May, on whose death in 1956 what remained of the estate was purchased by Johnstone Burgh Council for housing. The mansion, by this time lying derelict and abandoned, was declared unsafe, and demolition commenced, only to be halted before completion through the intervention of Major David R. Somervell, a relation of the family. In 1957 the 1,000-house Johnstone Castle Housing Scheme was built on the site for local people at a cost of £2 million. Of the original structure, only the three-storey central tower now remains. B-listed and standing in Tower Place, it has been renovated and is privately owned.

# Leethland

Leethland House was built in 1930 for James McMurchy Greenlees on an 8-acre plot of land, formerly part of Leitchland Farm, feued from the Elderslie Estates. Designed in simple Scottish style by Paisley architect Harry Cook, whose other credits included the Hugh Smiley Day Nursery (1911), Renfrewshire Education Offices (after 1919) and a number of villas in the Thornly Park area of Paisley, Leethland House was a large, rambling, 2-storey L-plan structure which had extensive views over open countryside. Greenlees, a partner in the coal exporters and colliery agents, Borland and Greenlees, was a son of Thomas Greenlees of Netherton in Castlehead, who made his money in textile manufacturing and shipping. Principal partner in Rule and Greenlees, large-scale producers of cotton and gingham clothing in Glasgow's East End, Thomas Greenlees was also a partner in the steamship owning and brokering business set up by another of his sons, John Greenlees. The family had

strong ties with the Coats dynasty in Paisley. James Greenlees' sister Jane married the eldest son of Sir James Coats of Auchendrane, Stuart Auchincloss Coats, who was a director and vice-president in the Coats thread business and later Unionist MP for Morpeth; his niece married the younger son of Sir Thomas Glen-Coats, Major Alexander Harold Glen-Coats of Gryffe (1883-1933), also a director in J. and P. Coats and Liberal MP for West Renfrewshire (1906).

James Greenlees died in August, 1941. On the death of his widow, Grace MacIntyre Darling, in September, 1963, the Leethland property, comprising the 12-roomed mansion, seven and a half acres of ground laid out in lawns, gardens and plantations, and a 4-room gardener's cottage was placed on the market. It was purchased by popular entertainer Calum Kennedy (1928-2006), who established his Glen Music Company there in

May, 1964. Kennedy was approaching his peak as a performer at the time. Born on the Isle of Lewis, he had taken the gold medal at the National Mod in Aberdeen in 1955, and followed this up by winning a gold medal at the World Ballad Championship in Moscow in 1957 and performing at the Bolshoi. With a pleasant voice and an engaging personality he became a popular figure during the Sixties, and was a regular presence on television. He hosted the first live show on Grampian Television and also starred in his own variety show on STV, presenting the long-running series, Calum's Ceilidh and Round at Calum's. Fortune proved fickle for Kennedy in the 1970s, however. His wife died suddenly in 1974, at the age of 39, and Kennedy, afflicted by throat problems, didn't perform for two years. When he made his comeback, he found that public tastes in music had changed and that his archetypal Scottish, kilted persona and sentimental repertoire were out of fashion. He diversified and became an impresario, bringing Shirley Bassey, Frankie Vaughan and the Billy Cotton Band Show to his two theatres, the Dundee Palace and Aberdeen's Tivoli Theatre. He continued to perform, and made a stage comeback in the 1990s. He died in 2006, having suffered a stroke the previous year.

The B-listed Leethland House was the scene of two serious fires. The first in 1977 saw gang slogans sprayed in red paint on the doors of the unoccupied gate house and on an office and store at the rear of the house, and the destruction of Kennedy's 10,000-strong record collection, a grand piano and the family's stage props, kilts and dresses. Then, in 1985, the building was virtually destroyed in a second blaze, amid reports that the fire was started deliberately. The damage led to the house being downgraded to C-listed status. Kennedy's troubles were compounded in 1992 when he lost a £1.75 million legal battle against his insurance company, who refused to pay out on the claim and were supported by a judge who ruled that Kennedy had failed to disclose that other insurers had declined to provide cover for the building. With funds unavailable for a restoration, the house lay derelict and abandoned, and by 1992 had become a drinking den for local youths. In May, 1999, to afford some degree of protection to the house, the Scottish Civic Trust placed it on its Buildings at Risk bulletin. Leethland House now stands in a ruinous and irretrievable condition within dense woodland in Glenpatrick Road, Elderslie.

# Merchiston

Around 1840 Sir William John Milliken-Napier (1788-1852) joined the ranks of landowners exploiting the cotton boom by opening the Barbush cotton spinning mill on his lands on the north bank of the Black Cart River near Johnstone. Merchiston House was built around 1855 by his second son John Stirling Napier (1820-91), founder and senior partner in the firm J. and W. Napier and Company, which managed the Barbush Mill. Surrounded by parkland and gardens, it was situated on rising ground north of the Kilmacolm Road and offered commanding views over the local countryside. Napier had additional interests in the cotton industry; he was also a partner in the Linwood Cotton Spinning Company owned by his father-in-law Andrew Brown of Auchentorlie, whose only daughter Janet he had married in 1845.

In 1870 Sir Robert John Milliken-Napier sold the mill property, including Merchiston House, to the Johnstone firm Finlayson, Bousfield, and Company, flax spinners and linen thread manufacturers, who had premises on the opposite side of the river. The company had first moved to Johnstone in 1849 taking over two existing cotton-spinning mills which were adapted and extended for the production of linen thread, extensively used in sail-making,

boot and shoe manufacture, and sack and bag making. When Charles Holehouse Bousfield retired from the business in 1876, the company became predominantly a Finlayson family business, with James Finlayson (1823-1903), who had taken up residence at Merchiston House in 1870, as principal managing partner, and three of his sons as partners. The company expanded into the growing American market in 1880 when his second son Archibald Watson Finlayson was despatched to the United States to establish a linen and thread mill in North Grafton, Massachusetts. James Finlayson was active in public affairs. He was a director of the Glasgow and South Western Railway for 30 years, chairman of the Scottish Imperial Insurance Company, and his standing in the Glasgow business community was reflected in his election as chairman of Glasgow Chamber of Commerce in 1889. He served briefly as a Liberal MP for East Renfrewshire in 1885, but did not seek re-election the following year. He supported many local causes, and in particular was instrumental in the building of a public hall, library and reading room for Johnstone's Working Men's Institute in 1867.

Glasgow architect Alexander Gardner made extensive additions to the house sometime between

1888 and 1911 for either James Finlayson or his eldest son William James Finlayson (1847-1925), who succeeded him at Merchiston and as chairman of the family firm. By this time amalgamation was the name of the game in the global thread market. In 1896 J. and P. Coats had taken over its three main British rivals, Clark and Company, Jonas Brook and Brothers, and James Chadwick and Brothers, to form a powerful global conglomerate. In 1898 a rival to Coats emerged when Finlayson and Bousfield merged with a number of other firms, including W. and J. Knox of Kilbirnie and the Northern Ireland concern, William Barbour and Sons, to form the Linen Thread Company, which effectively controlled the linen thread business in Britain and the United States. The Finlaysons all became directors in the merged company. Unlike his father, William James Finlayson, a keen amateur photographer, showed no interest in public affairs. He did, though, make improvements to the Merchiston property, commissioning Kilbirnie architect James Houston to design a lodge and cottage for the grounds in 1920. He died at Merchiston in April, 1925, to be succeeded by his only son Charles, on whose death, in 1939, the Merchiston estate, comprising the mansion, several cottages and between 50 and 60 acres of farmland, was put on the market.

Merchiston House, situated on the edge of the village of Brookfield, was used to accommodate Canadian soldiers during the Second World War, following which it was purchased by Paisley Burgh as a replacement for Broadfield Hospital, a facility for people with mental health problems which it sold to Port Glasgow Town Council in 1946. The patients were moved to Merchiston in 1948, the year the hospital was taken over by the National Health Service. An extension to Merchiston House was opened in 1955 to accommodate a further 34 patients, and a further wing added in 1958. A nine million pound redevelopment took place in 1985, when new education, therapy and recreational facilities were provided. Merchiston House was demolished the following year, in the face of protests from local residents. The hospital closed in 2007-2008, and was demolished in 2013.

The Finlayson, Bousfield and Company Flax Mills in Johnstone, which employed over 2,000 people at their peak, were closed down in 1957 as a result of a declining world market for linen threads in the face of competition from new synthetic threads such as nylon and polyester. Although B-listed, the mill complex was demolished in stages between the 1970s and 2007. The site is now occupied by a Morrisons supermarket and Linenmill Court, a new apartment development.

# Milliken

In 1729 the open farmlands of Over and Nether Johnstone were purchased from George Houston by Major James Milliken (1669-1741), recently returned from St Christopher Island (St. Kitts) in the Leeward Islands. The following year Milliken commissioned land surveyor John Watt, an uncle of the steam engine pioneer James Watt, to lay out a planned estate on the land, at the centre of which was to be an elegant mansion, built in 1733. He gave the family name to the estate and the house.

Around 1695 Milliken, the son of a West Indian merchant in Ayr, had travelled in the company of his friend William MacDowall to Nevis in the Leewards, a source of Glasgow sugar imports since 1640. Here he began to forge an affluent future, initially as a sugar plantation overseer but latterly as a plantation owner and agent managing various estates for absentee planters. He became a highly respected figure, serving in the island militia in campaigns against the French, marrying a wealthy widow, Mary Tovey, whose late husband Richard Tovey had owned one of the largest plantations on Nevis, and becoming an island councillor. He acquired a reputation as an uncompromising and ruthless individual at a time when the slave management regime in the Leewards was brutal and unforgiving and slave mortality rates were high due to maltreatment, malnutrition and neglect. When the French half of St Kitts came into British possession at the end of the war with France in 1712, Milliken and MacDowall were among the British beneficiaries in the sharing out of the spoils. Milliken was granted the 200-acre Lamberts estate on Monkey Hill, which he estimated at the time would return him between £2,000 and £3,000 annually. He returned to Glasgow a very wealthy man, and applied his wealth to cementing his place within the Glasgow business community. He and MacDowall, made burgesses of the city in 1730, brought their sugar and shipping businesses home with them, founding the West India firm James Milliken and Company. They became principal partners in Glasgow's South Sugar House and, diverting their ships from London in 1728, made Glasgow the market for their sugar and rum, in the process laying the foundations of the city's West India trade. Milliken took an interest in another of Glasgow's sugar establishments, the Easter Sugar House, and diversified into other businesses, becoming a partner in the Port Glasgow Rope-Works, the Greenock Rope and Sail Duck Manufactory, and the Glasgow Tanwork.

In 1736 Milliken transferred the Milliken estate to his only son James, on the occasion of the latter's marriage to Jean MacDowall of Garthland, a niece of his friend MacDowall. He also conveyed to his son half of the Monkey Hill Plantation with half of its slaves, horses, cattle, mules and equipment, although he retained overall management of the holding which, he reasoned, could not be conveniently divided. Born on Nevis and educated at Eton, James Milliken, junior (1710-76), had inherited his father's properties in 1741. He made improvements on the Milliken estate, adding a bowling green, eight acres of orchards and gardens, and a plantation of tall lime trees, and between 1745 and 1762 expanded the property, purchasing many local farms as well as the village of Kilbarchan. He began the mineral exploitation of Milliken, deriving revenue from at least two coal mines and one freestone quarry. He built up his real estate holdings in Renfrewshire with the purchase of the Gryffe Castle estate in 1754 and other land in Kilbarchan and Paisley, and invested in bridges and roads connecting his properties. Said to have spent more money on public roads than any man in Scotland, Milliken was also rector of Glasgow University (1759) and a partner in Glasgow's Ship Bank.

When Milliken's two sons both died unmarried, his Renfrewshire lands and St. Kitts estates were inherited by his grandson Robert Milliken Napier (1765-1808), the son of his eldest daughter Jean, from her marriage to General William Napier of Culcreuch. A professional soldier, he had a distinguished military career, serving in both the East and the West Indies, before the cumulative effect of his wounds forced his retirement. He died in 1808, second senior colonel in the Army. Milliken House had been destroyed in a fire seven years earlier, and it was left to his son and heir, Sir William John Milliken-Napier (1788-1852), to re-build Milliken House in 1836 about 250

yards from the site of the old house. Chopin was a guest of Sir William at Milliken in 1848. His son and successor, Sir Robert John Milliken-Napier (1818-84), began feuing estate land for housing, intimating in 1852 that the quarry on the lands would enable villas to be built more cheaply than anywhere in the Glasgow area, and in 1854 offering the inducement of a reasonably priced railway season ticket to feuars of land close to Milliken Park Station. He had ceased to live at Milliken by the time of his death, when the property was being leased by Charles Cayser of the Clan Line Steamship Company.

In March, 1887, his son, Sir Archibald Lennox Milliken-Napier (1855-1907), exposed the 1,564-acre Milliken estate for sale in lots. A 470-acre lot comprising Milliken House, extensive policies and the house farm was bought by Paisley starch manufacturer Archibald Mackenzie for £32,200. Provost of Paisley from 1894 until 1900, Mackenzie was a noted Paisley benefactor, gifting the burgh a fountain for the new Hawkhead Cemetery in 1891, and the Royal Victoria Eye Infirmary as a jubilee offering in 1897. In 1920 Mackenzie's trustees in their turn began to dispose of his Milliken property in lots. The main property, then including the White House, possibly a factor's house built by Mackenzie, was acquired by architect George Arthur Boswell, known for his cinema designs and for the extensions to Leiper's original Templeton's Carpet Factory in Glasgow in the 1920s and 30s. The old mansion, which had lain uninhabited for some time, was demolished in 1923 and much of the masonry used to modify and enlarge the White House, which became the new family home. The White House of Milliken is now the centrepiece of the 132-acre Milliken estate.

Milliken House stood south of the A761 Bridge of Weir road, west of Barochan Road. The former Lamberts plantation in Jamaica, the foundation of the Milliken family wealth, remains in the hands of the Napiers of Milliken to the present day. Sugar production continued on the site until 2006.

# Muirshiel

At the end of the 17th century Muirshiel and Queenside, north-west of Lochwinnoch, formed part of the estates of Balgreen, which were in the possession of Robert Semple, Sheriff-Depute of Renfrewshire. The Semples of Balgreen were descended from the Semples of Castle Semple, at one time one of the most influential families in Renfrewshire. The lands passed through a number of hands before being acquired early in the 19th century by Paisley banker Andrew Moody. Moody had been a thread manufacturer, but when steam was introduced to the cotton industry he turned his attention to banking, becoming a partner and manager in the Union Bank of Paisley. He was also appointed Chief Magistrate of Paisley, in which capacity he cut the first turf of the Glasgow and Paisley Canal.

The expansive moorlands of Muirshiel and Queenside provided a natural habitat for a range of

game birds and were long the haunt of the rich and idle classes in search of some recreational shooting. In 1821 Moody was leasing the shooting on his lands for 100 guineas for the season. Following his death in 1826, the 2,200-acre estate was acquired by Glasgow merchant John Miller (1778-1854) as a country retreat and possibly as somewhere to entertain associates. Sir Henry Pottinger, who negotiated the Treaty of Nanking which ended the First Opium War in 1842, and who later became the first Governor of Hong Kong, paid a shooting visit to Muirshiel in 1845. Miller had made his money in the West Indies as a merchant in Kingston, Jamaica, and joint-owner of the Staveley Park sugar plantation on the island. Around 1808 he married Mary Robinson McCook, the daughter of another plantation owner. Returning to Glasgow in 1816 they eventually took up residence in St. Vincent Street in Glasgow's New Town. Miller made early improvements on Muirshiel, planting nearly six acres of trees and putting twenty acres of soil under crops. In October, 1831, moreover, he built two servants' houses and a cattle shed. He also exploited the mineral resources of his estate, extending the mining of barytes, used in the production of paint, cosmetics, paper and porcelain, and establishing a barytes processing factory on the property. In 1843 Miller commissioned architect David Hamilton to build a handsome mansion at the foot of Mistylaw Muir. Deputy Chairman of the Glasgow, Paisley, Kilmarnock and Ayr Railway, Miller died at his St. Vincent Street home in December, 1854, leaving an estate valued at £42,150.

In June, 1855, the Muirshiel Estate, then extending to 2,500 acres, was placed on the market, where it remained until purchased by Captain Thomas Watson Greig in 1863. He sold it in 1873 when moving to assume his grandfather's estate of Glencarse in Perthshire. Greig's obituary of July, 1912, described him as a man with 'many-sided interests', an oblique reference to an unusual passion for ladies' shoes, about which he wrote two books, *Ladies' Old-fashioned Shoes* (1885) and *Ladies' Dress Shoes of the Nineteenth Century* (1900). Muirshiel's new owner was Francis Nathaniel, Marquess Conyngham (1832-80). A Royal Navy officer who served at the siege of Sebastopol, Conyngham was later Liberal MP for County Clare and a member of the Home Rule League. He died at Muirshiel in September, 1880. His burial place in Monument Wood on the estate is marked by a granite obelisk.

Conyngham's estate was placed in trust, and in 1882 Muirshiel was leased on a short tenancy for £300 to Liverpool shipbuilder Gilbert Thompson Bates (1847-1917), who was to acquire Muirshiel outright in 1890. Around 1910 he was followed at Muirshiel by his son-in-law Edward Lionel Fletcher (1876-1968), another prominent member of the Liverpool shipping community, who spent most of his business career with the White Star Company, eventually becoming a joint manager of the White Star, Dominion, and American Lines. He was a manager of the White Star Line at the time of the Titanic disaster in 1912. Chairman of the Liverpool Steamship Owners' Association, he was made an honorary commander in the Royal Naval Reserve in 1914 for his role in implementing an Admiralty scheme for having the food-carrying White Star colonial steamers fitted with guns for defensive purposes. A year later he received a knighthood, probably for services rendered in shipping the British Expeditionary Force to France. Fletcher was a noted marksman, winning the silver medal in the King's Prize at Bisley in 1898, and leading the British team in international competition. He had widely varied business interests, including the British Lion Film Corporation, Associated Greyhound Racecourses and Wells Brewery in St Albans. In 1920 he extended the Muirshiel estate when he acquired part of the adjacent lands of Tandlemuir, which he rechristened Conveth.

In 1935 the Muirshiel estate, by then covering 3,300 acres, was bought by Sir Bernard Edward Fitzalan-Howard (1885-1972), 3rd Baron Howard of Glossop, Derbyshire, for £7,250. A coming-of-age celebration for his eldest son Miles Francis Fitzalan-Howard, later Duke of Norfolk, was held at Muirshiel the following year. The Fitzalan-Howards came north with associates and staff every autumn to shoot grouse, pheasants and rabbits on the moors. Boys from the Kibble School in Paisley, a residential school for young offenders, assisted with the beating on shooting days, wearing red overalls and carrying red flags for safety and visibility. A number are known to have dispensed with their conspicuous clothing in order to go AWOL. In 1944 the Fitzalan-Howards sold the Muirshiel estate to Glasgow-based Keir and Cawder, who had reopened the barytes mine two years earlier. Colonel William Stirling, chairman of the company and a well-known figure on Scotland's grouse moors, was the last occupant of Muirshiel House from about 1945 till 1950. After his departure the house was demolished in 1952. In June of that year Keir and Cawder sold the estate to Renfrew County Council for £16,000. Muirshiel Country Park was created on the site in 1970.

No evidence remains of Muirshiel House, which stood in the car park where the new timber building stands today. The Muirshiel barytes mine closed in 1969.

# Spring Grove

The Quarry Park in Kilbarchan, part of the Milliken estate, stood directly west of a small freestone quarry which supplied much of the stone used in the construction of village houses in the 18th century. In March, 1850, Glasgow builder Edward Buchanan purchased two acres of the Quarry Park from the trustees of Sir William Milliken-Napier, and built on the site a modern mansion, which was known locally as Quarry House. Buchanan was a speculative building contractor who was not only involved in villa construction in Kilbarchan but was responsible for building development across Glasgow, including the construction of the elegant, serpentine Stobcross (later St. Vincent) Crescent in Glasgow, following the completion of which he was declared bankrupt in 1852. When his trustees placed Quarry House on the market, it was acquired two years later by the Glasgow merchant and commission agent Robert Bell, who acquired additional acres from the Milliken estate to extend the boundaries of his new property, which he re-christened Spring Grove. The south-facing Spring Grove House eventually sat within 8 acres of ground, complete with bowling green, extensive flower gardens, shrubberies, and plantations. Bell and Buchanan were to become business associates in the late 1850s, building tenements in Pollokshaws in Glasgow, but in due course Bell's business affairs followed the pattern of his partner's and in 1862 Spring Grove was again on the market.

Bell's elegant and substantial modern furniture was

auctioned off at Spring Grove in March, 1864, when Irvine lawyer John Smith (1801-66) purchased the property. Smith had come into a fortune on the demise of a client and distant relation, the Irvine businessman and philanthropist John Ferguson, who died in 1856 leaving almost £1.25 million. Ferguson left £100,000 to Smith, who was also appointed executor and principal trustee of the Ferguson Bequest Fund, set up with £400,000 to maintain and promote religious education and missionary activity. Smith gave up his legal practice in Irvine and moved to Kilbarchan, whence he commuted to his Glasgow office to administer the Ferguson Bequest. He died at Spring Grove in October, 1866, leaving twin daughters who were to achieve celebrity later in the century as the Westminster Sisters and the Sisters of Sinai. Agnes and Margaret Smith, students at Irvine Royal Academy before being sent to finish their education in England, mastered French, German and Italian while still quite young. After John Smith's "superior modern furniture" was auctioned off at Spring Grove House in 1867, the twins moved to London, where they continued to learn languages. Their travels in Europe and the Middle East in 1868, which included visits to Egypt, Palestine and Greece, led to Agnes' first book *Eastern Pilgrims*. Taking up residence in Cambridge, they subsequently spent three decades on academic research and acts of philanthropy. Agnes' discovery, on one of her many journeys to St Catherine's Monastery on Mount Sinai, of centuries-old Syriac manuscripts which shed fresh light on New Testament scholarship, and the contribution the twins made to cataloguing the monastery's Arabic and Syriac manuscripts, earned the respect of the academic world and gained them European recognition. Various academic honours ensued, this at a time when women were not allowed to study for degrees at the universities of Oxford and Cambridge. When the senate of Cambridge University rejected a motion to offer degrees to women in 1896, the twins proceeded to found a new Presbyterian college in Cambridge, Westminster College, now a centre for learning within the United Reformed Church.

The Spring Grove estate was marketed in 1874 with an asking price of £4,500, and was sold that year by Smith's trustees to the Glasgow timber, ship, and insurance broker, Arthur William Singleton. When he became insolvent in 1891, Spring Grove was purchased that June by Archibald Watson Finlayson, son of James Finlayson of Merchiston, and, like his father, a partner in the family's linen thread manufacturing concern, Finlayson, Bousfield, and Company. Finlayson, who had been instrumental in establishing the company's linen and thread mill in North Grafton, Massachusetts in 1880, served on Renfrew County Council and died in 1916, leaving an estate valued at £134,882, excluding his real estate interests.

The eight-acre Spring Grove was acquired from his trustees in 1921 by David Thomas Morrison, a Glasgow oil merchant and manufacturer who had been tenant of the house for a number of years. Morrison resurrected an old 18th century Kilbarchan industry when, in October, 1926, following the General Strike, he opened a coal mine in the grounds of Spring Grove. Morrison lived at Spring Grove until 1935. The house subsequently lay unoccupied until tenanted by the Home Guard during the Second World War. By 1950 it was uninhabitable and shortly afterwards demolished to make way for a new housing development.

# Auchentorlie

## 5

## *Paisley and Renfrew*

The lands of Whiteford, situated on the banks of the River Cart between Paisley and the Hawkhead estate, took their name from Walter de Whiteford, who was granted the property by Alexander III for his service against the Norwegians at the Battle of Largs in 1263. They later came into the ownership of the Dundonald family who in 1760 subdivided and feued Whiteford to a number of individuals, among them William Kibble. His daughter Margaret married the Paisley merchant Thomas Bissland in 1771. Bissland, a builder from Drymen, had come to Paisley in 1756, but soon abandoned the construction business for a career in commerce, joining forces in 1760 with Charles Maxwell of Merksworth, with whom he carried on an extensive timber business trading with the Baltic and the Mediterranean. Treasurer of Paisley in 1771 and a property owner in the town, Bisland in 1785 acquired a twenty-five acre plot of the Whiteford estate called Auchentorlie, upon which he constructed a castellated mansion house.

He was succeeded in 1804 by his only son, also Thomas Bissland (1772-1846), a merchant and cotton spinner, who six years earlier had purchased a few acres of the Ferguslie estate, which contained a house which he modified and extended in the same turreted style as his father's Auchentorlie mansion. In 1806 he purchased the remaining 156 acres of the Ferguslie estate from Paisley Town Council for £10,000 and began to designate himself Bissland of Ferguslie. Auchentorlie, which had become surplus to requirements, was sold the to brewer and distiller Matthew Brown (1756-1836) of Crossflat, who extended the property. Around 1828 Brown conveyed Auchentorlie to his eldest son Andrew Brown, a cotton merchant and manufacturer, and a partner with his brother Hugh Brown of Broadstone in the Linwood Cotton Spinning Company and in Browns, Malloch and Company, which operated mills at Johnstone and Elderslie. In 1828 Andrew Brown replaced Bissland's house with a modern residence. An elegant and commodious two-storey house with pleasure grounds and an extensive garden adjoining, Brown's mansion was pleasantly situated on elevated ground and was approached from the Seedhill Road by a long, winding avenue. Between 1838 and 1840 his fortunes were given a boost when he inherited his father's extensive business portfolio, which included the Port Glasgow Sugar House at Newark, the distillery at Portnauld near Inchinnan, a share in the Greenock Brewery of James Watt and Company at Cartsdyke, and various pockets of land on the Whiteford estate. Andrew Brown died suddenly at Bridge of Allan in September, 1856, and Auchentorlie became the property of his daughter Janet, wife of John Stirling Napier of Merchiston.

In 1858 the 16-acre Auchentorlie estate was purchased from Janet Brown for £5,000 by Alexander Cattanach (1829-88), manager of James Stewart and Company's Saucel Distillery in Paisley. One of the largest malt and grain distilleries in Scotland, the Saucel Distillery covered eight acres and had an annual output of one million gallons. Cattenach's only surviving son Lorimer sold Auchentorlie House and grounds in 1910 to the Parish Council of Paisley, which adapted it for use as a home for children and maternity cases, in due course providing accommodation for 77 inmates. The Council purchased Auchentorlie in order to rationalise its provision for the treatment of children in care. The acquisition of Auchentorlie facilitated the segregation of neglected and under-nourished children of parents who were in prison or in the poor-house from orphaned or abandoned children from respectable homes. The latter were

to be accommodated at Auchentorlie, whilst the former continued to be sent to the authority's other children's home at Largs. The home continued to operate on the Auchentorlie site until 1933, when Paisley Town Council established a replacement home at Woodside House and closed the Auchentorlie facility.

Prior to this, in 1929, Paisley Parish Council had sold the 15-acre Auchentorlie estate including the mansion and lodges to the Seedhill Finishing Company, whose expansive cloth dyeing and finishing factory buildings occupied the land adjacent to the property. When the home closed, the mansion reverted to a private residence and in due course became home to the Money family. The property was later acquired by Paisley Town Council, which in 1967 placed a contract worth £200,000 with Barrhead contractor Hugh Leggat to build 63 houses on the site. The mansion, which had been lying unoccupied for some years, was demolished to accommodate the development, which was completed in 1968.

Auchentorlie House was situated on the south side of Seedhill Road, directly south of Linside Avenue. Thomas Money, who lived at Auchentorlie House in the 1950s, had a distinguished academic career, culminating in appointment to the post of Professor Emeritus of Chemistry at the University of British Columbia in Vancouver, Canada, in 1997.

# Blythswood

The Renfield estate, located west of Renfrew on the right bank of the River Cart near its junction with the Clyde, was purchased in 1654 by Colin Campbell, a Glasgow merchant and future provost of the city, who proceeded to build a house on the land. He had earlier, around 1650, purchased the 470-acre Blythswood Estate, then on the western outskirts of Glasgow, at which point Blythswood became the family designation. Campbell's Renfrewshire estate was described at the beginning of the 18th century, as "one of the most singularly pleasant places in all this neighbourhood". The old house on Renfield was the rural residence of the Campbells of Blythswood until Archibald Campbell (1761-1838) began to replace it between 1820 and 1822 with an imposing neoclassical-style mansion to designs by the architect James Gillespie Graham. The north-east facing house, constructed of fine, white freestone, had 118 rooms and an Ionic, four column portico, which supported a pediment upon which the arms of the family were carved. The grounds surrounding the house contained gardens, parkland, trees, curling ponds, tennis courts, a cricket pitch and a golf course. Campbell, Tory MP variously for the Glasgow Burghs, the Elgin Burghs and the Perth Burghs, as well as rector of Glasgow University (1807), called the mansion Blythswood House after his Glasgow estate. Around the same time, one of the streets in the new town being built on Campbell's Glasgow lands was called Renfield Street. Campbell died unmarried in 1838, when his estates passed to his cousin, Archibald Douglas of Mains (1809-68), who assumed the family name and designation.

The new laird and his wife were involved in a tragic accident on 25 November, 1847, when travelling to dine with Sir Archibald Campbell at Garscube. As the carriage in which they were travelling was crossing a wooden bridge over the Forth and Clyde Canal, a bridge railing gave way and the whole party, including the coachman and two servants seated behind, was pitched into the canal lock. The sluices had to be opened to raise the water to the level of the bank, at which point the party inside the carriage was extricated with great effort, but Campbell's third son, only 6 years old, perished in the accident.

Campbell was succeeded by his eldest son, Archibald Campbell (1835-1908), a veteran of the Crimean War, in which he sustained severe wounds. A Lieutenant-Colonel, he retired from the army on the death of his father and turned his attention to politics and to physics. Staunchly Conservative like his father, he sat in the Commons as MP for Renfrewshire (1873-4) and for West Renfrewshire (1885-92). He was also active in the foundation of the Conservative Association and the Conservative Club in Glasgow, and in promoting the Scottish branch of the Primrose League, the organisation formed by Disraeli's admirers to support Conservative Party principles and imperialism. He was made a baronet in 1880, and raised to the peerage as Baron Blythswood in 1892. Two years later he was appointed aide-de-camp to Queen Victoria. Campbell, a close friend of Lord Kelvin, was passionate about scientific research and established a private laboratory in the grounds of Blythswood, where he constructed precision instruments and carried out experiments in the use of cathode rays, radioactivity and spectroscopy. He was a pioneer in researching what became known as X-rays, later achieved by Rontgen, and designed a speed indicator which was fitted to Royal Navy ships. Latterly he turned his attention to aerodynamics. "His kites were a subject of wonder and awe to the rural population of Renfrewshire", reported *The Times*, and his laboratory was used to conduct experiments into the efficiency of aerial propellers. Blythswood, who became significantly associated with the public life of Glasgow, was elected a Fellow of the Royal Society the year before his death from heart failure at Blythswood House in 1908, leaving no immediate heir and an estate valued at £776,272.

Within 32 years, and after six successors, the title was extinct. His immediate successor, his brother, the Rev. Sholto Douglas Campbell (1839-1916), who ended his clerical life as rector of St Silas Episcopal Church off Woodlands Road in Glasgow, also died childless at Blythswood, to be followed by another brother, Major-General Barrington Bulkeley Campbell (1845-1918), a career soldier and veteran of the Egyptian and South African wars, who held the title for only two years. His three sons then succeeded in turn. The eldest, Major Archibald Douglas Campbell (1870-1929), died

childless at Blythswood in November, 1929. Although he and his wife divided their time between the Renfrewshire seat, their house in Montague Square in London, and Lady Blythswood's Penrice Castle near Swansea, he was active in the life and social activities of Glasgow and was made a freeman of the city in 1922. The next brother, Barrington Sholto Douglas Campbell (1877-1937), died unmarried in an Edinburgh nursing home, to be followed by his younger brother, the Rev. Leopold Colin Henry Douglas Campbell (1881-1940), who lived and died at Beer, East Devon. Only six months later his son Philip Archibald Douglas Campbell, the 7th and last Lord Blythswood, was killed in a car accident in Surrey at the age of 21.

Blythswood House played host over the years to many well-known figures. Royalty stayed there as a matter of course when visiting the West of Scotland, as when the future King Edward VII and Queen Alexandra were guests in 1876, when laying the foundation stone of the new Post Office building in Glasgow's George Square, Queen Victoria in 1888, when inaugurating Glasgow's new Municipal Buildings, the future King George V and Queen Mary in 1907, when laying the foundation stones of the new buildings at the University and the Royal Infirmary, and the Duke of York, when performing the opening ceremony at the Scottish Motor Show in 1923. In the end, the house lost its appeal to the Blythswoods. After the death of the 4th Lord Blythswood in 1929, his widow decided to move to Penrice Castle. About the same time the 5th Lord Blythswood intimated that he would not be occupying Blythswood. In February and March, 1930, a sale of the furniture, paintings and general effects of the house took place. The mansion was then closed for an indefinite period, never to reopen. It fell into ruin and was demolished in 1935, much of the broken masonry used for the bottoming of suburban roads.

Blythswood House stood within the perimeter of the 15th hole of Renfrew Golf Club's new course.

# Brediland

Brediland in the south-west of Paisley came into the possession of a branch of the Maxwells of Caerlaverock in 1488, and remained in the Maxwell family until the 19th century. By then the family estates included Brediland, Meikleriggs and Merksworth, and the Maxwells of Brediland had become one of Paisley's oldest and most respected landed families. William Maxwell, who succeeded to the family estates at the end of the 18th century, seems to have been typical of the family. A quiet, unassuming type, with little interest in public affairs, his portly presence was regularly noted in the Paisley Coffee-Room where, with his hair powder, knee breeches and large silver shoe buckles, he was regarded as a fine specimen of the old country gentry. He died at Merksworth in 1837, to be succeeded by his son, Captain James Maxwell, who had acquired his rank serving in the Stirlingshire Militia during the Napoleonic Wars. Like his father, he preferred his Merksworth residence to the ancient house on the Brediland property, a single-storey thatched-roof structure with swept attic dormers and crow-stepped gables, situated just below the Candren Burn. His wife Anna achieved a minor celebrity on the back of a number of guides she wrote for the women of Victorian Britain, among them *The Lady's Guide to Epistolary Correspondence*, and *Letters from the Dead to the Living*. Marital guidance is the main topic of her book, *The Young Lady's Monitor, and Married Woman's Friend (1839)*, in which she offers the following advice to the newly married young mother:

*"Make yourself so agreeable to your husband, that he will see there is no true happiness absent from his home...Many a man has been mortified, broken down, and ruined, by having a slattern for his wife. It is very rare*

*that a man becomes intemperate and vicious when his wife is thoroughly neat and tidy in her person and house. As long as she is inviting and tasteful in her appearance, and fully retains her early attractions, serves him with sweet and wholesome food, and diffuses an air of comfort and purity around her, it is hardly in any husband, not previously brutalised by vice, to stray from the paradise she creates, in search of happiness elsewhere."*

James Maxwell, who obviously didn't stray, died at Merksworth in 1848, to be succeeded by his cousin William Maxwell, the last laird of Brediland, who died childless in 1858. The 300-acre Brediland estate was sold in 1866 to Patrick Comyn Macgregor of Lonend. The estate at the time was considered varied and picturesque, with excellent farmland, romantic burn-side banks and some evidence of industrial activity. The Maxwells of Brediland worked the coal, stone and clay on the land, and owned a brick-works and the Brediland pottery which produced cane, lustre and brown ware.

Patrick Comyn Macgregor (1824-85) had succeeded his father as manager of Leckie's Lonend Dye-works, before becoming a partner in the firm and then outright proprietor when he purchased the business on Leckie's death in 1853. He was active in local affairs, serving on the Town Council and in 1872 becoming a member of the original Paisley School Board and convener of its Works Committee, which oversaw the building of four new schools in a short space of time. He was also a director of Paisley School of Art, president of the Paisley Agricultural Society and secretary of the West of Scotland Burns Club. He disposed of parcels of Brediland, feuing land for housing and for railway development by the Glasgow and South West Railway. Like his immediate predecessors, Macgregor opted for life beyond Brediland and lived with his sisters at Lonend House, where he died unmarried in 1885.

His brother John Ross Macgregor (1837-1913) inherited the business and Macgregor's properties. He retired in 1899, and between 1902 and 1904 built the red sandstone Brediland House, where he died in 1913. His widow continued to live at the property until her death five years later. Whilst the Macgregor family retained the bulk of the Brediland estate for feuing, Brediland House and policies were sold in June, 1920, for £4,600 to the engineer William Young Fleming, later chairman and managing director of the ship and dredger builders Fleming and Ferguson, who turned a quick profit by selling it seven months later for £6,300 to Glasgow produce importer Thomas Noble. Noble retired from the family business Henry Noble and Son in 1925, and the following year Brediland House was put in trust for his family as Noble turned his attention more fully to civic affairs, becoming treasurer of Paisley Town Council in 1928. His death at Brediland in March, 1948, was followed three weeks later by the sudden death of his only son Thomas, aged 48, who had succeeded his father as managing director of the family firm some years earlier.

In May, 1948, Babcock and Wilcox of Renfrew acquired the house and over 3 acres of grounds for a hostel for engineering trainees from across the globe, and in September that year 12 student apprentices and graduate engineers were in residence at Brediland. Conversion work began on the house in 1949, and future modifications would turn the building into a 28-bed facility, the administration of which was entrusted to the local Y.M.C.A. By 1983 Brediland House, which was situated on Lounsdale Road, was no longer in use and lay vacant. That year Paisley Council Planning Committee gave Leech Homes permission for a £670,000 development of 62 homes on the site. Despite a local outcry the house was demolished in July, 1983, and Leech Homes Greenways Court development opened on the site the following year.

# Castlehill

The first Renfrew Castle, a wooden structure with stone foundations, was built around 1170 by High Steward of Scotland Walter Fitzalan on the Kings Inch, part of the lands of the burgh and territory of Renfrew granted to him by David I. It was replaced as the Stewart manor house by a second castle built in the 13th century on a small hill to the west, on the edge of the River Clyde. This structure, surrounded by a large moat, became for a period the main residence of the Stewarts and their successors. Reputedly the birthplace of Robert II, grandson of Robert the Bruce, it attained royal status on his accession to the throne.

In the late 15th century Lord John Ross of Hawkhead, made the hereditary constable of the original castle by James IV, built on its ruins a three-storeyed fortification known as the Inch Castle, which became the residence of the Hawkhead family. This building survived till the late 18th century when the lands of Kings Inch and other local properties were purchased by the tobacco lord Alexander Speirs for a country estate. It was demolished around 1777 when Speirs began the construction of an elegant mansion on his property. The path to the Renfrew Ferry ran through Speirs' land, and in 1787 his family agreed a deal to relocate the ferry to a spot on the Clyde half a mile west, offering in return to build two quays, a ferry house and a new road, which, constructed directly east of the hill on which the second castle had been constructed, became known as Ferry Road. By the time the ferry was operating from its new site in 1791, this castle had been long dismantled, the Castlehill site housing a soap-works, which had been constructed using much of the stone removed from the old fortress. For much of the 18th century Castlehill was in the possession of the Paterson family, merchants in Glasgow. It passed out of the family after the sequestration in 1795 of John Paterson of Castlehill, whose father and namesake had been provost of Renfrew in 1775.

Castlehill House, a compact 7-roomed villa with servants' quarters, set in large gardens and with an extensive frontage to Ferry Road, was built in 1832 on just over an acre of the lands of Orchard, where the orchards of the royal castle once stood. It was constructed by local starch manufacturer William Brock for his mother, Janet Crawford, the widow of Renfrew bleacher Walter Brock, who had established the family bleach and starch manufacturing works in neighbouring Orchard Street. Following his mother's death around 1851, the house reverted to Brock, who leased the property to a number of local industrialists. It was occupied briefly from 1852 by the engineer, iron-founder and shipbuilder James Ward Hoby, who had opened his London Works to the east of the River Cart, adjoining the nearby Renfrew Pier, in 1850. His business collapsed in 1854, forcing him to vacate Castlehill House, which in 1860 was leased by Brock to another shipbuilder, William Simons, who had taken over Hoby's former shipyard that year. When the house was placed on the market two years later, with an asking price of £1,700, it was purchased by yet another shipbuilder, James McLintock Henderson, who had opened his ship-building yard, James Henderson and Son, later Lobnitz and Company, on the River Clyde at Renfrew in 1847. Henderson rented out the house, which was occupied from the late 1860s by James Young Hamilton, Inspector of the Poor for Gorbals Parish.

The next resident of Castlehill House was the engineer, naval architect and shipbuilder Andrew Brown (1825-1907), who had taken over management of William Simons and Company in 1860. A native of Gorbals, Brown served an apprenticeship as an engineer in the Oakbank Foundry of John Neilson before working for William Craig and Company as a draughtsman and foreman pattern-maker, and then for Tod and Macgregor, where he assisted in the construction of engines for steamers. He had been engineering manager of the Anderston shipbuilders and engineers A. and J. Inglis prior to moving to Renfrew. Simons at the time was a small company in expansion mode,

eventually growing in size and output to rival many Glasgow firms. In 1862 it built the *Rothesay Castle*, the fastest boat of its time, but came to specialise in dredgers and ferry boats, constructing the first steam ferry boat for passenger and vehicular traffic at Govan, and becoming responsible for the introduction of steam ferries on the Mersey. Brown assumed full control of the company on Simons' retiral in 1886. In 1890 he purchased Castlehill from Henderson's trustees for £3,680 and rebuilt and enlarged the house. A noted figure in municipal affairs, Brown entered Renfrew Town Council in 1864, becoming provost for the first time in 1867 and eventually holding the office on 5 different occasions over the ensuing 15 years. He died in May, 1907, the oldest shipbuilder on the Clyde. His son William Brown (1850-1929) became chairman and managing director of the company, a position which he continued to hold until his death on Christmas Eve, 1929.

Castlehill House was continuously occupied until 1933, then lay vacant until 1936 when it was demolished. The site was subsequently levelled to create a playground.

The Brown Institute was gifted to the town of Renfrew by Andrew Brown four years before his death. Originally housing a library, reading room and a panelled billiard room, it has since 1997 housed the Renfrew community museum. Another local landmark, Montdyke House, was bequeathed to Renfrew Town Council by another of Andrew Brown's sons, Colonel Walter Brown, also a director in the family firm, who died in 1925. The Simons and Lobnitz yards, long-time rivals in the dredger-building business, eventually amalgamated. The Simons yard continued to operate until 1957 when it was taken over by the Weir Group, who then went on to buy out Lobnitz in 1959. Simons-Lobnitz closed in 1963 due to financial difficulties.

# Crossflat

In 1800 the road leading from Paisley to Glasgow cut through fine luxuriant countryside dotted with large estates. South of the road, to the east of Paisley Abbey, stood the lands of Crossflat (pronounced by the older inhabitants "Corslats"), a name which could denote either a level plot of ground where a cross once stood or "the cross of the king" in Gaelic. In the 1770s the owner of these lands, William Buchanan, a merchant and bailie of the town, began to dispose of them in lots. The brewer and distiller Matthew Brown (1756-1836) purchased part of the arable farmlands of Crossflat from Buchanan's trustees around 1800 and soon after built Crossflat House, a 3-storey, 14-roomed mansion fronted by a large park and approached by a neat, winding avenue from the Glasgow road.

Brown had owned one of the only two large breweries in Paisley in 1782, and, with the purchase of his rival twenty years later, came to have a virtual monopoly of brewing in the town. Over the ensuing thirty years he extended his business interests, acquiring the Portnauld distillery in Inchinnan, becoming a senior partner in James Watt and Company, which owned the Cartsdyke Brewery in Greenock, and purchasing the Port Glasgow Sugar House at Newark. His status was reflected in the company he kept as a director of the North British Fire Insurance Company, which included Richard Oswald of Auchincruive and Sir John Lowther Johnston of Westerhall. Brown augmented his position as a man of property with the purchase of the adjacent estate of Auchentorlie in 1805 and various parcels of the neighbouring lands of Whiteford. He died in 1836 leaving all his business and most of his property interests including the Crossflat estate to his eldest son Andrew Brown (1787-1856), a merchant and cotton spinner who, with his brother Hugh Brown of Broadstone, owned a number of cotton mills across the county. Matthew Brown's three unmarried daughters continued to occupy Crossflat House, their father's wealth ensuring the maintenance of an affluent lifestyle. The daughters were people of substance in their own right. Helen, Mary and Elizabeth Brown had the resources to purchase in 1836 one of Glasgow's landmark commercial premises, the Virginia Buildings in Virginia Street, the old headquarters of Glasgow's tobacco elite. They were to derive a steady rental income from this property well into the century.

After Andrew Brown's sudden death at Bridge of Allan in September, 1856, his sisters moved to Greenock and the compact Crossflat estate was placed on the market, the advertisement highlighting the dual attraction of the property - "Though quite in the country the house is within a mile of the Railway Station". In 1856 Crossflat was sold for around £3,600 to William Philips, a local yarn merchant actively involved in municipal and social affairs. Former provost of Paisley in 1853 and a long-serving magistrate, he was also president of Paisley Ragged and Industrial School, governor of the Paisley Cemetery Company, and chairman of the Paisley Gas Light Company, the Abbey Parochial Board and Paisley's Deaf and Dumb Society. He modernised the Crossflat mansion and is said to have put the estate in order. In 1869 Philips, having intimated his intention of moving to Glasgow, put Crossflat on the market with an asking price of £6,000. It was purchased the following year by Dr. James Hill of Garngad House in Glasgow, who planned to replicate at Crossflat the private asylum he had established on Garngad Hill. For whatever reason, Hill's plans failed to come to fruition and in August, 1872, Crossflat was purchased by the engineer and iron-founder Alexander Fullerton (1819-86), a partner in Fullerton, Hodgart and Barclay whose Vulcan Works on the Renfrew Road in Paisley employed between 700 and 800 people in the construction and manufacture of compressors, boilers, pumping machinery and engines. A speciality of the works was hydraulic machinery for railways, docks and steel works, which the firm supplied to many of the principal docks and railways in Britain and Europe.

Fullerton, often referred to as Major Fullerton because of his commission in the 3rd Renfrewshire Rifle Volunteers, retired from the business in 1885 and died the following year. His son William P. Fullerton, a solicitor, remained at Crossflat until 1888 when his father's trustees sold the 18-acre estate, including the mansion, to Govan builder Hugh Wilson, who sold it two years later to the Glasgow building contractor and property speculator David Macgregor, who in turn sold it in 1892 to yet another Glasgow builder, James Christie. Each of these contractors feued portions of Crossflats for tenement construction. Crossflat House was demolished around this time. In June, 1895, Christie concluded the sale of a 4-acre plot of Crossflat for £5,000 to the Paisley School Board for a site for a new school, the existing Paisley Grammar School on Church Hill being considered inadequate for the secondary education demands of an ambitious and expanding town. Part of the £34,000 cost of the new school was met by a £15,000 grant from the trustees of the former Liberal MP William B. Barbour, on condition that Barbour's name was associated with the building. The school, called the *Paisley Grammar School and William B. Barbour Academy*, opened in 1898. Tenement construction continued on the former Crossflat estate well into the 20th century.

# Elderslie

King's Inch, one of the eight islands which populated the River Clyde in the middle of the 17th century, was separated from the burgh of Renfrew by a river channel and was home to Inch Castle, a three-storey structure built by Sir John Ross in the latter half of the 15th century. When dredging, to deepen the river and facilitate the passage of ships to the developing port of Glasgow, stopped the river meandering and enabled submerged land to be reclaimed, King's Inch became an extensive parcel of land and was purchased by the Virginia merchant Alexander Speirs (1714-82) in 1760.

Speirs, the son of an Edinburgh merchant, had travelled to Virginia in the 1730s and become a plantation owner and an independent merchant on the James River. On his return to Scotland in the 1740s he settled in Glasgow and formed lucrative tobacco importing partnerships with Archibald Buchanan of Auchentorlie and John Bowman of Ashgrove, both members of the affluent Virginia merchant elite which dominated Glasgow society at the time. He was a founding partner in the Glasgow Arms Bank in 1750, and cemented his growing reputation five years later with a strategic marriage to Buchanan's daughter Mary. By 1772 he was the largest single importer of tobacco to Glasgow. Partnerships with other tobacco lords like William Cuninghame of Lainshaw and John Glassford of Dougalston enabled this triumvirate of merchant princes to dominate Glasgow's tobacco trade. By 1777 the syndicates they controlled dealt in eighty per cent of the city's tobacco export trade. Speirs invested his accumulating capital shrewdly, and became a partner in a range of businesses, including the Wester Sugar House, the Glasgow Tanwork, the Smithfield Ironworks, the Port Glasgow Ropework and the Pollokshaws Printfield Company. Active in the political life of the city, he was city treasurer in 1755 and served as a bailie in 1757 and 1762. In 1770 Speirs purchased for his town residence George Buchanan's mansion at the head of Virginia Street, then considered the finest house in Glasgow.

Speirs' acquisition of King's Inch was central to his grand design of creating a country estate commensurate with his position. It was the first of a number of property purchases between 1760 and 1782 which saw him accumulate over 10,000 acres of land in Renfrewshire, which he had consolidated by Crown Charter into a barony which he called Elderslie, after his most important purchase, the

330-acre Elderslie estate, which he acquired in 1767. In 1777, on his King's Inch lands, Speirs began to build a north-facing mansion to designs by architect Robert Adam. Located 40 yards north of Ross's old castle, which was demolished, the 4-storey, pavilion-roofed Elderslie House, embellished with pleasure grounds, parkland, trees and shrubs, and a private lake stocked with ornamental fish, was finished in late 1782, only months before Speirs' death on December 10th. He died before the end of the American War, which ruined a number of his trading contemporaries, having managed to save most of what he had made. His response to the loss of trade with Virginia and Maryland had been to divest himself of his tobacco interests and switch to trading in sugar, cotton, rice, tea and rum.

His extensive property holdings and business interests passed to his eldest son Archibald Speirs (1758-1832), MP for Renfrewshire (1810–1818), a founding partner in the Renfrewshire Bank, and chairman of the Board of the Forth and Clyde Canal. His name is recalled in Speirs Wharf in Port Dundas, Glasgow. Longevity then skipped a couple of generations of the family. His successor, his eldest son Alexander Speirs (1810-1844), MP for Richmond in Surrey, died suddenly at Roehampton when only 34, while his only son, Alexander Archibald Speirs (1840-1868), MP for Renfrewshire (1865-1868), was even younger when he died from typhoid in December, 1868. Shortly after his death his widow abandoned Elderslie House, moving in 1870 to the family's Houston estate with their son Alexander Archibald Speirs, born posthumously in 1869. Thereafter Elderslie House was leased out. From 1875 it was occupied by Glasgow businessman James Morton (1820-88), a key figure in the greatest financial disaster of the Victorian era. Son of an East Kilbride farmer, Morton as a young man sold his father's milk and butter from a cart in Glasgow before opening a stationery shop in Glassford Street. He prospered sufficiently during "the Australia Mania" of the 1840s to commence business as a merchant trading with Australia, exporting "every known and unknown article of merchandise, from the traditional needle to the equally mythical anchor",

and importing wool, hides and tinned meat. He then began to move into cattle breeding and land in Australia and New Zealand. In 1870 he founded the New Zealand Land Company to speculate in real estate in the colony, and persuaded the City of Glasgow Bank to purchase enormous quantities of company stock. He had gradually become a figure of substance in Glasgow and the biggest client of the City of Glasgow Bank, from whom he obtained a succession of unsecured cash loans for his businesses. When the bank failed in 1878 with losses of £5.19 million, it was found that Morton, their largest debtor with liabilities of £2.3 million, was bankrupt. The directors of the bank were jailed for their reckless mismanagement, but Morton avoided any punishment for his role in the collapse of Glasgow's premier bank. In 1879 he returned to his roots, forming an extensive dairy business, Public Dairy Supply, on Elderslie. The business had to be abandoned when disease struck his cattle, and by the time his lease on Elderslie expired the mansion and estate were in a depressed condition. He ended up living in a small flat off his Southern Coffee Rooms in Crown Street, Glasgow, and died in a Glasgow nursing home.

The last occupant of Elderslie House was William Peacock, head of a Paisley rope and cord spinning firm, who died there on 22 March, 1924. The mansion was demolished later that year. The following year the Elderslie Estates Company was established to manage the extensive estates of the Speirs family across Scotland. Descendants of the family continue to own and manage some 4,000 acres of land in Renfrewshire alone, mostly around Houston and Kilmacolm. The Braehead Power Station, one of the first to be built in Scotland after World War Two, opened on the Elderslie site in 1951 at a cost of £5 million. This was demolished in the early 1980s and in September, 1999, the property company, Capital Shopping Centres, opened a vast £285 million shopping and leisure centre on the site.

# Ferguslie

The lands of Ferguslie, to the west of Paisley, once part of the extensive possessions of the Abbey of Paisley, were secularised after the Reformation. In 1798 a few acres of Ferguslie were purchased from Paisley innkeeper John Gibb by Thomas Bissland (1772-1846), son of the Baltic merchant Thomas Bissland of Auchentorlie, who enlarged and modified an earlier house which had stood on the property for well over 100 years. His mansion, situated on rising ground, was surrounded by landscaped gardens and well-wooded parkland. Earlier the same year, in what was perceived as a very good marriage, Bissland had married Margaret White Houston, eldest daughter of Andrew Houston of Jordanhill, one of Glasgow's most prominent West Indian merchants. Houston lived with the young couple at Ferguslie until his death in 1800, the year his business collapsed in the most spectacular commercial failure in Glasgow's history.

A merchant like his father, and a partner in the West Arthurlie cotton spinning firm Stuart, Locke and Company, Bissland in 1806 purchased the remaining 156 acres of Ferguslie for £12,000 from Paisley Town Council which had acquired the lands in 1747. When his extensive business succumbed to the general commercial malaise of 1810 and insolvency followed, Ferguslie was sub-divided and sold off. The 15-acre division containing the house passed through several hands before being purchased in 1845 for around £3,000 by Paisley thread manufacturer Thomas Coats, who quickly turned the mansion into a home befitting a captain of industry. An American visitor in 1848 described it as "a princely residence...fitted up in the most costly, convenient, and elegant style; (with) furniture of the richest and newest fashion." Coats and his wife brought up their family of 11 children at Ferguslie House, across the road from the family's expanding mills.

Thomas Coats (1809-83) was the fourth of the ten sons of James Coats who, in 1826, had built a small thread mill at Ferguslie, which he transferred on his retiral in 1830 to his sons James Coats (1803-1845) and Peter Coats (1808-1890), who formed the firm J. & P. Coats. Two years later Thomas joined the partnership and helped to spearhead the rapid expansion which saw Ferguslie become a global thread production centre. New markets were opened up at home and overseas, and when high customs duties threatened foreign exports, the company began building mills abroad, resulting in a short time in branches in the United States, Russia, Germany, Austria, Hungary and Spain.

Thomas Coats was a noted philanthropist and Paisley

benefactor. In 1866 he purchased the Hope Temple Gardens and, at an estimated cost of £20,000, transformed them into the Fountain Gardens, which were opened to the people of Paisley two years later. His interest in science and meteorology – he ran his own weather station at Ferguslie – saw him spend an estimated £12,000 building, equipping and endowing an observatory which he presented in 1882 to the Paisley Philosophic Institute. Active in education, he became the first chairman of Paisley's School Board in 1873, retaining the post until his death. During his tenure he donated £1,000 to each of the 4 new board schools on condition that their accommodation footprint exceeded the regulation minimum. A keen numismatist, he collated the large and extensive Ferguslie Collection of Scottish Coins. He was also a devout Baptist, a former president of the Baptist Union of Scotland, and after his death the Coats family built the Thomas Coats Memorial Baptist Church in his memory. A commemorative statue was also erected by public subscription outside Paisley Town Hall. He died in 1883, leaving an estate valued at £1,308,734. The following year the firm became a private joint stock company of family shareholders, a structure which was to assure significant wealth for succeeding generations of the family.

The eldest of his six sons, James Coats (1841-1912), also a director in the company, followed him at Ferguslie, where he lived with other members of the family. Considered reclusive and eccentric, James Coats was a powerfully-built individual who spent a great deal of time aboard his various yachts. His eccentricity was best exemplified in his yacht, *Syren*, a 250-ton craft which was built without engines, boilers or propellers, the space normally allocated to these occupied by a gymnasium for himself and his friends. This handsomely-fitted vessel, no more than a glorified houseboat, had to be towed about the Clyde by smaller craft. His philanthropy was of the practical sort. He gifted libraries and bookcases to about 4,000 Scottish towns, villages and schools, and engaged two Glasgow University lecturers to visit these places to stimulate their use. When he identified a dearth of popular Gaelic literature in the Highlands and Islands he commissioned Gaelic literature and published it at his own expense. He employed opticians to go around the country testing the eyes of the elderly unable to read print and providing free spectacles. Every Christmas he sent a boatload of toys, games, books and provisions to the inhabitants of Fair Isle, and every New Year's Day a parcel of books, 2 pounds of tobacco and 2 pipes found their way to every lighthouse on the Scottish coast. He provided pupils across the country with free leather school bags, and teachers with gifts like dressing cases and travelling bags, and spent an annual £1,500 on boots, shoes and stockings for Paisley's needy children. At the other end of the age spectrum he paid to send Paisley's elderly citizens to seaside locations such as Arran for a month at a time. Coats was also the largest subscriber to the Scottish National Antarctic Expedition of 1902-1904, which named a one hundred and fifty mile stretch of the Antarctic continent Coats' Land in his honour.

He died unmarried at Ferguslie House in 1912, leaving no will and an estate valued at £1.96 million. The Ferguslie property passed to his brother Sir Thomas Glen-Coats, through whom the family continued to occupy the mansion. Another brother, William Allan Coats (1853-1926), of Dailskairth in Dumfries, died there in August, 1926, leaving £3.9 million, the eighth millionaire estate left by a member of the Coats family up to that time, overshadowed only by the £4.64 million left by his brother George Coats, Lord Glentanar, in 1918. In line with William's wishes, the most valuable work in his art collection, Vermeer's *Christ in the House of Martha and Mary*, was presented to the National Gallery of Scotland on his death.

In May, 1933, Ferguslie House and 17 acres of policies were gifted by the two remaining Misses Coats to Paisley Town Council for a public park. The council accepted a further 19 acres of the estate offered on reasonable terms. The house was demolished around this time and the policies opened to the public. The old stables of Ferguslie House have been converted into apartments and part of the park turned over to housing, while the stone lions which welcomed visitors to Ferguslie House now stand sentry at Blackhall Manor in Paisley.

# Ferguslie Park

In 1872 Thomas Coats (1809-83), senior partner in the thread manufacturers J. and P. Coats, acquired an additional 208 acres of grounds of the former Ferguslie estate, situated north of his home, Ferguslie House. On this land in 1889 his second son Thomas began to build a palatial residence, which he named Ferguslie Park House. Surrounded by mature woodland and gardens, and landscaped around two artificial ponds, the mansion was completed in 1890 in Scottish Baronial style, to designs by architect Hippolyte J. Blanc, who was also responsible for the stables and the lodge. Additions were made to the house in 1900 by Thomas Graham Abercrombie, and in 1908 again by Blanc.

Thomas Coats (1846-1922), born at Ferguslie House, had entered the family firm after completing his education at Queenswood College in Hampshire, and had trained in various aspects of the business before becoming a director of the company and in due course chairman in 1912. This was a period of rapid expansion for the firm, the growth enhancing turnover and profitability. In 1910 Coats, Britain's largest textile company, returned profits of £3.2 million, greater than the combined earnings of the second and third most profitable British industrial concerns, Imperial Tobacco and Guinness. Thomas Coats adopted the additional surname of Glen (his mother's maiden name) in 1894, the year he was created Baronet Glen-Coats of Ferguslie Park. The conferment of the baronetcy coincided with the opening of the Thomas Coats Memorial Baptist Church, built by the family as a memorial to his father, Thomas Coats. Glen-Coats' political sympathies were with the Liberal Party. He was Liberal MP for West Renfrewshire from 1906 until 1910, and a member of various Liberal clubs and organisations in Glasgow, Edinburgh, and London. He could count Lord Roseberry, Herbert Asquith and David Lloyd George among his friends; all were recipients of his hospitality at Ferguslie Park at one time or another. As with almost all members of the Coats family, he was a generous benefactor to Paisley and to national charities and causes. He gifted the land and made other provision for Paisley Technical College, and made significant donations to the

Royal Alexandra Infirmary, to Quarrier's Homes, where in 1910 he built the Elise Hospital (now the Marcus Humphrey Care Home) at a cost of £10,000 in memory of his wife who died that year, and to the King Edward VII sanatorium at Midhurst. He also funded construction of the Paisley YMCA building. He succeeded his father as chairman of the Paisley School Board, founded Paisley's Association for Improving the Condition of the Poor and was active in his support of the new Sunday Schools and of the Renfrewshire branch of the Red Cross, founded in 1910. His contribution to Paisley was recognised in 1916 with the freedom of the burgh. Like most of the Coats family, he was a yachting enthusiast and for a long time was commodore of the Royal Northern Yacht club.

Glen-Coats died at Ferguslie Park in July, 1922, following complications from a fracture of the right thigh the previous month. His estate was valued at £1.72 million. His elder son Thomas Coats Glen Glen-Coats (1878-1954) succeeded to the title and his father's estates. A naval architect and yachtsman, he designed and was at the helm of the *Hera*, which won the 1908 Olympic gold medal for Great Britain in his home waters of the Clyde. A staunch Liberal like his father, he entertained the Asquiths, Lloyd George and Lady Bonham Carter at Ferguslie Park in 1926, when Asquith described the house as "a typical millionaire's villa with some Corots, a Sir Joshua Reynolds and a Hoppner intermixed with family photographs and some sentimental mezzotints." The baronetcy was to become extinct on his death childless in 1954. The mansion had been surrendered much earlier.

Major Alexander Harold Glen-Coats (1883-1933), his younger brother, was the last member of the family to live at Ferguslie Park, which he relinquished upon acquiring Gryffe Castle near Bridge of Weir early in 1931. A director of the family business for 21 years, he died in October, 1933, in London, leaving estate valued at £596,000. The following month the mansion and policies of Ferguslie Park were presented to the Royal Alexandra Infirmary by the second baronet as a memorial to this father, mother and younger brother, together with a sum of £22,500 towards the cost of alterations, furnishings, maintenance and operational expenses. After modifications by architects Abercrombie and Maitland, the Glen-Coats Auxiliary Hospital opened in Ferguslie Park House in July, 1934. An unexpected bonus feature of the gift turned out to be the spectre of Lady Glen-Coats, who, it was said, could be heard playing the piano in the upper part of the building when not actually standing watch over sleeping patients. In September, 1934, Paisley Town Council acquired the remainder of the 142-acre estate, which became earmarked for a housing scheme.

The hospital closed in 1972. Renfrew District Council applied for permission to demolish the listed building in November, 1979, and it was taken down the following year. Glencoats Park was formed on parts of the hospital grounds. Glencoats Lodge Nursery, established in 2005, occupies the mansion's original lodge house.

J. and P. Coats underwent a number of corporate transformations during the 20th century before becoming Coats plc in 2001. A billion-pound global enterprise, Coats plc, the world's largest supplier of industrial thread, is now owned by the London-based Guinness Peat Group. The last member of the Coats family to head the company that still bears the family name was Sir William Coats (1924-2009).

*John Wilson (Townhead)*

*James Richardson (Ralston)*

*George F. Boyle (Hawkhead)*

*Sir Archibald Campbell (Blythswood)*

*Sir Peter Coats (Woodside)*

*James Morton (Elderslie)*

*Sir Stewart Clark (Kilnside)*

*Sir Thomas G. Glen-Coats (Ferguslie Park)*

# Gallowhill

Gallowhill, about a mile north-east of Paisley, passed out of the possession of the Cochranes of Dundonald in the 1730s when Thomas, 6th Earl of Dundonald, gifted it to his daughter Catherine on her marriage to Captain William Wood. Towards the end of the 18th century the estate was subsequently divided into Over and Nether Gallowhill. In 1831 the smaller, northern portion of the lands, the 49-acre farm of Nether Gallowhill, together with a dwelling house built only eight years earlier, was purchased by William Sim, owner of the Paisley Soap Works in West Croft Street, on whose death in 1842 his Gallowhill property was rented out, initially to shawl manufacturer James Robert MacArthur.

Sim's Gallowhill estate, then extending to 62 acres, was purchased from his trustees in 1864 by Peter Kerr (1818-69), who had made his money in Paisley's thread manufacturing industry. He had succeeded his grandfather and father in 1836 as a manufacturer of thread and of the heddle twines used in weaving shawls, and greatly improved product quality, facilitating the shawl-weaving process by glazing the materials. In 1850 he formed Kerr and Company with his brother-in-law George Clark, second son of John Clark, one of the founders of the Paisley thread-makers, J. and J. Clark. In 1865 Kerr and Company amalgamated with J. and J. Clark and Company to form Clark and Company, and two years later the Paisley thread manufacturer, J. and R. Clark, was absorbed for £24,000. Clark and Company was to become one of the leading competitors to J. and P. Coats. Kerr, who made many improvements in the machinery used in the manufacture of thread, and invented a very successful thread-polishing machine, visited the United States in 1866 with a view to expanding the business by establishing works in New York for spinning and glazing thread. Returning to Paisley in 1867, he began the construction of the French Chateau-style Gallowhill House to designs by Glasgow architect William Forrest Salmon, but was destined never to live in the house, which cost around £12,000 to build. On another visit to the United States to visit to the firm's extensive factory in New York, he was seized with cramp and drowned while bathing in the River Hudson at Longbranch on 2nd August, 1869, only months before the completion of his Paisley mansion.

His widow inherited the house where she lived until her death in 1904. Their daughter Elizabeth Anne Kerr (1853-1930) married Hugh Houston Smiley (1841-1909) in 1874. Of an old Ulster-Scots family, Smiley, principal proprietor of the liberal/unionist newspaper, *The Northern Whig*, made his money in the Irish linen industry and in commercial ventures in Egypt. After their marriage, the Smileys took up residence with the bride's mother at Gallowhill, where alterations were made to the house in 1892 and again in 1902 when, at a cost of £1,300, the stable and coachhouse were converted into a three-car garage and workshop, one of the first examples of its type in the country, and a four-room house was built for the chauffeur. Smiley was actively involved in the public and social life of the town. He was variously chairman of Paisley School Board (1880-3), a director of Paisley Savings Bank and vice-president of Paisley Art Institute. A prominent Clyde yachtsman from the early 1890s, he would sail his craft to his Irish seat, Drumalis, near Larne, in summer. It was near Drumalis in 1901 that he built and endowed at a cost of £17,000 a cottage hospital for Larne. He was created Baronet Smiley of Drumalis and Gallowhill in October, 1903. Three years after his death at Drumalis in 1909, his widow financed the establishment of a nursery school in Paisley to carry her late husband's name. Lady Smiley remained at Drumalis, which is thought to have been where the 1914 Larne gun-running operation for the Ulster Volunteer Force was planned. A long standing friend of Sir Edward Carson and an enthusiastic supporter of his "Keep Ulster British" campaign, Lady Smiley

had six months previously donated £10,000 to the Ulster Volunteer Indemnity Fund.

In 1915 she loaned Gallowhill to the War Office as an auxiliary hospital for wounded soldiers. When her health began to fail, she decided to return to Scotland in 1928 and died two years later, predeceased by her son, the 2nd baronet, Major Sir John Smiley (1876-1930), a career soldier. Among numerous bequests she left £10,000 to both the Royal Alexandra Infirmary in Paisley and the Royal Victoria Hospital in Belfast to endow and name a ward to be known as the Smiley Ward, and £10,000 to the Hugh Smiley Day Nursery in Paisley. All the bequests had to be halved because of increased taxation and heavy death duties. Her grandson, Sir Hugh Houston Smiley (1905-1990), the 3rd baronet, married Nancy Beaton, sister of noted photographer Cecil Beaton, in the society wedding of the year in 1933. They lived in London and Hampshire, where he held the offices of High Sheriff and Vice-Lieutenant. A Grenadier Guards officer, he also served as honorary secretary of the Jane Austen Society without, he liked to jest, ever having read the author's works.

The 71-acre Gallowhill estate was sold by Sir Hugh Smiley's trustees in May, 1930, to Paisley Town Council for housing. The mansion was demolished around 1932 to accommodate the construction of 264 homes, swiftly augmented when the council took a decision in 1934 to build a further 900 houses. The Gallowhill Housing Scheme was not completed until tower blocks were constructed in 1968. Gallowhill House was situated near Priory Avenue close to the high flats. The Hugh Smiley Nursery remains operational today.

# Glen

The Glen estate, formerly part of the Barony of Thornley, was situated on the southern outskirts of Paisley at the foot of the Gleniffer Braes. In 1797 Paisley manufacturer Robert Barclay purchased a 7-acre portion of the lands of Glen from London merchant William Wallace, whose father James Wallace of Caversbank had acquired the estate in 1755. Barclay augmented his holding seven years later when he purchased four acres of Muirdykes from the Wallace family. Part of the land was converted into a bleachworks, where around 1835 William Fulton (1801-68), the son of a Paisley weaver, established a dyeing, shawl washing and scouring business. At his Glenfield Works Fulton invented a method of manufacturing starch from East Indian sago and marketed the product as *Glenfield Patent Double-refined Powder Starch*. In January, 1847, he sold the business and the exclusive right to manufacture his Glenfield starch for £700 to William Wotherspoon, who turned the product into a household name. Wotherspoon's marketing claimed it was the only

starch used in Queen Victoria's laundry. A few years later Wotherspoon moved operations to a factory in Maxwellton in Paisley, while retaining the Glenfield Starch copyright, which he aggressively defended against imitators. Rivals passing off inferior products as Glenfield Starch were pursued through the courts. One such copyright case in 1870 eventually reached the House of Lords, which ruled in Wotherspoon's favour.

In 1850 William Fulton acquired the 11-acre Glen estate, complete with the Glenfield Works, from Barclay's trustees and re-entered the industry, where he came to establish a reputation as a progressive employer. Around 1852 he was among the first industrialists to introduce the 60-hour week, and in 1866 he established an early works canteen, fitting up a room where employees could have a substantial meal in comfort for a few pence. Although a wealthy man, Fulton was mindful of his roots. When he took over the Glen estate he declared that the people of Paisley would have licence to wander the braes and glens as if they were their own. Groups like the Sabbath Schools took him at his word, organising an annual excursion to the grounds. As a former weaver, Fulton had an affinity with Paisley's old weavers, especially the "characters" and amateur bards, and revelled in their company He would often despatch his works carts into Paisley to collect groups who would spend pleasant summer days at the Glen, being rewarded for their verses with curds and cream. This interest in poetry was reflected in his construction in the 1850s of a stone-canopied fountain on his lands to commemorate his friend Robert Tannahill, Paisley's weaver poet.

Fulton extended the boundaries of his property, where around 1859 he built the Glen mansion on the site of an earlier house. He died there in November, 1868, to be succeeded in the business and the Glen estate, then extending to 40 acres, by his eldest son, also William Fulton (1837-96), who expanded the company and largely rebuilt the works in 1879. He was also responsible for facilitating an event that was to become a regular feature of the Paisley social calendar. In 1874 the Glen hosted a concert to commemorate the centenary of the birth of Robert Tannahill, whose work makes frequent reference to the landscapes of the Gleniffer Braes. Such was the success of the original recital, when 2,000 people walked out from Paisley to hear the music, that concerts were held on a regular basis until 1936. Money raised from the concerts financed the construction of statues commemorating Robert Tannahill at Abbey Close in 1883 and Robert Burns in Fountain Gardens in 1896. Cash was also raised for deserving causes in the town, including the Royal Alexandra Infirmary. These concerts were on an impressive scale, probably the equivalent of modern pop concerts. At their peak the choir numbered around 700, mainly mill girls and other working women of the town, and the concerts, presenting a mainly Scottish repertoire, were performed to large audiences of around 30,000, many arriving by train from Glasgow and Greenock.

William Fulton died at the Glen in 1896, to be succeeded by his brother Joseph, who took the firm public later that year in order to repay some of William's financial obligations. His son Charles William Fulton, as well as being a partner in the family firm, was a prolific inventor who between 1908 and 1933 lodged patents in the fields of textile manufacturing, motor vehicle design and furnace construction. In 1924 he facilitated the resurrection of the Glen concerts which had lapsed during the war. The last Fulton to reside at the Glen was James Fulton. He died in January, 1933, bequeathing his impressive art collection, including works by Boudin and Corot, to the Paisley Arts Institute. In November that year the Glen estate was placed on the market. It was acquired by Paisley Burgh Council in May, 1934. The house was demolished shortly after and the policies turned into a park, the Glen Policies area of the Gleniffer Braes Country Park on Glenfield Road. The house lodge now serves as Glen Lodge Visitor Centre for the park.

William Fulton and Sons' Glenfield dyeing and finishing works grew to become the biggest concern of its kind in the Paisley area, at its peak employing 800 to 900 people. The Fultons remained active in its management until 1940. The works were taken over by Viyella International in 1965 and closed the following year.

# Hawkhead

The Hawkhead estate, which stood on the left bank of the White Cart River, south-west of Crookston and just over a mile south-east of Paisley, was in the possession of the Ross family from 1390 until the death of William, the 13th and last Lord Ross, in 1754. Hawkhead House, considered an elegant structure at the time, consisted of a large, old tower with walls six to eight feet thick, to which lower buildings had been added in 1634 and again in 1737, as indicated by a Ross crest above the main doorway. It stood in an extensive landscape of orchards and large gardens. When the last laird's sister Elizabeth Ross (1725-1791), widow of the 3rd Earl of Glasgow, succeeded to the property in 1777, she renovated the mansion interior to designs by architect Robert Adam, formed a new four-acre garden directly south of the house and built a large 120-foot green-house.

In 1791 Elizabeth Ross was succeeded by her son George Boyle, 4th Earl of Glasgow (1766 - 1843), whose paternal ancestors were the Boyles of Kelburn. He was made a peer in 1815 with the title of Baron Ross of Hawkhead. When his son James Boyle (1792-1869), the 5th Earl, died in 1869, the estate was inherited by his half-brother George Frederick Boyle, 6th Earl of Glasgow and third Baron Ross of

Hawkhead (1825–1890). With the title came all the Boyle property which, in addition to Hawkhead, included Crawford Priory in Fife (the family seat), the Kelburn estate near Largs, most of Great Cumbrae, land in Dalry, Stewarton, Corsehill and Fenwick, estates in Dunbartonshire and Northumberland, and town houses in Perth and Edinburgh. Boyle was deeply involved in the religious controversies of the day. A follower of the Oxford Movement, he was a prominent supporter and financier of the drive to rejuvenate the Scottish Episcopal Church, in the course of which he accumulated massive debts building and endowing Episcopal churches across Scotland, including St Ninian's Cathedral, Perth, the first cathedral to be built in Scotland since the Reformation, and the College of the Holy Spirit at Millport, built and endowed at a cost of £17,000, and later to become the Cathedral of the Isles. His over-generous support combined with a dramatic fall in land values caused his bankruptcy in 1885 with debts of almost £1million. The insolvency forced him to sell all his properties, the disposal of which had raised around half a million pounds by February, 1887. Boyle died in comparative poverty in Edinburgh in April, 1890, and was buried at the church he founded on Millport.

Boyle lived for much of his life on Great Cumbrae, and Hawkhead House was leased to a succession of Glasgow businessmen. His last tenant was John Lye, head of Copland and Lye's drapery warehouse in Sauchiehall Street, Glasgow, who modernised the house and added two large portable green-houses. In June, 1886, the 3,400-acre Hawkhead estate was placed on the market. Attracting no buyers it was subsequently exposed for sale in lots in December that year, when the mansion house lot and three fields lying to the south, about 1,000 acres in total, were purchased by quarry-master William Stevenson, who had paid £40,000 for the neighbouring estate of Househill in 1872. Stevenson's company Baird and Stevenson owned quarries all over Scotland, and was considered the largest business of its kind in Britain. Like many quarry-masters, Stevenson was also a building contractor and property speculator. In 1859-60, with builder John McIntyre, he had feued land from Sir John Maxwell of Pollok on which they constructed the suburb of Regent's Park in Strathbungo, Glasgow. On his retiral from business Stevenson turned his attention to public affairs, and in 1883 was returned as a local councillor for Gorbals, a post he held for 17 years. A Glasgow bailie and senior magistrate, he also owned a string of racehorses. His purchase of Hawkhead was followed by a lawsuit, when Lady Georgina Boyle won a court decision against him in 1891 for the return of three valuable oil paintings on the walls of Hawkhead House which Stevenson had refused to return claiming they were part of the structure of the mansion.

In January, 1890, Stevenson sold 190 acres of his Hawkhead lands for £15,200 to the Govan District Lunacy Board for an asylum and hospital. Designed by Glasgow architect Malcolm Stark, the asylum, a large Scottish Baronial structure dominated by an Italianate water tower, opened on 23 January, 1896, at a cost of £141,161, while the hospital was completed two years later. The Stevenson family lived at Hawkhead House until 1912. Two years later the mansion was sold to Paisley Parish Council, who used it as an out-station of Riccartsbar Mental Hospital in Paisley to provide for patients able to benefit from an outdoor life and work on the adjacent farmlands. At the time of the takeover a dungeon dating back to the 14th century was found under the house, as well as an ancient tunnel, said to stretch from the house to the White Cart River about four hundred yards away, presumably used as a means of flight to the river where a boat to Paisley Abbey or Crookston Castle would ensure assistance or sanctuary. Paisley Town Council returned to Hawkhead in 1932 when acquiring 25 acres of the estate from Stevenson's trustees for an infectious diseases hospital which, designed by local man Thomas Tait of 1938 Glasgow Empire Exhibition fame, opened in 1936 at a cost of £150,000. A further 51 acres adjoining were purchased in 1935 for a maternity hospital, also designed by Tait. Plans were prepared and contractors appointed in July, 1939, but the outbreak of hostilities precluded any building. Following the war Paisley proceeded with the project, spending £26,000 on construction and preparation of the hospital, and were naturally aggrieved when, after the advent of the National Health Service, the Western Regional Hospital Board decided that the building, the first stage of which was completed in 1954 and named Ross Hospital, should be used for Glasgow maternity patients.

In early 1953, with little regard for the ghost known as the White Lady, said to haunt many rooms in the mansion, Hawkhead House, which was showing the effects of age and dry rot, was demolished by the Board of Managers of Renfrewshire Mental Hospitals, who had assumed responsibility for the building in 1948. It stood directly north-east of Hawkhead House Farm and east of Ben Lawers Drive in the private, residential Hawkhead estate.

# Kilnside

In 1788 James Kibble of Whiteford feued part of the lands of Kilnside of Seedhill, on the north bank of the White Cart River, south-east of Paisley Abbey, to Thomas Whitehead, who proceeded to build an extensive tannery on his property. Whitehead conveyed the tannery and the grounds in 1827 to his son Joseph Whitehead (1780-1859), who built Kilnside House on a site adjacent to the family business. An imposing two-storeyed mansion with a pedimented porch, pillared portico, stone balustrades and pavilioned roof, it stood within seven and a half acres of policies, entirely contained within a wall which offered seclusion from the tan-works and other local industries. Trees, shrubs, lawns and flowers adorned the grounds, and Kilnside's gardener was a regular prize-winner at horticultural events in Paisley and beyond. On his father's death, Joseph Whitehead, junior, succeeded to the tannery business and to Kilnside House, where he lived till his death in September, 1872. Six months later the property was purchased for

£6,110 by thread manufacturer Stewart Clark (1830-1907), who improved and extended the house in the 1880s, adding a large conservatory to the right of the structure and installing many ornamental stained-glass features to the interior of the house, one room having a series of full-length classical figures grouped together in panels.

Clark was the fourth son of John Clark, who in 1812, with his brother James, built a two-storey mill at Seedhill to mechanise thread production. When they retired from the business in 1852 the fortunes of the company, J. and J. Clark, were entrusted to the ensuing generation of Clarks. Stewart Clark joined the family firm in 1854 and six years later became a partner in the company which, under the aggressive management of his elder brother John, was about to embark on a spectacular growth spurt. In 1865 the firm merged with another thread-making company, Kerr and Company, to create Clark and Company and two years later swallowed up another thread manufacturer, J. and R. Clark. When new machinery and new methods of production called for new mills, the Linside Mill and the Burnside Mill were taken over in 1867. Modern mill buildings were also erected at Seedhill; the Atlantic Mill in 1872, the Pacific Mill in 1878, and a huge domestic finishing mill in 1886. In the 1870s the Clark mills were renamed the Anchor Mills, and the company's anchor logo was to become an internationally recognised trade-mark. The company had also opened a large mill in New Jersey in 1860, where they manufactured cotton thread for the United States market, and in due course established a global range of factories, in the process becoming one of the most profitable textile concerns in Britain. In 1896 Clark and Company merged with their great rivals J. and P. Coats to become the dominant force in global thread-making.

Stewart Clark was Liberal MP for Paisley from February, 1884, until September, 1885, when he stood down citing business commitments. He took an active interest in a number of Paisley institutions, and was president of the Royal Alexandra Infirmary, the Victoria Eye Infirmary and the town's Industrial School. He was also involved with various other charitable and educational movements, such as the local Association for Improving the Condition of the Poor. In his later years he became fond of sailing. He raced his steam yacht *Vanduara* in Europe and the United States, and used it to sail to his Cairndhu estate in County Antrim, where the family spent each summer. Until 1900 he divided his time between Kilnside House and The Cliff, another home in Wemyss Bay. In February that year he purchased the 2,000-acre Dundas Castle estate near South Queensferry for £135,000 and left Paisley the following year. He was granted the freedom of the burgh of Paisley in 1902, in recognition of the family's generosity to the town, best exemplified in the Clark brothers' gift of £100,000 to construct the George A. Clark Town Hall, named for their brother George Aitken Clark who died in Newark, New Jersey, in 1873. When Stewart Clark died, he left an estate valued at £1.95 million, exclusive of his property portfolio.

The Clark family continued to live in the mansion for a number of years, but around 1910 it became part of the Anchor Thread-works complex, initially being converted into a canteen capable of seating 800 workers at a time. The Anchor footprint expanded as the century progressed and by 1951 it covered 51 acres. Recession claimed many of the buildings in the 1970s, however, and, after the closure of the mills in 1983, the London-based building contractors, the Wiggins Group, acquired most of the site, but failed in their plans to build a hotel and a housing and shopping development on the site. The iconic domestic finishing-mill building lay abandoned and neglected until 2005, when a regeneration project, funded by a private-public partnership at a cost of £12 million, saw it reopen as business premises and private apartments.

Kilnside House, which was located at 8 Seedhill Road, was sold in 1983 to the Cue Ball Group, a subsidiary of Ladbroke's Leisure Group, who soon after secured approval from the Council for a change of use from a listed building to a private licensed leisure club. After renovation it opened as a snooker club. The B-listed building was destroyed by fire in 1992. Miller homes purchased the grounds and opened its Millstream Court flatted development on the site in the 1998.

A memorial window to Joseph Whitehead, junior, presented by his sister Mary Whitehead or Philips, can be found on the north wall of Paisley Abbey.

## Netherhill

The Netherhill estate on the east side of the Renfrew Road, north-east of Paisley, was created by Paisley solicitor and procurator fiscal Robert Rodger from a 13-acre portion of the lands of Nether Gallowhill which he purchased in 1855 from the trustees of the sequestrated James Kibble of Greenlaw. The following year he built the Gothic-style Netherhill House to designs by Glasgow architect Charles Wilson. Standing on the summit of a low hill within a well-wooded environment it was accessed from the Renfrew Road via a long sweeping tree-lined avenue. It was purchased shortly after Rodger's death in October, 1864, by John Baird (1814-83), principal partner in the long-established Paisley wine and spirits merchants James Harvey and Company. Baird, who lived at Netherhill with his brother Alexander, a co-partner in Harvey's, died at Netherhill House in April, 1883, only months after his brother, and in June that year the property was sold to the trustees of the deceased thread manufacturer and merchant James Clark, formerly senior partner in Clark and Company of the Anchor Thread Works, who had died two years earlier.

Netherhill, which became home to Clark's widow and four surviving sons, witnessed a sequence of premature deaths in the Clark family. Of the four sons who were living there in the mid-1880s, all directors in Clark and Company, only one survived to the turn of the century. John George Clark, the eldest son, an enthusiastic yachtsman who built yachts and steamers with portentous names such as *Cassandra* and *Lady Cassandra*, was only 30 when he died in June, 1892, at Wargrave Hill, the home of his in-laws in Berkshire. Seven months later his brother James Alexander Clark (1868-1893) was killed in a road accident in Colorado Springs, caused when his horse bolted and his carriage collided with a heavier vehicle. Typhoid, which had swept through Paisley shortly before, claimed the life of their youngest brother Norman who died at Netherhill House in December, 1898. He was only 29, and five weeks earlier had contributed funds to provide for a short coastal or country break for poor people who had had the misfortune to catch the disease. He left an estate valued at £326,000. Following the death of James Clark's widow at Netherhill in 1893, the property was sold the following March for £12,000 to another thread manufacturer, Peter Mackenzie Coats, son of Archibald Coats, chairman of J. and P. Coats, who in turn sold the property in February, 1902, to the Smileys of neighbouring Gallowhill.

During this period the tenant of Netherhill was James Clark's surviving son, Kenneth Mackenzie Clark (1868-1932), who was 22 when he joined the family business. When J. and P. Coats paid £2,585,913 in 1896 to acquire the Clark interest in Clark and Company, Kenneth M. Clark was one of the four members of the Clark family who benefitted. The buy-out money, together with shares in the new, enlarged J. and P. Coats, guaranteed an affluent future. Clark made improvements to Netherhill House, installing electric lighting in 1897 and earning a fine of £2 in the process, for failing to secure the necessary permissions. He lived at Netherhill until around 1902, when his rented flat in Grosvenor Square beckoned, after which he moved on to the 13,800-acre Sudbourne estate in Suffolk, which he bought in 1904. He eventually retired as a director of the merged firm in 1909, and proceeded to live the life of a man of leisure. His pleasures included yachting in lavish purpose-built craft, shooting and fishing at his Sudbourne estate and in Scotland, principally at the 75,000 Acharacle estate at Ardnamurchin which he bought in 1919, and gambling. He broke the bank at Monte Carlo several times before World War 1, and this may have helped to pay for the house he built at Cap Martin on the Riviera. He is said to have played billiards every night of his life and to have loved whisky, which eventually killed him. His only child, the noted art patron and historian, Kenneth Mackenzie, Baron Clark (1903–1983), wrote in his autobiography, 'My parents belonged to a section of society known as 'the idle rich', and although, in that golden age, many people were richer, there can have been few who were idler." Alan Clark, the military historian, diarist and Conservative politician, was his grandson.

In 1906 Netherhill was leased by William Andrew Young, managing director of the Renfrew engineering and boat building firm Lobnitz. Eleven years later the Archdiocese of Glasgow earmarked Netherhill as a possible site for a second Roman Catholic Teacher Training College, in anticipation of a demand for more teachers following the passing of the 1918 Scottish Education Act. The training was to be undertaken by the Society of Sisters of the Faithful Companions of Jesus, a religious order founded in Amiens in 1820 which had established a house in East Buchanan Street in Paisley in 1889, where they had established St. Margaret's Convent School. When the opening of Craiglockhart College in Edinburgh in 1919 made the Paisley college plan redundant, the 13-acre Netherhill estate was purchased in May the following year from Hugh Smiley's trustees by St. Margaret's Convent, who built a new school in the grounds in 1922. Around 1930 a substantial annexe was added. St. Margaret's Convent School continued on the site as a boarding and day school, becoming a Senior High School in 1967 and merging with St. Mirin's Academy in 1976, following local authority reorganisation.

In 1978 the Faithful Companions of Jesus left Netherhill House and moved into a smaller house in Riccartsbar Avenue, from which they travelled to teach in the school until 1981. After the pupils moved out of the building in 1979, the derelict and boarded-up Netherhill House became subject to several attacks of vandalism and was eventually demolished in 1982. Eight years later St. Mirin and St. Margaret's School vacated the property, which was purchased in May, 1993, by Cala Homes, who the following year obtained planning permission to build 66 houses on the site.

# Ralston

Straddling the Glasgow Road just over a mile east of Paisley, the Ralston estate took its name from the family which occupied the lands from the 13th century until 1704, when Gavin Ralston sold the property to John, Earl of Dundonald. In 1755 Ralston was bought from his grandson by West Indian merchant William MacDowall of Castle Semple, whose son and namesake sold most of Ralston in 1800 to William Orr (1747-1812), who had made his fortune in the Irish linen industry. Three years earlier Orr had purchased the adjacent lands of Ingleston from the Earl of Glasgow for £10,000, and built a villa on the property. He called his combined estates Ralston, and in 1810 commissioned architect David Hamilton to enlarge and redesign the earlier house to create an elegant country residence.

Financial difficulties led his eldest son Robert to market the 442-acre Ralston estate in 1833 with an asking price of £32,000. It was eventually purchased in 1840 by sugar merchant and ship-owner James Richardson (1790-1860). His firm James Richardson and Sons, one of the largest sugar businesses in Glasgow, sourced sugar supplies from producers in the West Indies and arranged their distribution to refiners across Scotland. A capacity for risk-taking was central to his success. When he saw, for

example, that supplies of West Indian sugar were failing to meet the increasing domestic demand for the product, Richardson, against the prevailing wisdom, turned his attention to Mauritius, where his firm succeeded in increasing its production of sugar from around 30,000 tons in 1839 to about 160,000 tons by 1860. The prosperity that ensued owed much to the use of indentured labourers recruited mainly from India, a practice which flourished in the years following the abolition of slavery throughout the British Empire in 1833. Ralston was Richardson's first important property acquisition. At the time of his death, he also owned the estates of Hartfield, near Greenock, and Gartconnell in Bearsden. His estate was valued at £213,658, and included shares in Lancashire Railway, East Lancashire Railway and Lancashire and Yorkshire Railway; a sugar house in Greenock; and five Glasgow ships.

Ralston was inherited by his eldest son Thomas Richardson (1816-72) who, having joined the family business at the age of 17 on an annual salary of £25, graduated to become chairman of the family firm and a major figure in the Glasgow sugar trade. Like his father he was attracted by the investment opportunities offered by the fledgling railway industry, and was a director of the Glasgow and

South-Western Railway, as well as a shareholder in the Caledonian, London and North-Western, North British, Great Western, and Budapest railway companies. He was also heavily involved with the Port Washington Iron and Coal Company of Ohio. He extended the Ralston estate with the purchase of nearby Hillington, made improvements to the house in 1864 to designs by Glasgow architect Campbell Douglas, and added two lodge houses on the Glasgow Road the following year. He died in Budapest while returning from a tour of the Middle East in June, 1872, and was buried overlooking the Danube. He left an estate valued at £274,612. Richardson was succeeded in turn by his sons Robert Young Richardson (d. 1884) and George Wood Richardson, the latter a cotton manufacturer and property developer. Owner of the Linwood Cotton Mill, George W. Richardson was responsible for much of the early tenement construction off Seedhill Road in Paisley, including the laying out of Violet Street and Lang Street around 1900. Richardson regularly leased Ralston, preferring life on his Kirn estate in Argyll. James Clark, senior partner in Clark and Company of the Anchor Mills in Paisley, occupied the house from 1879 until 1881, and John Henderson of the Anchor Shipping Line from 1882 until 1887.

In November, 1890, Ralston House and around 260 acres of the extensive Ralson estate were purchased by Sir Charles William Cayser (1843-1916), who commissioned architects J. and J. Hutchinson to modernise and improve the property. Electric lighting and a well-stocked library were installed, and a winter garden and an aviary created. Cayzer, the son of a London school teacher, had amassed a fortune in the shipping business. The firm he founded in Glasgow in 1878, Cayzer, Irvine and Company, had become a significant force in Anglo-Indian commerce by the late 1880s, enabling him to expand his mercantile horizons within and beyond the Indian sub-continent, and to establish the Clan Line as one of the world's great shipping companies. In 1892 Cayser was returned as the first Conservative MP for the English ship-building constituency of Barrow-in-Furness. A knighthood followed in 1897 and a baronetcy in 1904. Cayser's wealth enabled him to purchase a Scottish estate for each of his six sons and permitted acts of philanthropy, such as when he donated £10,000 in 1895 towards the erection of the Sailors' Orphan Home in Kilmacolm. When two of his daughters married Royal Naval officers, Admirals Sir John Jellicoe and Sir Charles Madden, household names during the First World War, Cayser was popularly referred to as "the father-in-law of the British Navy".

Ralston was the Cayser residence for a short number of years. When creeping suburbanisation began to threaten the leafy environs of the estate in the final years of the 19th century, Cayser decided to move the family home to Gartmore, near Aberfoyle, which he bought in 1900 from Robert Bontine Cunnighame Graham for £130,000. Two years later he began to build Kilpurnie Castle on 8,000 acres of land he acquired near Newtyle near Forfar. Cayser died in late 1916, leaving an estate valued at £2,204,148. Just before he died he placed Ralston House and policies at the disposal of the War Executive. *The Red Cross Hospital for Paralysed Sailors and Soldiers,* fully equipped by Cayser at a cost of £1,500, occupied the house until 1936, the Red Cross Society terminating its lease in June that year. The hospital closed, its remaining 40 inmates transferring to Erskine Hospital, and the house was quickly demolished to make way for a private housing development. Cayser, Irvine and Company entered into an arrangement with the Johnstone building contractor James Y. Keanie to exploit the contemporary demand for self-contained homes, and by 1954 had developed 183 acres of the Ralston estate and built around 1,283 houses for owner occupation.

Ralston House was located at the east end of Strathmore Avenue. Of the estate buildings the East and West lodges on the Glasgow-Paisley Road still stand, having been converted into private homes, while the stables serve as the clubhouse of Ralston Golf Club.

# Townhead

In 1732 John Wilson, a Paisley merchant and future bailie of the town, purchased the properties at No. 40 and 41 High Street, Paisley, and on the steading of the former built a town residence. A spacious mansion, two-storeys high over a half-sunk basement, it was recessed from the line of the High Street by a wide courtyard and a railing-topped stone wall. On his death in 1764, his properties were inherited by his second son John Wilson, a gauze manufacturer. Silk gauze production had been introduced into Paisley in 1759 and had rapidly become the principal industry of the town. By 1781 around twenty Paisley firms were engaged in the trade, and the silk gauzes of Paisley, worth an annual £350,000, were exported to markets in London, Dublin and Paris. John Wilson, who made a sizeable fortune in the trade, was considered one of the richest and most respected members of Paisley's business community. He became a town councillor in 1772, and may have been the John Wilson, merchant, who is listed among the founders of the Paisley Bank in 1773. He married Margaret Sym (1753-1824), daughter of Glasgow merchant Andrew Sym and Grizel, eldest daughter of James Dunlop of Garnkirk, and they had a family of 10 children. The fourth child and eldest son, John Wilson (1785-1854), was to achieve celebrity as an advocate, philosopher, author, literary critic, and poet. His daughter, in a memoir of her father, noted that he was born in a gloomy looking house in a dingy court adjacent to the family mansion, which may have been undergoing modifications at the time and to which the family removed after his birth on May 18, 1785. She described the three-storey, 10-roomed Townhead House as "a stately building, with large gardens, and an imposing entrance". The windows to the rear commanded extensive views over beautiful, undulating countryside, while the immediate prospect was marked by a wooded vale and rich, sloping fields.

After the death of his father in 1796 and his mother's move to Edinburgh, Wilson's maternal uncle, the lawyer Robert Sym, occupied Townhead. Educated in Paisley and the Mearns, where he was a school mate of Sir John Maxwell of Pollok, Wilson seems to have gone directly to Glasgow University where he studied from 1797 until 1803, before entering Magdalen College, Oxford, where he took several college honours and showed an aptitude for sports and athletics before graduating in 1807. About this time he inherited around £50,000 from his father's estate, which allowed him to live the life of an independent gentleman, and, having sold the Townhead property, he purchased in 1805 the small property Elleray on the banks of Lake Windermere. At Elleray, which became his home, he boated, shot, fished, walked and generally amused himself, composing a volume of poems published in 1812 as *The Isle of Palms*, and entertaining friends and acquaintants such as William Wordsworth, Samuel Taylor Coleridge and Robert Southey. His original inheritance was augmented by a dowry in 1811 when he married Jane Penny, the daughter of a Liverpool merchant, but the mismanagement of his financial affairs by his uncle, and his own extravagance and profligacy, resulted in the loss of his fortune and he was compelled to consider a career in law. He moved to Edinburgh to live with his mother and begin his legal studies. Though elected to the Faculty of Advocates in 1815, his passion for literature ensured a short-lived legal career and drew him to join the staff of Blackwood's Edinburgh Magazine, as an editor and contributor, and the writer most frequently identified by the pseudonym Christopher North. Wilson was appointed to the chair of Moral

Philosophy at Edinburgh in 1820, more for his Tory principles, it would appear, than his background as a philosopher, and held the post until 1851 when he resigned due to ill-health and was granted a civil-list pension of £300, on the recommendation of the Prime Minister, Lord John Russell. He died three years later at his Edinburgh home. A statue to his memory, raised by public subscription, stands in Princes Street Gardens.

Townhead House was to know many owners and occupants throughout the 19th century. The last individual to be sole occupant of the property was probably Paisley merchant William Fulton, who lived there from 1834 until 1839. Around 1848 John Gilmour opened a plumber and gas-fitter's business on the premises, subdividing the mansion for occupancy. In the latter half of the 19th century a succession of Paisley businessmen tenanted Townhead House, from grain merchant James Young in 1848 to the cabinetmaker and upholsterer James Hunter in 1886. A school for the general education of young ladies shared the premises from the late 1860s until 1897. For much of this time the principals were the Misses Pattinson, whose brother James Pattinson, organist at Maxwell Parish Church and self-professed Professor of Music, taught organ, piano, singing and harmony in the house.

In 1897 the Townhead House property was sold for £6,500 to a property developer, who demolished the old buildings and began to erect several tenements on the site in 1898. Townhead House was located opposite the Museum and Central Library on High Street. A bronze relief plaque commemorating John Wilson's birthplace adorns the building opposite at 63-65 High Street.

# Woodside

The tree-covered lands of Woodside, about one mile west of Paisley Abbey, were in the hands of the Stewart family from 1445 until 1680, when they were sold to Ezekiel Montgomerie, Sheriff-Depute of Renfrewshire. Montgomerie appears to have been a bit of a rogue. In 1684, having faced 24 charges of misconduct in public office, including extortion and oppression, he was sentenced to imprisonment, but managed to escape. He also managed to hold on to Woodside, which he sold in 1688 to Thomas Crawford of Cartsburn, with whose family it remained until acquired in 1751 by Paisley merchant Robert Sheddan, who was probably responsible for the original house on the property. The estate, with its panoramic views over the Kilpatrick Hills, Ben Lomond, and Goatfell in Arran, was purchased in 1846 from the trustees of his second son John Sheddan by the Paisley Cemetery Company, who sold it three years later to the thread manufacturer Peter Coats, the sitting tenant of Woodside since 1844. In 1850 Coats replaced the old house with a grand mansion, built to designs by Glasgow architect Charles Wilson.

Peter Coats (1808-1890) and his brother Thomas took over the running of their father's Ferguslie thread-works in the 1830s, and were largely responsible for growing the company, J. and P. Coats, into one of the world's leading thread manufacturers. Coats supplied thread to both the domestic and foreign markets. The American market in particular was to become vital to their prosperity. In 1840 three-quarters of the company trade was with America, and Peter Coats is credited with the move into the American manufacturing market in 1870, when the company established mills in Pawtucket, Rhode Island, which came to rival Ferguslie in size and significance. The Coats were noted philanthropists; Peter supported many local causes and made generous donations to the town of Paisley, including the Public Library and Museum, which he founded in 1869 at an estimated cost of £18,000. He was also active in public affairs and was a director of Paisley Infirmary and of Glasgow's Deaf and Dumb Institution, and a Fellow of the Royal Society of Edinburgh. His public services were acknowledged with a knighthood in July, 1869. After the death of his wife Gloriana in 1877, Coats, who had been a central figure in the company for 47 years, retired from the business and moved to his South Ayrshire estate of Auchendrane, purchased in 1868. Here he stayed for half the year, spending the winter season in Algiers, where he died on 9th March, 1890, leaving a personal fortune of £2.5million. In memory of his wife, Coats in the 1880s provided a Presbyterian Church at Minishant, close to his Auchendrane home; he also built a church in Algiers, which he bequeathed to the United Free Presbyterian Church of Scotland, on the understanding that they would always supply the pulpit there with acceptable preachers during the season.

After Coats removed to Auchendrane, his second son Archibald Coats (1840-1912) added an extension and winter gardens to Woodside House in 1881 to designs by Edinburgh architect Hippolyte Jean Blanc. Electric lighting was introduced at Woodside in 1882, perhaps the first domestic installation in Paisley. Coats became the first chairman of the company when it went public in 1890, shortly after his father's death. Under his leadership the firm carried out an aggressive and extensive policy of direct investment in foreign countries, especially after 1896 when it took over its three British rivals, Clark and Company, Jonas Brook and Brothers, and James Chadwick and Brothers. By 1905 J. and P. Coats had become the largest textile business in the United Kingdom and, by the time of Archibald Coats' death in 1912, leaving an estate valued at £1,365,132, the largest in the world. The following year his unmarried elder son Peter Mackenzie Coats died prematurely at Woodside following a bout of pneumonia. His twin brother William Hodge Coats (1866-1928) followed him at Woodside and in 1922 became chairman of the company. His only son, Lieutenant Eric Coats of the Scots Guards, was killed in action in 1918, and when William H. Coats died in 1928, leaving an estate valued at £1.3

million, he left Woodside to Paisley Town Council, which decided in March, 1932, to convert the house into a children's home to replace an existing facility at Auchentorlie House. During the war Woodside House doubled as a Civil Defence HQ, and an air-raid shelter and a large purpose-built first-aid post were built in the grounds. On May 6th, 1941, tragedy struck when a landmine dropped from a German plane struck the first-aid post, killing 92 medical and civil defence staff. The mansion was destroyed by fire in September, 1952. Initial plans to rebuild the house at an estimated cost of £10,000 were jettisoned and the house was demolished.

Woodside House was situated to the east of what is now Woodside Crematorium, close to King Street. The site is now occupied by two rows of council flats. A statue to the memory of Sir Peter Coats, erected by public subscription in 1898, stands in Dunn Square adjacent to Paisley Town Hall, while Paisley Abbey contains a memorial window to William H. Coats and his wife.

The wealth of the Coats family stemmed from the vice-like grip they kept on company affairs in the years leading up to the outbreak of war in 1914. For sixty years after the company's founding in 1830, the business was managed solely by three members of the first generation of the Coats family and eight of the second. When the partnership was converted into an unlimited liability company in 1884, eight members of the family formed the board, with all the capital in family hands. When this became a limited company in 1890, with declared capital of £5.75 million and Archibald Coats as chairman, the board consisted of eight members of the Coats family and four outsiders. With the 1896 merger the number of directors increased to eighteen, half of whom were family members. Until 1914 the founding family either held a majority or was equal to the number of outsiders on the Board and always held the chairmanship; it also owned 30-40 percent of the company shares.

# 6

## *Port Glasgow, Greenock and Wemyss Bay*

Balclutha House was built between 1856 and 1857 for Greenock iron merchant James Morton (c.1822-1890) at a cost of £17,000. It was designed by James Boucher and James Cousland, the architects who played an influential role in shaping ecclesiastical, commercial and domestic building design in and around Glasgow for almost 30 years, and who were among the most sought after architects for the emerging middle-class suburbs of Dowanhill and Kelvinside. Morton named his property Balclutha, from the Gaelic *Baile Cluaidh*, meaning "a settlement or home on the Clyde". The substantial and elegant mansion, situated in the west end of Greenock amidst spacious grounds featuring fine lawns, ornamental shrubbery and tennis grounds, contained over 20 rooms, a large conservatory and vineries.

Son of James Morton of the Shotts Iron Works, Morton acquired the Greenock Iron Works around 1848. He expanded his interests in the industry in 1861 with the acquisition of the Glasgow iron merchant business of Andrew Thompson and Company. Actively involved in the business, political and ecclesiastical life of Greenock, Morton was chairman of the Greenock Chamber of Commerce (1860), provost of Greenock (1868) and president of the Greenock Bible Society and the Greenock Working Boys and Girls Religious Society. He was also a member of the inaugural Greenock School Board in 1872. He is also reported to have given his name to the local football club, of which he was the first patron. Misfortune seemed to have dogged his steps from 1879 onwards, however. That year his son Sidney died at Balclutha, to be followed in quick succession by his wife Margaret and eldest daughter Maggie in 1881, and his eldest son James three years later. Towards the end of 1883, moreover, his business fell victim to the recession that gripped the Clyde that year. The failure of the long-established Govan shipbuilding firm Dobie and

Company proved calamitous for Morton, who had over-extended credit to them. His two companies became insolvent and Morton was compelled to put Balclutha on the market in 1887 at a knock-down price of £2,000 and move into smaller premises in Forsyth Street.

The 4-acre property was purchased at auction in December that year by Charles Cameron (1841-1924), who immediately took steps to modify and extend Balclutha with a view to hosting visitors attending the British Medical Association Congress in Glasgow in August, 1888. Son of a newspaper owner, Cameron was editor of the radical and crusading *North British Daily Mail*, Scotland's first daily newspaper, from 1864 until 1874, when he was elected Liberal MP for Glasgow. He represented various constituencies in the city between 1874 and 1900. Cameron was active in the Commons, being responsible for the Inebriates Acts of 1898 and other legislation abolishing imprisonment for debt in Scotland and conferring the municipal franchise on women. A temperance campaigner, he was a member of the Royal Commission on the Liquor Licensing Laws (1895), which secured various reforms in the Scottish Liquor Laws. His contributions to journalism and to Parliament were recognised with a baronetcy in 1893, while, more prosaically, his services to Glasgow and Scotland were marked by the Cameron Memorial Fountain at Charing Cross (1895/6).

In 1902 Cameron left Balclutha, which was occupied between 1904 and 1909 by the builder and railway contractor Robert MacAlpine. Nicknamed "Concrete Bob", his company Robert MacAlpine and Sons in the previous twenty years had constructed nearly 150 miles of railway in Scotland and Ireland, pioneering the mass use of concrete in railway construction, most famously on the 40-mile Mallaig extension railway and on the Glasgow Subway, which opened in 1896. He also built houses, public buildings and industrial premises, including the Singer Sewing Machine Works in Clydebank. In the 20th century the firm became a giant of the construction and civil engineering world, building docks, power stations, Wembley Stadium and the Dorchester Hotel.

In May, 1911, Cameron, then residing at Virginia Water in Surrey, sold Balclutha to the shipbuilder, collector and big-game hunter Robert Lyons Scott (1871-1939). A director, and later chairman of Scott's Shipbuilding and Engineering Company, Scott still found the time to undertake over 20 hunting expeditions and make over 290 kills in places as far apart as Canada and Kenya, Norway and the Sudan, some even, despite restrictions, in the early years of World War One. His trophies - animals, birds and fish - were presented to Greenock's Natural History Museum in the 1920s and 1930s. Scott died unmarried at Balclutha in July, 1939, leaving a personal estate valued at £376,410 and bequeathing his collection of arms and armour and a library of over 3,000 related books and manuscripts, "the most considerable collection in private hands at that time", to the people of Glasgow.

On the outbreak of war in 1939 Balclutha was purchased by the Admiralty. It was used to accommodate members of the Women's Royal Naval Service before being converted in 1945 into a hostel for civilian staff workers from the Fort Matilda Torpedo Factory. When this closed in 1955, the Admiralty sold the property for £2,255 to a local building contractor named McEwing, who subsequently secured planning permission from Greenock Corporation to construct 45 houses on the site. Demolition of the mansion was well advanced in December, 1956, when Renfrew County Council made a compulsory purchase order for Balclutha as a site for a new academy. A legal wrangle over compensation ensued, which was not settled until a Court of Session ruling in 1959 rejected Ewing's compensation claim of £25,337. A new Greenock Academy was built on the site in 1964 by local architects Frank Burnet Bell and Partners. Closed as an educational establishment in 2011, the building was then used as the school location for the BBC drama series Waterloo Road, filming of which ended in August, 2014. The school was subsequently demolished in 2015.

# Boglestone

Port Glasgow, it has been said, begins at Boglestone, and as the 20th century dawned Boglestone was dominated by Boglestone House. Standing on Clune Brae about a mile and a half from Port Glasgow, with commanding and unbroken views across the Clyde estuary to Dumbarton, the peaks of Ben Lomond and the Cobbler in the north, and to Gareloch and Loch Long in the west, Boglestone House was built around 1874 by John Hamilton on a one-acre plot of ground feued from Colonel David C.R. Carrick-Buchanan of Drumpellier, who had paid £90,000 for the Finlaystone estate in 1863. A plain, square, three-storey structure with an ornate tower on its south-east corner, it contained four public rooms, a library, smoking-room, and nine bedrooms, and was originally built as a hotel to serve the Upper Port Glasgow

passenger station directly south of the house. The station opened in 1869 on the Greenock and Ayrshire Railway line, which ran from Bridge of Weir to Greenock's Princes Pier, where the Glasgow and South Western Railway steamers connected with Dunoon, Kilcreggan and Helensburgh.

John Hamilton (1827-1893), the son of an impoverished Paisley weaver, was a self-educated and self-made man. In his twenties he spent eight years as a commercial traveller, working on commission for three of Edinburgh's largest firms. Around 1860, following pleadings from a wife who was increasingly disgruntled at being left at home with 5 children, he settled down and opened a successful photography business, which he sold ten years later. Using the proceeds and his savings, augmented with extensive borrowings from the City of Glasgow Bank, he decided to enter the property development business, with a view to settling down and retiring on the rents of the buildings he would construct. In addition to his hotel, which he called Boglestone Castle, he built a theatre, Mr Hamilton's Music Hall, and a range of houses and tenements in Port Glasgow. His business affairs unravelled, however, with the spectacular collapse of the City of Glasgow Bank in 1878. Financially bereft and in debt, he abandoned his family and in 1879 emigrated to New Zealand where he prospered in Dunedin, making advertisements for the stations on the South Island Railway Lines. He did not entirely neglect his family in Scotland, however, sending home monthly sums of £5. He returned to Scotland in 1882 in a vain attempt to persuade his family to return with him to New Zealand, only to encounter further misfortune when he lost a protracted law suit with the Salvation Army over the lease of his theatre. In 1885 Hamilton returned to Dunedin where in due course he built a home which he named Boglestone House, published a book of his own poems entitled *The Lay of the Bogle Stone*, and became one of the founding members of the Dunedin Burns Club.

Boglestone House was never occupied as a hotel. After Hamilton absconded to New Zealand in 1879, the house reverted to Carrick-Buchanan who placed it on the market for sale or rent. Unoccupied for most of the following decade it became something of a white elephant, perhaps because of its proximity to the nearby local landmark, the Bogle Stone, a "black granite" deposit from the ice age, long associated with strange occurrences around which local myth and stories of the occult and haunting developed. Parts of Boglestone House were occasionally let to workmen. One November afternoon in 1894, a blaze broke out in the house. The fire brigade summoned from Port Glasgow failed to respond to the alert because it did not possess a fire engine and the property was out-with the burgh boundaries. The fire subsequently raged unchecked until the building was totally gutted. Boglestone House was insured, however,

and subsequently rebuilt. It was acquired in 1902 by Port Glasgow provision merchant and property speculator Samuel Greer, whose daughter Agnes and her husband, Greenock dentist W. Nance Alexander, shared the property in the first decade of the new century. Greer lived at Boglestone House until his death in 1915. The house was abandoned as a family home in the early 1920s. At some point it was sub-divided into four self-contained apartments, which became popular with railway staff, despite the absence of facilities such as gas and electricity.

After the Second World War Port Glasgow's housing needs became critical as a result of the number of properties lost in the Blitz. Boglestone became part of the land bank brought into public ownership by the burgh council as it sought to implement its post-war housing strategy. By 1954, 500 homes had been built on Boglestone and on nearby Broadfield. Boglestone House, which was demolished in 1969 to accommodate the construction of Boglestone and St. Michael's Primary Schools, was situated west of the A761, roughly where Newark (formerly Boglestone) Primary School now stands.

# Broadfield

In 1762 Port Glasgow surgeon Dr. Alexander Molleson took a fifty-seven year lease of 135 acres of the lands of Broadfield and Blackstone, part of the Finlaystone estate, from William Cunningham, the 13th Earl of Glencairn, and set about developing a country estate. Situated two miles east of Port Glasgow, with picturesque views across the River Clyde to Dumbuck, Dumbarton, and Dunoon, the lands extended southward about 1 mile from the Clyde, its northern boundary, and were intersected by the Glasgow to Greenock Road. Molleson, the first bailie of Port Glasgow and Newark in 1775, built a house on the property, enclosed the land with thorn-hedges, sowed a wide range of crops and established a garden that was both attractive and functional, providing many exotic plants and flowers which were useful in his profession. William Cunninghame Cunninghame Graham of Gartmore, who had inherited the Finlaystone estate in 1797, sold the property in 1806 for £3,000 to Paisley merchant James Sym, who sold it on the following

year to James Crawford, a partner in John Crawford and Company, a Port Glasgow company which, with branches in Lisbon and Newfoundland, was one of the largest and most profitable mercantile businesses on the Clyde. Crawford was also Commander of the Revenue cutter *Royal George* and owner of Garrison House on Millport. In 1810, following Crawford's death, all his properties, including Broadfield, passed to his brother John Crawford (1747-1813), the founder of the family firm, who spent over £5,000 building an elegant new mansion to the front of Molleson's earlier house. John Crawford retired from the business in 1811 and died two years later, property rich but cash poor, in debt to the tune of £45,000. The family business was declared bankrupt three years later. To help recover something for the creditors, Crawford's trustees put his lands of Broadfield, Park and High Holm on the market. Broadfield was acquired in 1822 by Port Glasgow merchant James Anderson who resold it the following year to the Glasgow grain merchant

John May, who extended the boundaries of the property by purchasing a considerable portion of the nearby Newark estate. John May of Broadfield, who achieved a certain celebrity in Glasgow for the prominent role he played in organising balls, assemblies and theatrical displays, died in Glasgow in January, 1839. His family retained the 443-acre Broadfield estate until 1866, leasing the mansion and policies and disposing of parcels of land over time for feuing. That year May's daughter Lillias sold the property to Colonel David C.R. Carrick Buchanan of Drumpellier and Finlaystone.

Andrew Wingate, a Glasgow textile merchant, took a lease of Broadfield House from 1848 until his death in 1862. The year before he died his youngest child was born. Francis Reginald Wingate (1861-1953), educated at a private school in Jersey before undergoing military training at Woolwich, was to have a distinguished military and political career, almost all of which was associated with Egypt and the Sudan. He served with Kitchener for 40 years. From 1896 to 1898 he was director of military intelligence under Kitchener in the campaign to retake the Sudan, and in 1899 succeeded him as Sirdar of the Egyptian Army and Governor General of the Sudan, a post he held until 1916, when he was appointed High Commissioner to Egypt. One of the most decorated men in the British Army, and an acquaintance of Lawrence of Arabia, General Sir Francis Reginald Wingate, aide-de-camp to Queen Victoria and to King Edward VII, retired from the service in 1922.

The Wingates removed from Broadfield in 1864 and the tenancy was taken over by carpet manufacturer Arthur Francis Stoddard (1810-82). The son of a Massachusetts minister, Stoddard started his business career as an importer of foreign goods in New York before moving to Glasgow in 1844 when he became a partner in the Manchester firm, A. and S. Henry, which had opened a Glasgow office targeting the American market. The business prospered, and in 1862 Stoddard retired relatively well-off, intending to return home. That year, however, despite having no background in the industry, he

purchased and began to overhaul the Glenpatrick Works near Elderslie, taking on a new career as a manufacturer of tapestry carpets. Within five years he was exporting 75% of his output to the United States. Stoddard subsequently purchased Broadfield House and estate from Carrick-Buchanan in 1875. His family continued to live on at Broadfield after his death, before selling the mansion and 59 acres of grounds for £17,000 in 1887 to J. P. Harrington, owner of a wholesale warehouse in Glasgow. It may have been Harrington who renovated and modernised the house around this time, adding a new porch, Corinthian pillars and sheet glass windows. Broadfield was home to Harrington until his death there in 1917.

The last owner of Broadfield was George Anderson Tombazis, who purchased the Broadfield estate in 1918. A great-grandson of the Port Glasgow merchant and ship-owner, James Anderson of Highholm, Tombazis was Greek Consul in Glasgow for thirty-six years and was considered the doyen of the consular corps. Latterly he became a partner in B. Sheriff and Company, formed in Glasgow in 1920 to acquire and operate sugar and rum estates in Jamaica. Tombazis died at Broadfield in 1923, leaving an estate valued at £36,568, excluding his real estate interests. Two years later Broadfield was acquired by the Paisley District Board of Control which opened the mansion that year as the *Broadfield Certified Institution*, a centre for male psychiatric patients, or "male mental defectives" as they were referred to in the terminology of the period. Four years later the adjoining 35-acre Broadstone estate was acquired from Harland and Wolff for £8,500 to accommodate "mentally deficient females and juveniles", and the two mansions were administered as a single hospital. In 1946, Broadfield was acquired by Port Glasgow Town Council which cleared the site in preparation for the Broadfield housing estate which followed. Broadfield House was situated on the land above Holy Family RC Church.

# Cardell

Immediately after Charles Wilsone Brown purchased the 127-acre Wemyss Bay portion of the Kelly estate in 1850, he began to feu the ground for villa development. At the time of purchase the estate already contained four large and elegant marine villas, built around 1790 when the property was owned by the Stewarts of Ardgowan. Leased from season to season to wealthy Glasgow merchants and referred to as "New Glasgow", they were quickly joined by new buildings of more elaborate design. By 1852 noted architects like James Salmon, John T. Rochead, R. W. Billings and Charles Wilson were building houses around the bay, and by 1855 "New Glasgow" contained thirty-six houses.

Among them was Cardell House, which stood on a 3.5 acre site above Wemyss Bay, with an open outlook over the Firth of Clyde. Attributed to Robert William Billings (1813-1874), the architect of Castle Wemyss, Cardell was purchased in 1858, on the death of the original owner Donald Blair, by the banker John Gilchrist (1803-66), who had made his fortune in Australia. Arriving in Sydney in 1828, he worked in the whaling trade before setting himself up as a general merchant and mercantile agent in

1835. His firm Gilchrist and Alexander introduced large numbers of Scottish immigrants to the colony, transporting 900 to Sydney between 1839 and 1842 alone. One of the most active and prominent businessmen of his day, Gilchrist held directorships in many public companies, mainly banking, insurance and shipping ventures, and was a founder member of the first board of directors of the Sydney Exchange Company in 1851. He returned to England in 1854, becoming a member of the Union Bank of Australia's London board, and generally extending his banking connections. His interest in Cardell may have been related to his passion for sailing. A yachting enthusiast, he purchased the famous racing craft *Kilmeny* in 1865 and began alterations to equip it for a sea voyage to Sydney, but died at his Bayswater home in November, 1866, before making the trip.

Cardell was purchased from Gilchrist's trustees in 1867 by Glasgow merchant John Hatt Noble Graham (1837-1926), son of John Graham of Skelmorlie Castle. Graham and his father were partners in William Graham and Company, the East India firm founded by his grandfather William Graham in 1784. It was his father who established in Oporto the port house which continues to connect the firm's name with Portugal's wine trade to this day. Graham sold Cardell in 1871 for around £3,500 to Catherine MacFarlane, wife of Port Dundas distiller Daniel MacFarlane, who commissioned architect John Honeyman to make alterations to the house at a cost of £1,789. Cardell was purchased from Mrs. McFarlane in 1881 by the noted shipbuilder and engineer William Pearce (1833-88). Pearce had trained as a designer and naval architect at Chatham Dockyard and in 1860 was in charge in of the Achilles, the first iron warship ever constructed in the royal dockyard. He had moved to the Clyde in 1863 and the following year became general manager of R. Napier and Sons, then building most of the ships for the Cunard line. In 1869 he became a partner in John Elder and Company, and sole owner of the business in 1878 on the retirement of the other partners. Under his chairmanship the business was converted to a limited liability company, the Fairfield Shipbuilding and Engineering Company, which became a global leader in ship design and marine engineering. Employing up to 5,000 workers in its Govan shipyard, it built ships for the major shipping lines, including the Pacific Steam Navigation Company, in which Pearce was a major shareholder. Pearce was also chairman of the Guion Steamship Company and of the Scottish Oriental Steamship Company. Elected as Conservative MP for the new Govan constituency in 1885, Pearce was raised to the peerage as Baronet Pearce of Cardell in July, 1887. He died suddenly at his Piccadilly home in December, 1888, leaving an estate valued at £1,069,669. His only son William George Pearce (1861-1907) succeeded to the baronetcy, the chair of the company, and Cardell. More noted for the shooting parties at his Berkshire estate, Chilton Lodge, than for his business acumen, he died childless in 1907 at his Park Lane home.

Cardell was acquired from his trustees in 1908 by stock-broker and collector Bernard Buchanan Macgeorge (1845-1924). A partner in S.N.Penney and Macgeorge, stockbrokers and agents for the London, Liverpool and Globe Insurance Company, and a former chairman of the Glasgow Stock Exchange, Macgeorge is reported to have had many of Glasgow's merchant princes as his clients. He was also one of Glasgow's best known and wealthiest art and book collectors. His Glasgow home in Woodside Crescent housed works by Byron, Shelley, Tennyson and Burns, perhaps the most complete collection of Ruskin literature then in existence and a number of important works by William Blake, including the whole of the Blake collection formerly in the library of Lord Beaconsfield. His eye for literary and artistic treasures made him a wealthy man. His collection of Whistler's etchings was sold in New York in 1902 for £3,000; a rare collection of four Shakespeare folios was sold to America three years later for £10,000; while an unrivalled collection of etchings and drawings by French artist Charles Meryon was sold for over £10,000 in 1916. After his death in February, 1924, his collection of engravings raised £12,281 at auction, while his library of first editions raised £32,062. The Macgeorge family occupied Cardell well into the 20th century. By the early 1980s the house lay unoccupied and semi-derelict. In 1983 the three-acre Cardell property, marketed with an asking price of £55,000, was acquired by Largs building contractor Patrick McAlindon, who demolished the mansion and built a luxury flatted development on the site.

Sir William Pearce is celebrated in a number of Glasgow memorials. In 1887 Glasgow's Old College High Street entrance was removed to the new University campus on Gilmorehill, where it was reconstructed and re-modelled by Alexander George Thomson and named Pearce Lodge for the man who had donated funds for the building. A statue of Pearce, designed by Edward Onslow Ford and erected in 1894, stands at Govan Cross. Affectionately referred to locally as the Black Man, it stands opposite the Pearce Institute, which was donated to Govan by his widow in 1906.

# Cartsburn

The land on which the town of Greenock was originally founded comprised two estates: Easter and Wester Greenock. When Lady Margaret Crawfurd of Kilbirnie came into possession of Easter Greenock in 1661, she found the property burdened with debt and decided to dispose of it. In 1669 she sold it in two portions, one to Sir John Schaw of Wester Greenock, the other, that part of Easter Greenock surrounding Crawfurdsdyke or Cartsdyke, to her cousin Thomas Crawfurd (d.1695), a merchant and former town clerk of Glasgow, and second son of Cornelius Crawfurd of Jordanhill. Crawfurd's division was considered the more valuable. Skimming the sea shore about a mile east of Greenock, Cartsdyke, a small one-street, fishing town established sometime prior to 1592, had grown in importance in the 17th century as a shipping port and a convenient place

for discharging cargoes and transferring them to small vessels for the onward journey upriver to Glasgow.

Crawfurd's right to the lands, which he called Cartsburn, was confirmed in July, 1669, by a Royal Charter which erected Cartsburn into a free barony. Crawford then lived in Cartsburn House, a plain, small, two-storeyed building on rising ground, surrounded by trees. The date 1672, once visible above one of the windows, indicated the likely date of construction. Crawfurd soon began to feu his lands, particularly to the merchants, shipmasters and craftsmen who were increasingly settling in and around Greenock as the town expanded. They built houses of good quality close to the shore in a thriving Cartsdyke, some distance from the mansion house to the north. Among them was John Spreull, a Glasgow apothecary, surgeon, ship-owner and merchant, who feued a piece of land on both sides of High Street in 1667. Spreull, who came from a prosperous and well-established Glasgow family, was known as Bass John for the 6 years he spent imprisoned on the Bass Rock around 1680 for his Covenanting sympathies. He was for many years the largest dealer in pearls in Scotland, and became the main curer and exporter of red herrings in Greenock. The herring trade, the keystone to the prosperity of the local fishing industry at the time, induced a number of Glasgow merchants to open herring processing factories in the area. As the 18th century progressed, however, attention turned to whale fishing. A whale fishing station was established at Cappielow in 1752, and several expeditions were equipped at Cartsdyke for whaling in the Greenland seas. This venture eventually proved unprofitable, however, and was totally abandoned by 1788.

Cartsdyke, which had a population of 629 in 1735, could boast among its inhabitants James Watt, the eminent engineer, whose grandfather Thomas Watt, a teacher of mathematics and navigation, was for a time baron bailie of Cartsdyke, the official appointed by the Crawfurds to collect government taxes, the minister's stipend, the voluntary assessment for the poor, and the funds for repairing the kirk, the bridge and the clock. He also adjusted weights and measures and generally acted as factor on the estate. Another who lived in Cartsdyke was the schoolteacher and songstress Jean Adams, credited by some, on not entirely convincing evidence, with being the composer of the well-known Scots song, *There's nae luck about the house.*

The Crawfurds continued to reside at Cartsburn until the end of the 18th century when Christian (Christina) Arthur Crawfurd, who inherited Cartsburn in 1796, moved the family residence to Ratho, the estate of her husband Thomas MacKnight. Cartsburn House was destined to be rented out thereafter and the feuing of the estate grounds accelerated. By the beginning of the 19th century industry was well developed on Cartsburn

with foundries, shipyards, sugar refineries, engine manufacturing works, glass and bottle works established, as well as housing for a growing industrial workforce. Christian Crawfurd died at Ratho House in 1818, to be succeeded by her son William McKnight, who assumed the surname Crawfurd. In 1846 McKnight Crawfurd was described in the local newspaper as a non-resident landlord who was almost totally unknown in Greenock and never visited the town nor engaged in any undertaking in it for the public good. He did however continue to feu the lands for public works and for railway development. Following his death in Edinburgh in 1855, Cartsburn was inherited by his elder son Thomas, who had joined the 93rd Highlanders as a lieutenant but sold out when succeeding to the family estates.

In the latter half of the 19th century what remained of the old tree-covered Cartsburn estate rapidly disappeared before sprawling industrialisation. When the 88-year old Thomas McKnight Crawfurd, 8th Baron of Cartsburn, died in 1909 at his Torquay residence, the Crawfurd family had long forsaken the grime, squalor, and pollution of the industrial suburb they had created for the more rarified air of their rural and marine retreats. At the time of his death Crawfurd owned, through purchase or inheritance, the country estates of Kirkland House in West Kilbride and Fulwood Park in Cheltenham, as well as Argyll Hall in Torquay.

Cartsburn House was demolished around 1907 to accommodate Cartsburn School, which opened in Inglestone Street in 1908 and was destroyed during the Greenock Blitz of May, 1941. The last remnant of Cartsburn House is the sundial in the gardens of Lauriston Castle, Edinburgh, which was transferred from Cartsburn House by Thomas McKnight Crawfurd after his purchase of Lauriston Castle in 1871.

# Castle Wemyss

When the creditors of the bankrupt Australian merchant James Alexander divided and marketed his 900-acre Kelly estate in Wemyss Bay in 1850, Charles Wilsone Brown acquired the 127-acre Wemyss portion for £15,000. He immediately began to recoup some of his investment between 1851 and 1854 by accepting £2,500 for 4 villas which then stood on the property, and feuing several lots of land for building. He commissioned architect Robert William Billings to build a mansion high on Wemyss Point, about 1 mile south of the pier. Billings spent three years in Wemyss Bay between 1850 and 1853 building the red-sandstone house, which cost around £6,000. Brown, a partner in his father's oil and paint business and in the Western Bank, became insolvent shortly after the family business went bankrupt in 1857, and having to dispose of his assets, he sold Castle Wemyss in 1860 to the shipbuilder John Burns (1829-1901), who that year employed Billings to make additions to the house. Castle Wemyss was actually built in three stages, and was only completed by Billings shortly before his death in 1874, when he added a new

floor, new wings and a clock tower to the existing building to create a grand, castellated structure of imposing dimensions.

John Burns was the son of George Burns (1795-1890) who in the 1830s with his brother James had established a shipping business which held a near-monopoly of mail deliveries between Britain and Ireland, before helping to found the British and North American Royal Mail Steam Packet Company (later the Cunard Line). In 1858, on the retirement of his father, he assumed his father's roles in both G. and J. Burns and in the management and development of the Cunard Line, where he became a key figure as Cunard replaced its fleet of wooden paddle steamers with iron and then steel ships and established a reputation for high speed vessels. Created 1st Baron Inverclyde of Castle Wemyss in July, 1897, Burns entertained lavishly at Castle Wemyss. Among many notable guests were the social reformer Lord Shaftesbury, to whom Castle Wemyss was his "home in the North", the explorer Henry Morton Stanley and the Duke of Cambridge.

A frequent visitor was the novelist and post-office official Anthony Trollope. Claims that Trollope wrote much of *Barchester Towers* at Castle Wemyss can be dismissed; the novel was written in 1857, three years before Burns bought the property. However some part of the later three novels of the Barchester Chronicles, written after 1860, may have been composed at Burns' home. Trollope was a guest of Burns in January, 1870, while beginning *The Eustace Diamonds*, in which he based 'Portray Castle' on Castle Wemyss. In June, 1878, moreover, Trollope accompanied John Burns and his wife, and a party of sixteen guests, on a sixteen-day cruise to Iceland aboard Burn's new steamer *Mastiff*, and chronicled the trip in a record of the cruise, *How the Mastiffs Went to Iceland*.

In 1890 John Burns and his wife passed away within 24 hours of each other at Castle Wemyss after 40 years of married life. He was succeeded in the business and at Castle Wemyss in turn by his two sons, George Arbuthnot Burns (1861-1905) and James Cleland Burns (1864-1919), before the property and the title fell to the latter's son John Alan Burns (1897-1957), who had served in the Scots Guards during World War One prior to his succession. He took no active role in the running of Cunard, but after two failed marriages - the first in 1926 to Olive Sylvia Sainsbury, daughter of Arthur Sainsbury, millionaire owner of a large chain of grocery shops, and the second in 1929 to June Howard-Tripp, a well-known star of silent films who gave up her show-business career on marrying - showed a commitment to public service, serving as Dean of Guild in Glasgow, president of the Scottish Council for Physical Recreation, chairman of the Scottish branch of the British Sailors' Society, governor of the Royal Scottish Academy of Music, and treasurer of the Homoeopathic Hospital of Scotland. In 1936 he gifted Inverclyde House in Largs to the nation for a sports centre, and in 1944 endowed Greenock's Inverclyde Centre as a hostel for sailors. At the time of his succession Castle Wemyss had only 2 bathrooms, a deficiency he rectified by converting half of the mansion's bedrooms into bathrooms, no doubt to the delight of his guests, who included the actress Gladys Cooper, exiled King Peter of Yugoslavia in 1943 and the Royal Family in 1947 when reviewing the fleet. Haile Selassie, Emperor of Ethiopia, first visited Castle Wemyss in May, 1936, and lived there throughout the war until his country's liberation from the Italians.

The 4th and last Lord Inverclyde died in 1957, leaving an estate valued at £1,026,320, of which £810,326 went in death duties. He left no heir and the title became extinct. The Castle Wemyss estate, including the house, then containing 7 public rooms, 14 bedrooms, and 11 staff bedrooms, and set in 41 acres of lawns, gardens and woodland, was put on the market later that year. A 3-day sale in 1958 saw most of the furniture and other artefacts sold to the general public. That year Glasgow Corporation declined an offer to bid for the property, which, under Inverclyde's will, had already been offered in turn to his four nieces, along with £20,000 for upkeep and management, on condition they lived in it for at least 10 years. All declined the offer because of the prohibitive costs of maintenance. Castle Wemyss was purchased in 1959 by Glasgow building contractor John Lawrence, who the following year announced plans to build 500 flats, bungalows and villas on the estate, and, having decided against converting the castle into a hotel, declared his intention to demolish the house in the spring of 1961. The house survived, however, though left abandoned and neglected. The roof was removed to avoid the payment of housing rates and it steadily deteriorated until it was eventually demolished in 1984. In the late 1990s the grounds were further developed for an estate of executive homes.

*James Gammell (Garvel Park)*

*Col. D.C.R. Carrick-Buchanan (Broadfield)*

*Sir Michael R. Shaw Stewart (Greenock)*

*Sir George Burns (Wemyss)*

*James Morton (Balclutha)*

*Sir John Burns (Castle Wemyss)*

*James Young (Kelly)*

*Sir William Pearce (Cardell)*

# Garvel Park

Garvel Park House once stood at the end of a long, tree-lined avenue in its own estate on the eastern shoreline of Greenock. The three-storey mansion was built in 1777 by prosperous Greenock merchant and banker James Gammell (1735-1825), who had built on the commercial foundations laid by his father, the merchant and shipmaster William Gammell, to become a major figure in West of Scotland business circles. The firm he formed in 1768, James Gammell and Company, had trading links with Virginia and the Carolinas, Jamaica, Scandinavia, Lisbon and Rotterdam. A major importer of tobacco, with property and stores in the colonies, Gammell sustained significant losses during the American War of Independence when the colonists confiscated British property and repudiated their debts. It is estimated he was owed £15,000 in North Carolina alone. His trading operations appear to have been well enough diversified to enable him to continue

to prosper, however, and by the early 1780s he had acquired a considerable number of properties in Greenock, as well as having established a rural retreat at Garvel Park on the outskirts of the town. Active in local politics, he was elected to Greenock Town Council in September, 1769, and became a bailie four years later. He resigned from the Town Council in 1784, by which time his business horizons had widened. A year earlier he had been a founder member of Glasgow's Chamber of Commerce, an organisation that was to consume much of his time. In 1785, moreover, he became a founder director with James Dunlop of Garnkirk and Andrew Houston of Jordanhill in Dunlop, Houston, Gammell and Company, the first bank to be established in Greenock, later known simply as the Greenock Bank. In addition to being a large shareholder, Gammell was appointed the bank's first manager. By that time he had also become a partner in James Hunter & Company, an early

Greenock entrant into the Newfoundland timber trade.

Like many of his business contemporaries Gammell invested his trading gains in more permanent assets like property. In 1811 he purchased the estate of Countesswells, near Aberdeen, the first in a series of property acquisitions in the north-east. He followed up in 1816 with the 2,600-acre Ardiffery estate for his grandson James and the 830-acre Portlethen estate for another grandson, Ernest, and in 1823 and 1824 respectively purchased the 6,700 acre Drumtochty estate and the 1,200-acre Lethendy estate in Perthshire for himself. Given that Lethandy cost £37,000 it is not unreasonable to assume that his total outlay on these properties was around £150,000, a significant sum for the period. Gammell continued to live at Garvel Park House until after the death of his wife in 1818, but he left Greenock for Aberdeenshire in 1822 and died at Drumtochty Castle in September, 1825, having outlived his two sons, Lieutenant-Colonel William Gammell (1765-1802), who died of yellow fever in the West Indies, and Lieutenant-General Andrew Gammell (1764-1815), who died in Bloomsbury and was buried in Westminster Abbey, although it is unclear why he merited such an honour, his military career being far from distinguished.

After Gammell's death his trustees began to dispose of his Greenock tenement properties and estates. Garvel Park was sold in 1832 to Greenock shipbuilder John Scott (1752-1837), principal partner in John Scott and Sons. Scott installed his eldest daughter Margaret at Garvel with his son-in-law, Robert Sinclair, managing partner in the firm's engineering arm Scott, Sinclair and Company, which manufactured marine engines at their Westburn Shipyard for the company's own hulls, as well as for other shipbuilders and for the Royal Navy. In 1855, following Mrs. Sinclair's death, Garvel Park passed to her brother, the shipbuilder Charles Cunningham Scott (1794-1875) of Scott and Company, who had established his Cartsdyke yard on open land on his sister's Garvel Park estate in 1850.

In 1868 the Greenock Harbour Trust purchased the 53 acres of Scott and Company's Shipbuilding Works at Garvel Park for £80,000 in order to extend the town's harbour accommodation. At an additional cost of over £60,000 a new graving dock opened in 1874. Five years later, at an estimated cost of half a million pounds, construction of a wet dock at Garvel began. The James Watt Dock, designed to compete with Glasgow's new Queen's Dock, failed to dissuade ships from proceeding upstream to Glasgow, but did serve Greenock's needs, especially for the importation of raw sugar for refining in local refineries. Garvel House was destined to be leased out as shipbuilding came to dominate the landscape. The mansion was invariably occupied by people associated with shipbuilding, including contractors, harbourmasters and engineers. It was latterly used as offices linked to George Brown and Company, who occupied the Garvel yard from 1900, building a wide range of coastal ships, carrying out ship repairs and manufacturing cargo handling equipment.

Garvel House was vacated around 1983 when the firm went into liquidation and it soon became derelict. In 1997 Clydeport, the Glasgow-based ports and property development company, having failed to sell either the historic A-listed Garvel House or the large sugar warehouse adjacent, and quoting a feasibility study showing that it could cost more than £18m to save both buildings, applied for consent to demolish both structures, believing the land could be used more productively. Planning permission was granted subject to the condition that the facade of the mansion, with its fine Corinthian door-piece, would be stored so that it could be resurrected at some future date. Six years later, there having been no action in the intervening period, Clydeport again applied for consent to demolish, claiming the building was in such a poor and dangerous condition that there was no point in retaining any part of it. Planning permission was granted and on December 21, 2004, Garvel House was demolished.

# Gourock

In 1784 the lands and barony of Gourock, comprising Gourock House and 2,500 acres of land, were purchased for around £20,000 from Sir John Stewart of Castlemilk by West Indian merchant Duncan Darroch (1740-1823). The mansion, built about 1747 by Sir Archibald Stewart using stones from a dilapidated old castle nearby, occupied a prominent position above the Bay of Gourock and had commanding views of the Holy Loch, Loch Long, and the Argyllshire Hills. Darroch, a farmer's son from the Isle of Jura, is thought to have been educated in a school attached to Paisley Abbey, and travelled in his late teens to Jamaica, where in due course he was a partner in a merchant firm in Kingston, married Mary Rowan, the daughter of his business partner, and subsequently gained sole control of the business. After more than 20 years trading he returned to Scotland with considerable capital which he applied to the purchase of property.

Following the purchase of Gourock, Darroch acquired the adjacent lands of Fancyfarm in 1792. Like many of the new landowners of the period he improved his property, enclosing and draining the lands, planting woodland and building better and more spacious houses for his tenants. Darroch's thirst for property extended to beyond the grave. The year before his death in 1823, he made a trust disposition conveying all his assets to trustees whom he directed to purchase other estates for the benefit of his heirs. Subsequently, around 1825, they purchased the lands of Park Erskine, Gleddoch and Drums, near Langbank, for a reported £49,000.

Darroch had a large family in Jamaica but they all died in infancy except for one son, Duncan, who was brought to Scotland after his mother's death. Prior to his second marriage, to Janet McLarty, the daughter of a Greenock merchant, Darroch signed a prenuptial contract on 8th April, 1791, conveying Gourock on his death to any heirs of this marriage. Accordingly the Gourock estate was inherited by their only surviving son Angus Darroch, a London merchant, who died childless in 1827, when Duncan Darroch (1776-1847), the son from his first marriage, succeeded to Gourock and Drums. A career soldier, he had seen service in Ireland, South America, Portugal and Canada, before retiring with the rank of Major-General in 1815. He and his wife moved from their Surrey home to take up residence in Gourock House about 1830. He extended the mansion in 1841 and made improvements to the grounds and estate, including building the tower on Tower Hill, completed the year he died. Darroch was known to drive from London to Gourock House in his own carriage, apparently taking 8 days for a journey which cost £35. His son and successor Duncan Darroch (1800-1864), known as Major Darroch by virtue of having raised a local volunteer company, lived at Gourock House and took an active interest in local affairs, becoming provost of Gourock in 1863. He in turn was followed by his son, also Duncan Darroch (1836-1910), a barrister, who showed less commitment to the Gourock property. He sold Drums and in 1873 bought the 32,000-acre Torridon estate in Ross-shire for £83,000. He made London his home, and alternated between the capital and his highland retreat, where he undertook extensive planting to create a deer forest, cleared the land of sheep and returned crofters to land from which they had been evicted during the Highland Clearances. At this time his Gourock estate, extending to 2,700 acres, was providing him with an annual income of around £4,000 and occasional windfalls, as in 1867 when he disposed of estate land to the Caledonian Railway Company.

For the remainder of the century the 26-room mansion and estate grounds were leased, a letting notice of 1865 extolling the virtues of the game shooting possible on the estate, indicating that it contained roe-deer, grouse, partridges, black game, pheasants, woodcocks and snipe. An early tenant was James Tennant Caird, senior partner in the engineering and shipbuilding works of Caird and Company. A bailie of Greenock Town Council for many years, Caird entertained the Japanese ambassador to lunch in Gourock House in 1872. In the closing decades of the 19th century the house was home to banker David Macduff Latham, local agent for the Royal Bank of Scotland in Greenock, a position from which he retired in 1905 having held the office for 60 years.

Gourock was inherited in 1910 by yet another Duncan Darroch (1868-1923), son of the laird of Torridon, who reoccupied the mansion. In 1913 he gifted Darroch Park (later renamed Gourock Park) to the Town Council for popular recreation. During the First World War he served with the Argyll and Sutherland Highlanders at Gallipoli, where he sustained serious injuries from which he never fully recovered. Lieutenant-Colonel Darroch was a member of Renfrewshire County Council, and the first chairman of Renfrewshire Education Authority. His son Duncan Darroch (1899-1960) left Gourock House in April, 1924, having sold the house and policies to Gourock Town Council for £10,000. The grounds were laid out as a park, and facilities including a bandstand provided for public recreation and entertainment. The house was used for social gatherings, dances and parties, and even housed a popular tearoom in the late 1920s and 1930s. In September, 1939, on the outbreak of war, the band room in Gourock House was converted into an Auxiliary Fire Station; two additional rooms were allocated to the National Fire Service two years later. A centre for the decontamination of possible gas attack victims was constructed in the grounds at the beginning of hostilities. By the end of the war general apathy, neglect and lack of investment had taken its toll and a dilapidated Gourock House was subsequently demolished in 1947.

# Gourock Castle

The original Gourock Castle, which stood sentinel over the town of Gourock, was the stronghold of the Douglas family until the reign of James II, when it was forfeited by the Earl of Douglas in 1445 and passed to Archibald Stewart of Castlemilk. It subsequently became the seat of the barony of Finnart-Stewart, before being demolished about 1747. The name was later revived for a turreted marine villa built by Captain James Dalzell (d.1855) on a piece of ground on top of Kempock Hill, shortly after he feued the land from Duncan Darroch of Gourock in 1831. Commanding a panoramic view of the Firth of Clyde, the house was surrounded by a strong wall which also enclosed fine gardens and pleasure grounds. On the adjacent ground beyond the wall, standing between the edge of the cliff and the villa, was located the Kempock

Stone, a prehistoric monolith 6 feet high and 2 feet in diameter, believed to exercise a mysterious influence over the winds and waves. Also known as Granny Kempock, it is said that sailors and fishermen would pace around it seven times, carrying a basketful of sea-sand and chanting an eerie strain in order to ensure a prosperous breeze. The titles of the feu of Gourock Castle apparently prohibited any building on the plot of land on which the stone stood.

One of the first commanders of steam vessels in Scotland, Dalzell engaged in the West of Scotland shipping trade, making weekly passages between Glasgow and Belfast. In September, 1826, his steam trader *Eclipse* was said to have made the fastest passage then recorded between Belfast and Greenock

– 10 hours and 10 minutes. Dalzell retired from sailing in 1830. The last vessel he commanded on the Glasgow to Belfast route was the steam packet *Frolic* which was to founder off Porthcawl in the Bristol Channel in March, 1871, with the loss of 88 lives. He moved to Glasgow on becoming the agent and marine surveyor for the Association of Underwriters in Glasgow, in which capacity he was frequently called as an expert witness to testify in cases of shipping disasters on the west coast, as when the paddle steamer *Orion* sank off the Portpatrick Lighthouse in June, 1850, with the loss of 41 lives. Dalzell had a town property in Glasgow and seems to have rarely resided at Gourock Castle, which was occupied in the 1840s, perhaps as a summer residence, by the Frankfurt-born John Frederick Zoller, who had established himself in Glasgow around 1825 as a commission agent and Belgian consul. In his time it is recorded that the Belgian flag flew over Gourock Castle. Another tenant of the property in the early 1850s was Adam Roxburgh, who became a senior magistrate and provost of Gourock in 1859.

In 1854 Gourock Castle was purchased by James Panton, founder in 1825 of the Glasgow music and musical instrument selling firm James Panton and Company. In the same year that he acquired Gourock Castle, Panton purchased the estate of Garthamlock in the east of Glasgow for £16,750. Panton immediately began to exploit the coal reserves on Garthamlock and turned his attention to becoming a coal-master. He became embroiled in expensive litigation over the coal-works on Garthamlock in 1859, and this may have led him to put his Gourock property on the market that year. Panton, like his predecessor Dalzell, appears not to have occupied his seaside retreat, which was let during his tenure.

The property was bought from Panton in 1860 by Thomas Longlands (1798-1870), who had recently returned from Russia, where he had spent upwards of 20 years manufacturing beetroot sugar. Originally from the Falkirk area, Longlands had occupied the farm of Kersiebank, near Polmont, but when differences with his landlord resulted in lengthy litigation and financial ruin, he emigrated to Russia in search of new opportunities, leaving behind a considerable amount of debt. Apparently his first actions on returning prosperous to Scotland were to settle all his old obligations. Longlands was credited with discovering the site for the Coves reservoir in Gourock, opened in 1862, and assisted the burgh commissioners in securing the land. He died at Gourock Castle in 1870, following which his unmarried sister continued to occupy the house.

The last owner of Gourock Castle was the Parkhead wine and spirit merchant John Aitchison, who purchased it when it came on the market in 1883, possibly as a retiral home. When Aitchison died in May, 1895, with no family and an estate valued at £6,705, the burgh commissioners attempted to buy the property as part of a programme of burgh improvement, planning to use the house as burgh chambers and to establish a recreation ground on the site. When Gourock Castle and grounds came up for auction in January, 1896, however, their bid of £2,070 was well trumped by the £2,580 bid made by a property syndicate which planned to develop the site for housing. The house was subsequently demolished and replaced by the tenements at Castle Mansions and Castle Gardens, which were constructed in 1897.

# Greenock Mansion

Greenock Mansion, which stood on rising ground above the town, overlooking the Clyde estuary, was the ancestral seat of the Schaw (later Shaw) family. In 1540 Sir Alexander Schaw obtained a grant of the forfeited lands of Wester Greenock-Schaw on which stood an old castle and a newly constructed manor house, set within extensive grounds which swept down to the river. This manor house was significantly modified during the following century. The dates 1635 and 1674 were discernible on stones on or near the old house, while the date 1629 could be traced on the nearby manorial well. A western addition was added to the house in 1694 and the last extension took place around 1740, when James Watt, the father of the engineer, constructed a rectangular block on a part of the house which had been allowed to decay.

Sir John Schaw (d.1693), 1st Baronet Greenock, purchased the neighbouring barony of Easter Greenock from Lady Margaret Crawfurd of Kilbirnie in 1669 and the following year was granted a Crown Charter uniting his two properties into a single barony, the Burgh of the Barony of Greenock. In 1718 the house became the residence of Marion Schaw (d.1733), only child of the 3rd baronet, Sir John Schaw, and her new husband Charles, afterwards 8th Baron Cathcart. Sir John granted his daughter, then Lady Cathcart, the feuing rights over portions of the lands of Greenock and during her life-time and that of her son Charles Schaw, the 9th Baron Cathcart, extensive feuing took place, swallowing up much of the wooded and rural landscape and the pleasure gardens surrounding the house. According to an old statute, in order to protect the amenity of the family home, no feuing was allowed within 300 yards from the mansion and this was enforced while it remained a family residence.

The male line of the Schaws of Greenock ended in 1752 with the death of Sir John Schaw, who was succeeded by his great-nephew, John Stewart of Blackhall (1739-1812), who assumed the surname Shaw. By this time little ground remained to feu within what were termed the Cathcart boundaries. However, Sir John had reserved lands from his daughter's feuing rights and in 1780 John Shaw Stewart, MP for Renfrewshire (1780-1796), had a survey and plan made of the town, disposed of much of the adjacent ground around the mansion house for building, and feued a number of farms on which the new town of Greenock would be built. He also sub-let the manor house. In 1793 a John McKechnie was leasing three rooms in the building. Around this time Shaw Stewart commissioned Hugh Cairncross, former clerk of works and assistant to Robert Adam, to design a new mansion house at Ardgowan, which was started in 1797. On its completion around 1801, Ardgowan House became the family home and the tenancy of the old mansion, described by a contemporary writer in 1803 as an elegant and modern building, transferred to the baron bailie, the individual trusted with the management of the laird's business affairs. He was also the magistrate appointed by the laird, and his influence and judicial powers only stopped short, it was said, of the gallows and transportation. The baron bailie would no doubt have had a use for the vaulted ground floor of the mansion, known to have been used as a prison, a popular story being that during the Napoleonic Wars some French prisoners were confined there.

In 1846 the local paper noted the absentee landlord status of the Shaw Stewarts. It was reported that neither Sir Michael Robert Shaw Stewart (1826-1903), the 7th Baronet, who had succeeded to his father's Greenock estates and sugar plantations in Trinidad and Tobago in 1836, nor his family were well known to the inhabitants of Greenock: "They have no residence whatsoever in the place. Their splendid old mansion is let in flats to sundry tenants. Their beautiful seat of Ardgowan, except for a short period in winter, is unoccupied and its portals barricaded, the very gardens being let out for rent." The family was known to the people of the town mainly through their representative in the mansion house. The baron bailie at this time, one of the Shaw Stewarts most respected factors as well as the last, was David Crawford (1790-1861), who held the post until his death. In addition to accommodating various estate officers, Crawford apparently found room in the old house for members of his own family. An Arabella Crawford (1779-1845) operated a boarding house for gentlemen and respectable businessmen in the mansion before her death there in 1845. Her spinster sisters died there, Anna in 1855 and Marion in 1856. The mansion continued as the administrative headquarters, or the "factory office", of the Shaw Stewarts into the 1880s, albeit part of the building was leased for commercial and residential purposes.

The mansion was eventually demolished by the Caledonian Railway Company in 1886 to accommodate a tunnel being built under the house as part of the extension of the railway from Greenock to Gourock. Handsome new estate offices were opened on the north side of Ardgowan Square in August the same year. By this time Sir Michael Robert Shaw Stewart was staying at Fonthill Abbey in Salisbury and had been appointed High Sheriff of Wiltshire.

The Greenock Mansion stood on the site now occupied by the Well Park.

# Kelly

The lands of Kelly, directly south of Inverkip village, were owned by the Bannatyne family from the late fifteenth century until 1792, when the estate was sold to Glasgow merchant John Wallace. The Bannatynes built the original Kelly Castle, which was destroyed by fire in 1740 and never rebuilt. John Wallace (1712-1805) was an extensive property owner in the west of Scotland. Tobacco and sugar were the sources of his wealth. A Virginia merchant, he was also a principal partner in the King Street Sugar House which received the produce of his 3 sugar plantations in Jamaica, named Glasgow, Ruglen and Cessnock, which provided an annual income of around £20,000. In 1793 Wallace built a plain mansion on a natural terrace overlooking the Firth of Clyde and surrounded it with thick woodland. His son Robert Wallace (1773-1855) greatly enlarged the house and improved the estate, reclaiming wastelands and planting woodland. In 1814 he acquired the adjacent property of Wemyss Bay from Sir Michael Shaw Stewart in exchange for his Finnock lands. A popular and accomplished orator, Wallace supported the 1832 Reform Bill and was elected MP for Greenock in 1833, the first of four successive electoral triumphs. He was an early advocate of Chartism, and a major player in the agitation for postal reform. He began the campaign for the Penny Post, and it was by his casting vote in the House of Commons that the measure was carried. His public service gained him the Freedom of Paisley in 1844. At Wemyss Bay, he prepared ambitious plans for a marine village comprising 200 villas, a hotel, an academy, three churches, a harbour and steamboat quay. His ambition out-stripped his reach, however. Depreciation in the value of his West Indian assets led to his bankruptcy, and in 1846 Kelly was sold by his trustees to James Alexander, a London merchant trading with India and Australia. He in turn became insolvent before he had paid Wallace for the property. Alexander's creditors put the 900-acre Kelly estate on the market in 1848 for £52,500. Finding no purchasers, they divided the estate and in 1850 sold it in two lots. The Wemyss part of the estate was bought by Charles Wilsone Browne, while James Scott paid £28,000 for the 774-acre Kelly portion.

James Scott (1810-84), a calico printer, became heavily involved in railway and property speculation in Glasgow in the 1840s. He was head of the business syndicate which purchased the Stobcross estate in 1844 and proceeded to make huge profits by exploiting it for railway, dock and housing development. He served on Glasgow Town Council, latterly as city treasurer, played a leading role in the formation of Kelvingrove Park and, as deputy-chairman of the Clyde Trust, was instrumental in many of the improvements made to develop the port of Glasgow. Locally, he was prominent in promoting the Greenock and Wemyss Bay Railway, which he facilitated by selling it part of Kelly for £10,000. Scott spent generously improving his Kelly property, before accepting £52,500 for it in 1867 from James "Paraffin" Young, (1811-83). Young was in property acquisition mode at the time. Four years later he paid £300,000 for the estate of Durris on Deeside.

Son of a Glasgow cabinet-maker, Young had made his fortune selling paraffin oil and paraffin wax, which were in universal demand for lighting, heating and for many industrial processes. Having discovered and patented a process for obtaining oils and paraffin products from shale and coal, he established a commercial oil-works at Bathgate in 1851, before beginning to build extended works at nearby Addiewell in 1863. In 1866, shortly after the expiry of his patent rights, Young sold his whole operation at Addiewell and Bathgate for £400,000, while retaining a large holding in the Paraffin Light and Mineral Oil Company which took over his business. Young enlarged Kelly House by adding a picture gallery and a large conservatory. Closely associated with David Livingstone (1813-73) from their days as young students of the eminent chemist Thomas Graham at Anderson's College (now Strathclyde University), he financed many of Livingstone's journeys to Africa. In 1875 two of Livingstone's African servants built a replica of Livingstone's African hut in the Kelly grounds, where it remained before being overtaken by shrubbery in the 1930s. Young donated £10,500 to found the Young Chair of Technical Chemistry at Anderson's College in 1870, and erected the statues of David Livingstone and Thomas Graham which now stand in George Square, Glasgow. He died at Kelly in May, 1883.

Five years later the Kelly estate was purchased for £35,000 by Linthouse shipbuilder Alexander Stephen (1833-99), who demolished the mansion and built a new, extended Kelly House on a higher site overlooking the pier to designs by William Leiper. This large, Gothic-style pile, with its tall chimneys and turrets, completed in 1890 at a reported cost of £70,000, was constructed in red sandstone to be more 'in keeping with the style of the district'. The new house was ultimately to suffer the same fate as the original Kelly Castle. While on the market for £40,000, it was leased by James Clark Neill, a director of J. and P. Coats, from 1908 until May, 1913, when he vacated Kelly to move to Curling Hall in Largs. The unoccupied Kelly House was gutted by fire on 5th December that year in suspicious circumstances. Fire services, summoned to a fire in the house at 5.39 a.m., took one hour to arrive from Johnstone, by which time the blaze had taken hold and the roof had collapsed. Poor water pressure hampered their work, and it was late forenoon before the fire was completely under control, by which time only the shell of the building remained. The cause of the fire was never established, but a presumption emerged that it was the work of militant suffragettes. The fire occurred the day following the incarceration of Mrs. Pankhurst in Exeter jail, and two newspapers, *Votes for Women* and *Women's Suffrage*, and a sheet of paper with the message "Retaliation; an answer to the Cat and Mouse Act", were found nearby.

The ruins of Kelly House occupied the site until 1940, when they were removed for the construction of Home Guard defences. During the war Canadian and American troops were billeted in the grounds of Kelly while preparing for Operation Torch, the invasion of North Africa. A proposal to use the Kelly grounds for a 500 bed TB hospital was rejected in 1949, and the estate was eventually sub-divided and sold in the 1950s. The site is currently occupied by a caravan park.

# Rothmar

The villa known as Rothmar, initially called Fern Cliff, was one of the earliest villas built upon the Wemyss estate when Charles Wilsone Brown began developing the property in 1850. It was built in 1851 at a cost of £1,783 by Mary Wilsone Davidson on a two-acre plot feued from Brown. The architect, John T. Rochead, was also responsible for the Davidson Mausoleum in the Glasgow Necropolis, built for her late husband James Davidson (d.1850), the muslin manufacturer and merchant who had owned the large Ruchill estate in the north of Glasgow. Situated on an elevated strip of land between the public road along the shore and a high range of red sandstone cliffs, Rochead's design ensured the house took full advantage of the panorama of the Firth of Clyde. The dining room window looked north to Loch Long and the entrances to the Holy Loch and Loch Goil, while the bay window of the drawing room faced west and offered an extensive prospect of Cowal, the Isle of Bute and peaks of Arran. The house was considered distinguished enough to be included, with Alexander "Greek" Thomson's Double Villa at Langside and Holmwood House in

Cathcart, in Blackie's *Villa and Cottage Architecture* (1868), which profiled selected examples of recently erected British country and suburban residences. Mrs Davidson spent most of the remainder of her life at Fern Cliff, where she died in August, 1875, aged 87.

The property was occupied from 1880 by Bryce Allan, who subsequently purchased it for around £3,000 in 1887, the year following his marriage to Annie Smiley, eldest daughter of Paisley thread-maker Stewart Clark of Kilnside. He immediately changed the name of the property to Rothmar. Bryce Allan was a partner in the merchant and shipping business James and Alexander Allan, part of the Allan Shipping Line. His father James Allan (1808-80), who had owned Ashcraig House in neighbouring Skelmorlie, was the eldest of the five sons of Captain Alexander Allan, who had founded the Allan Steamship Company in 1819, trading and transporting between Glasgow and Montreal. Consistent with his father's conviction that his five sons should have a grounding in the business, James was trained as a mariner and commanded his own ship before leaving the sea to turn his attention to managing the Scottish side of the business from an office in Glasgow. The captain's second son, Hugh Allan (1810-82), had gone to Montreal in 1826 and over time developed a successful shipping concern. In 1854 he launched the Montreal Ocean Steamship Company as part of the Allan Line and two years later won the government mail contract between Britain and North America. The following year the Allan Royal Mail Line started regularly scheduled sailings fortnightly between Liverpool and Quebec City and Montreal, and in 1861 inaugurated the first scheduled steamship service between Montreal and Glasgow. The company continued to expand throughout the second half of the 19th century until by 1884 it was the seventh largest shipping line in the world, and the largest privately owned. Its success owed much to its innovative flair; it boasted the first steel liner to sail the Atlantic, the *Buenos Ayrean* in 1880, the first ocean liner to have steam turbine engines, the *S.S. Victorian*, and the first liner with a promenade deck. It also transported emigrants under government subsidy, and was said to have carried more young Scots migrants to Canada than any other shipping line.

Allan remained at Rothmar until 1904, when he moved to an adjacent Wemyss Bay property, The Cliff. Rothmar was home from 1907 until 1921 to accountant William H. Jamieson, following which the property was sold. In 1924 the mansion was converted into a private hotel, a two-storey bedroom wing being added. Rothmar was acquired in 1927 by the Cunnison family, who made further alterations to the house in the 1930s, adding a sun lounge which linked the 1920s wing to the main house. During World War Two, when Skelmorlie became the headquarters of the 1st Army which landed in North Africa, and the beach at Wemyss Bay was concreted to facilitate loading and unloading of amphibious vehicles and landing craft, a number of local properties including Rothmar were requisitioned for military and naval purposes. Eventually derequisitioned in 1946 and restored to the Cunnisons, Rothmar resumed operation as a

family hotel, closing in due course in 1952 when Mrs Cunnison retired. The two-acre Rothmar property was then placed on the market.

The 39-bedroom hotel was acquired by Lanarkshire and District Miners' Welfare Convalescent Homes, who modified the building before opening it as a convalescent and rehabilitation facility. This operated on the premises until 1968, when it was judged surplus to requirements. Sold in 1970, it housed a Christian guest house and conference centre in the decade which followed, when it was renamed Seaside Heights. The property hosted meetings of local groups such as the Wemyss Bay Baptist Church and the Wemyss Bay Evangelical Church before being demolished in July, 2001, when the site was cleared in preparation for a new block of 24 flats. Rothmar was located at 2 Undercliff Road.

In 1891, the Allan Line took over the State Line and was often referred to as the Allan & State Line. Six years later the various branches of the Allan shipping empire were amalgamated under one company, the Allan Line Steamship Company of Glasgow. The company began to experience difficulty financing new ships after the turn of the century and was sold in 1917 to Canadian Pacific Steamships, which integrated the Allan ships with their own fleet and the Allan name was lost to sea transportation.

# Wemyss

Wealthy shipping magnate George Burns (1795-1890) began to plan for his retirement in 1856 when he joined Glasgow's mercantile and industrial elite in purchasing a new townhouse, 1 Park Gardens, in the prestigious new development on Woodlands Hill in Glasgow. He then turned his attention to a summer residence, and in 1860 purchased Charles Wilsone Brown's 127-acre Wemyss estate, following it up a year later with the purchase of the Wemyss Bay villa known as Wellesley from James Playfair, a prosperous West Indian merchant and Glasgow magistrate. He demolished this house and replaced it with a striking white sandstone structure to designs by Glasgow architect James Salmon. A picturesque mansion lying back from the road and nestling under a luxuriantly wooded cliff, it stood 30 or 40 yards from the shore and

commanded extensive views over the Firth of Clyde to Innellan, Toward and Bute. Large conservatories adjoined the house, one of which came to contain one of the largest specimens of New Zealand Tree Fern in the country. On the cliffs behind the house were fine terraced gardens which a *Gardeners' Chronicle* article in 1888 effusively compared to the Hanging Gardens of Babylon. Burns initially retained Wellesley House as the house name, but changed it to Wemyss House later in the century.

Burns and his brother James had set up as general merchants in Glasgow in 1818. By 1824, in partnership with Hugh Mathie of Liverpool, they established a small shipping line of six sailing vessels trading between Glasgow and Liverpool. Steamers quickly replaced these ships, and in

1830 the brothers moved into mail delivery, joining with two Liverpool-based Scots, David and Charles MacIver, to form the Glasgow Steam Packet Company, which ran passenger and mail services between Glasgow, Liverpool, Belfast and Londonderry. When in 1838 the Admiralty invited tenders for a steamer service to Halifax and Boston to carry the American mails, Samuel Cunard, a Nova Scotian merchant, decided to compete for the contract. Having failed to attract funding in New York or London for his planned steamer service between Liverpool and the United States, he came to Glasgow with a letter of introduction to Robert Napier, the Clyde shipbuilder and engineer, who introduced him to George Burns, who quickly created a consortium which raised £270,000 to back Cunard's project, Burns personally contributing £10,500. The Admiralty deal was secured and George Burns' name, with that of David MacIver and Samuel Cunard was on the contract. In 1839 The British and North American Royal Mail Steam Packet Company (later the Cunard Line) was established. Burns, who became the first chairman of the company, managed the Glasgow end of the business and was particularly involved with the ordering and building of the ships, which came to develop a high reputation for technical innovation and for the quality of service. With its highly lucrative and fully guaranteed government contracts, the Cunard Line expanded rapidly. Sailings to and from New York were soon added, as were Mediterranean trade routes. The original shareholders were gradually bought out by the founders until the whole business became vested exclusively in the three families of Cunard, Burns, and MacIver.

When Burns retired from G. and J. Burns and from Cunard in 1858, his son John Burns (1829-1901), who came to own the adjacent Castle Wemyss estate in 1860, became chairman of Cunard and sole partner in G. and J. Burns. George Burns spent the remainder of his life between Glasgow and Wemyss Bay, where in 1878 he erected the English Episcopal Church of Wemyss Bay (now demolished) in memory of his wife who died the previous year. He was created 1st Baronet Burns of Wemyss Bay in June, 1889, the oldest ever recipient of this award, and died the following year, leaving personal estate valued at £91,357, exclusive of real estate.

Wemyss House passed to his grandson James Cleland Burns (1864-1919), who became 3rd Baron Inverclyde on the death of his elder, bachelor brother George Arbuthnot Burns in 1905, at which point he switched residence to Castle Wemyss. When his son John Alan Burns (1897-1957), who had been born in Wemyss House, succeeded to Castle Wemyss in 1919, Wemyss House became the home of the 3rd Baron's widow, Charlotte, Lady Inverclyde (1865-1950). She appears to have preferred life in her Berkeley Square residence, and the Dower House, as it came to be known, lay untenanted for long periods, its heavy Victorian furniture shrouded in dust-sheets. The house was demolished in the 1940s and an apartment development, Undercliff Court, now occupies the site at the end of Undercliff Road.

By the turn of the 20th century, the Cunard Company owned 78 steamers and G. and J. Burns 107, all Clyde-built, with a total contemporary value of over £10 million. G. and J. Burns and its rival Laird Lines were acquired by Coast Lines in 1919 and were amalgamated in 1922 to form Burns & Laird.

# Woodhall

In 1860 the Paisley shipbuilding firm Blackwood and Gordon, attracted to Port Glasgow by the prospect of building larger vessels than was possible in their Paisley yard, began to develop the Castle Street Shipyard near Newark Castle. Seven years later, the shipbuilder and engineer Thomas Blackwood (1819-91) acquired around 40 acres of the Broadfield estate, situated roughly half way between Langbank and Port Glasgow, from Colonel David C. R. Carrick-Buchanan of Finlaystone and began to build an elegant, baronial-style mansion to designs by Edinburgh architect Frederick Thomas Pilkington. Beautifully situated amid gardens and well-laid out grounds, with a conservatory and vineries adjoining, Woodhall House commanded extensive views of the Clyde estuary. The lodge which marked the entrance to the estate from the Greenock road was considered a substantial and artistic building in its own right.

Under Blackwood's direction the shipyard proceeded to build over two hundred ships, including six iron steamers for George Gibson of Leith and eight steamers for William Burrell and Son, including SS *Strathclyde* in 1871 and the SS *Strathleven* in 1875. *Strathleven* earned a place in the history books when on February 2, 1880, she berthed in London's East India Dock with the first cargo of frozen meat from Australia. A group of Australian businessmen had chartered the vessel and fitted her with an adapted, dry-air refrigerating machine built by Glasgow's Bell-Coleman Mechanical Refrigeration Company. Sheep and cattle carcasses were taken on board for freezing, and with 40 tons of frozen beef, mutton and lamb, as well as a cargo of butter, *Strathleven* had sailed from Melbourne on December 6, 1879. Blackwood, a well-known and respected figure in Clyde shipbuilding circles, died in 1891.

The Woodhall estate was put on the market soon after, the advertisement noting that the land was mostly occupied for agricultural and market garden purposes while the foreshore was used as timber ponds and leased out. Blackwood's widow and grown-up family moved to Greenock, and the mansion was rented out. Iron merchant Archibald Young, son of James "Paraffin" Young, died at Woodhall in April, 1895. In the first decade of the 20th century Woodhall House was occupied by Glasgow businessman John Stevenson. Stevenson was principal partner in J. and B. Stevenson, the pre-eminent name in British bread manufacture at this time. Founded in Glasgow in 1865, by the end of the century the firm was considered unrivalled in the United Kingdom in terms of its size, scope and organisation. It did much to revolutionize the business of bread-making, manufacturing it on a large scale by modern processes which, it was claimed, excluded the possibility of manual contamination. On a daily basis its enormous seven-storey bakeries at Cranstonhill in the north of Glasgow and Plantation in the south produced 100,000 two-pound loaves of their widely advertised "machine-made bread". Bread, rolls and other products were distributed to bakeries and hotels across Scotland using a fleet of fifty large vans and about seventy horses, as well as steamers and railways. The company also had a huge factory at Battersea in London which served an extensive network of around twenty local depots.

Newspaper reports in November, 1905, that Yarrows of London had purchased the Woodhall estate with a view to transferring their shipbuilding business to the Clyde were to prove inaccurate, but only in terms of the location of their new yard. The company was to opt for an alternative green field site on the Scotstoun estate on the north bank of the Clyde the following year. Woodhall lay unoccupied for some time in the 1920s. In June, 1934, Port Glasgow Town Council, determined to address the problems of slum dwellings and overcrowded housing conditions, purchased the 58-acre estate, which directly adjoined the Council's existing eastern boundary. Work began immediately on a plan to build 400 houses on the 30 acres of the estate considered suitable for housing; the remainder consisting of wooded and rocky glen. Provost Andrew Wilson admitted publicly that he had been surprised to learn that between 50% and 60% of houses in the town had only one or two apartments, and for this reason he gave a commitment that no house in the new Woodhall scheme would have fewer than three apartments. In October of the following year Port Glasgow extended its boundaries to include the estate. Woodhall House stood for a time abandoned and derelict amid the house-building. Representation was made to the council to preserve the mansion with its ornate, hand-carved staircase, wood panelling and stained-glass windows, but the cost of restoration and maintenance was considered prohibitive and it was demolished shortly after.

The new community of Woodhall was devastated on May 5th, 1941, when a high explosive bomb exploded in Woodhall Terrace during the Inverclyde blitz of 1941, killing thirty people taking refuge in a bomb shelter. A plaque of remembrance for the seventy-four Port Glasgow people who perished in the blitz is a feature of the new Woodhall Park in the area.

The 1930s Woodhall Housing Scheme began to be demolished in 2006. The Blackwood and Gordon yard was taken over in 1900 by the Clyde Shipbuilding and Engineering Company, which modernised the works and built over 100 ships in the following quarter century, including gunboats during World War One and coastal passenger ships for Australian and British companies. It later became part of the John Slater group, which failed in 1927 when the yard was sold to James Lamont who closed it in 1938. Woodhall House stood where St Martin's Church now stands on Mansion Avenue.

# Glossary

**Aide-de-Camp:** a military officer who acts as a personal assistant or secretary to a person of higher rank.

**Bailie:** town magistrate. (The office of bailie was eliminated in law in Scotland in 1975 and today the position of bailie is an honorary title given to a senior councillor.)

**Baron Bailie:** the individual appointed to be steward of an estate.

**Burgess:** holder of a burgess's ticket. (Any person wishing to carry out business as a merchant or shopkeeper in a burgh had to obtain a burgess's ticket from the burgh.)

**Dean of Guild:** the head of the Merchant's House. (The Dean of Guild's Council managed the business of the Council.)

**Feuing:** the former term for the legal process under Scottish law of selling land. (A purchaser or feuar gained possession of his property in perpetuity for a fixed annual payment (a feu duty) to the land owner or superior. The feudal system of land tenure, including feu duties, was ended by the Abolition of Feudal Tenure etc. (Scotland) Act, 2000.)

**Feu Plan:** plan of the layout of an estate showing the allocation and disposition of all feus.

**Life-rent:** the right to use and enjoy the benefits of a property or other asset during life, without the right to sell the property or asset.

**Lordship:** a royalty paid to the landowner, often in coal, relative to the volume of coal produced on the estate.

**Preceptor:** the presiding officer of a board or organisation.

**Provost:** the senior magistrate and leader of the Council.

**Sequestration:** a process of bankruptcy where the person's estate is ring-fenced for the use of his creditors.

# Bibliography

In addition to the archives of the Glasgow Herald and the wide range of heritage resources held in Giffnock Community Library, East Renfrewshire, Paisley Central Library and the Watt Library, Greenock, the following sources were consulted in the preparation of this book.

*Academy Architecture, 1901*
Alexander, D. and McCrae, G.: *Renfrewshire: A Scottish County's Hidden Past, 2012*
Anderson, J.F.: *Bishopton and Langbank in Old Picture Postcards, 1992*
Anderson, J.F.: *Johnstone in Old Picture Postcards,* 1992
*The Bailie*
Blackie's *Villa and Cottage Architecture,* 1868
Blackwood, William and Sons: *The Recreations of Christopher North, Volume 2, 1842*
Blair, M.: *The Paisley Shawl and the Men Who Produced It,* 1904
Bowie, J.: *The Port - Past and Present* 1775-1975
Brown, R.: *The History of Paisley from the Roman Period down to 1884, Volumes 1 and 2,* 1886
Burgess, M.: *Discover Linwood,* 1993
Cathcart, W.M.: *Sketches of Greenock and its Harbours in 1886,* 1886
Clark, K.M.: *Another Part of the Wood,* 1974
Clark, S.: *Paisley: A History,* 1988
Crawfurd, G. and Semple, W.: *History of the Shire of Renfrew,* 1782
Crawfurd, G. and Robertson, G.: *A General Description of the Shire of Renfrew,* 1818
Dong-Woon Kim: *J. and P. Coats as a Multinational before 1994 (Business and Economic History, Volume 26, No. 2),* 1997
Dunn, J.A.: *A History of Renfrew,* 1971
Eastwood District Libraries: *Calico, Cotton and Character: A History of Busby,* 1988
Eastwood District Libraries: *Crossroads Community: A History of Clarkston,* 1988
Eastwood District Libraries: *Crum's Land: A History of Thornliebank,* 1988
Eastwood District Libraries: *Fairest Parish: A History of Mearns,* 1988
Eastwood District Libraries: *Sandstone to Suburbia: A History of Giffnock,* 1988
Eyre-Todd, G.: *Who's Who in Glasgow in 1909,* 1909
Factories Inquiry Commission Report: *Supplementary Report of the Central Board of His Majesty's Commissioners, Part 2,* 1834
Gardner, A.: *A Guide to Wemyss Bay, Skelmorlie, Inverkip, Largs and surrounding districts,* 1879
Gordon, Mrs.: *Christopher North: A Memoir of John Wilson,* 1863
*Greenock Herald*
Groome, F.H.: *Ordnance Gazetteer of Scotland (1882-4)*
Hamilton, D.: *Scottish Trading in the Caribbean: The Rise and Fall of Houston and Company (in Nation and province in the first British Empire: Scotland and the Americas 1600-1800, N.C. Landsman, ed.).* 2001)
Hector, W.: *Selections from the Judicial Records of Renfrewshire,* 1876
Hill, A.R.: *A Short Account of the Gilmours of Eaglesham,* 1991
Hill, J.C.: *Linwood, Paisley and District,* 1953
Hughson, I.: *Barrhead and Neilston in Old Picture Postcards,* 1985
Irving, J.: *The West of Scotland in History*
Leighton, J. M.: *Strath-Clutha; or, The beauties of Clyde,* 1840
Macarthur, W.F.: *History of Port Glasgow,* 1932
McClelland, R.: *The Church and Parish of Inchinnan: A Brief History,* 1905
Macrae, D.: *Notes about Gourock, Chiefly Historical,* 1880
McKelvie, J. and Sons: *Views and Reminiscences of Old Greenock,* 1891
McKenzie, B.: *A History of the Village of Langbank, Renfrewshire,* 1981
MacKenzie, R.D.: *Kilbarchan: A Parish History,* 1902
Maclehose, J.: *Memoirs and Portraits of One Hundred Glasgow Men,* 1880

McWhirter, J.: *Mine ain grey toon: The story of Barrhead from pre-historic times to 1914,* 1970

Metcalfe, W. M.: *A History of Paisley (600-1908),* 1909

Metcalfe, W.M.: *A History of the County of Renfrew from the earliest times,* 1905

Miller, A. H.: *Castles and Mansions of Renfrewshire and Buteshire,* 1889

Monteith, J. and McPherson, R.: *Port Glasgow and Kilmacolm from Old Photographs,* 1981

Moore, J.N.: *The early cartography of Renfrewshire to 1864,* 1999

Mort, F.: *Renfrewshire,* 1919

Mure, W.: *Selections from the Family Papers Held at Caldwell,* 1854

Murphy, W.S.: *Captains of Industry,* 1901

Murray, J.: *Kilmacolm: A Parish History,* 1898

Murray, R.: *The Annals of Barrhead,* 1941

Native, A.: *An Ecclesiastical Sketch of Lochwinnoch Parish, embracing a period of about three hundred years,* 1878

Nisbet, S.; A Sufficient Stock of Negroes: *The Secret Lives of William MacDowall of Castle Semple and James Milliken of Kilbarchan, (Renfrewshire Local History Forum Journal, Volume 14),* 2008.

Nisbet, S.: *The Growth of Port Glasgow in the 18th Century, (Renfrewshire L.H. Forum Journal, Volume 3),* 1992

Nisbet, S.: *Castle Semple Rediscovered, (Renfrewshire L. H. Forum Journal),* 2009

Nisbet, S.: *Busby and Dovecothall Cotton Mills, (Renfrewshire L. H. Forum Journal, Volume 2),* 1989

Nisbet, S.: *A History of Stamperland,* 2000.

Oliver, V.L.: *Caribbeana; Miscellaneous Papers,* 1914

*Paisley Herald and Renfrewshire Advertiser*

*Paisley and Renfrewshire Gazette*

Parker, D.: *A History of Muirshiel Mansion and Shooting Estate,* 2007

Parkhill, J: *The History of Paisley,* 1857

Paton, D.: *Sketches In and Around Johnstone,* 1884

Pride, D.: *A History of the Parish of Neilston,* 1910

Ramsay, P.: *Views in Renfrewshire, with Historical and Descriptive Notices,* 1839

Rankin, J.: *A History of Our Firm: being some account of the firm of Pollok, Gilmour and Co and its offshoots and connections,* 1920

*Register of Sasines for the County of Renfrew*

Reilly, V.: *Coats and Clark: The Binding Thread of Paisley's History, (Renfrew L.H. Forum, Volume 15),* 2009

Reilly, V.: *Paisley in Old Picture Postcards,* 1988

*Report of the trial of the Directors of the City of Glasgow Bank before the High Court of Judiciary,* 1879

Rogers, C.: *The Scottish Branch of the Norman House of Roger,* 1872

Semple, D.: *Local Memorabilia, Volumes 1-5,* 1871

Skillen, B.S.: *Old Mines and Miners of Renfrewshire: Glimpses of the Past (British Mining No. 1),* 1990

Smart, W.: *Skelmorlie: The Story of a Parish,* 1968

Smith, J.G. and Mitchell, J.O.: *The Old Country Houses of the Old Glasgow Gentry,* 1870

Smith, R.M.: *History of Greenock,* 1921

Strang, J. A.: *A History of Mearns Parish,* 1939

Stratten and Stratten: *Glasgow and Its Environs: A Literary, Commercial and Social Review Past and Present: With a Description of its Leading Mercantile Houses and Commercial Enterprises,* 1891

Taylor, C.: *The Levern Delineated,* 1831

The New Statistical Account of Scotland, Volume 7 (Renfrew), 1845

Webster, A.: *The Richest East India Merchant: The Life and Business of John Palmer of Calcutta,* 2007

Weir, D.: *History of the Town of Greenock,* 1829

Welsh, T. C.: *Eastwood District: History and Heritage,* 1989

Williams, L., and Loudon, A.: *Mearns Matters,* 2003

Winters, J.: *Images of Scotland - Linwood,* 1999

# House Index

# General Index